Reflective Practice:

A Guide for Nurses and Midwives

Second edition

Beverley Taylor

Open University Press

Open University Press
McGraw-Hill Education
McGraw-Hill House
Shoppenhangers Road
Maidenhead
Berkshire
England
SL6 2QL

email: enquiries@openup.co.uk
world wide web: www.openup.co.uk

and Two Penn Plaza, New York, NY 10121-2289, USA

First published 2006

A catalogue record of this book is available from the British Library

ISBN 10: 0335 21742 7 (pb)   0335 21743 5 (hb)
ISBN 13: 978 0335 21742 7 (pb)   978 0335 21743 4 (hb)

Library of Congress Cataloging-in-Publication Data
CIP data applied for

Typeset by RefineCatch Limited, Bungay, Suffolk
Printed in the UK by Bell & Bain Ltd, Glasgow

Reflective Practice WITHDRAWN

Second edition

In loving memory of my father, Leonard Frederick Bugg, and my brother, given the same name, but known as Bobby.

Contents

Introduction   1

1   The nature of reflection and practice   7
    Introduction   7
    Definitions and perspectives of reflection   8
        Practice and practice development   9
        Clinical supervision   11
        Education   12
    Criticisms of reflective practice   14
    Types of reflection   15
    Sources of reflection   16
    The nature of nursing and midwifery   18
        Nursing   18
        Midwifery   18
        Summary   21
    The nature of work constraints   22
        Cultural constraints   22
        Economic constraints   24
        Historical constraints   26
        Political constraints   28
        Social constraints   29
        Personal constraints   30
        Summary   31
    Issues nurses and midwives often face   32
        Engaging in self-blaming   32
        Wanting to be perfect and invincible   33
        Examining daily habits and routines   35
        Struggling to be assertive   36
        Struggling to be an advocate   37
        Differentiating between ideal and real practice expectations   38
        Playing the nurse/midwife-doctor game   40
        Managing collegial relations   41
        Dealing with organizational and health care system problems   42
        Managing self-esteem and worthiness problems   44
    Ensuring quality practice through reflective processes   44

Summary	45
Key points	46
2 Preparing for reflection	**48**
Introduction	48
Qualities for reflecting	48
Taking and making the time	48
Making the effort	49
Being determined	49
Having courage	49
Using humour	50
Summary	51
A kitbag of strategies	51
Writing	52
Audiotaping	53
Creative music	54
Dancing	55
Drawing	55
Montage	56
Painting	56
Poetry	57
Pottery	57
Quilting	58
Singing	58
Videotaping	58
Summary	59
Hints for reflecting	59
Be spontaneous	60
Express yourself freely	60
Remain open to ideas	60
Choose a time and place to suit you	61
Be prepared personally	61
Choose suitable reflective methods	61
Summary	62
A reflective exercise	62
The role of a critical friend	64
Encouraging reflective questioning	65
Conclusion	68
Key points	69
3 The Taylor model of reflection	**71**
Introduction	71
Explanation of the diagrammatic representation	71

Readiness 73
Exercising thought 75
Following systematic processes 76
Leaving oneself open to answers 79
Enfolding insights 80
Changing awareness 81
Tenacity in maintaining reflection 82
Summary 83
Key points 83

4   Types of reflection 86
Introduction 86
Caution about categories 86
Knowledge in nursing and midwifery 88
Empirical knowledge 91
Interpretive knowledge 92
Critical knowledge 95
Knowledge and human interests 98
Technical interest and work 98
Practical interest and interaction 99
Emancipatory interest and power 99
Three types of reflection 100
Technical reflection 101
Practical reflection 102
Emancipatory reflection 103
Choosing a type of reflection 103
Critical thinking and reflection 105
Definitions of critical thinking 105
Component parts 106
Skills and attitudes 107
The relation of critical thinking to reflection 109
Other ways of 'thinking' in reflection 109
Summary 111
Key points 111

5   Technical reflection 116
Introduction 116
Review of previous ideas 119
The process of technical reflection 122
Assessing and planning 124
Implementing 125
Evaluating 126
An example of technical reflection 126

Assessing and planning	127
Implementing	128
Evaluating	130
Summary	131
Key points	132

6 Practical reflection 133
Introduction 133
Review of previous ideas 135
The process of practical reflection 137
Experiencing 138
Interpreting 139
Learning 140
An example of practical reflection 140
Experiencing 141
Interpreting 141
Learning 144
Summary 145
Key points 145

7 Emancipatory reflection 147
Introduction 147
Review of previous ideas 150
The process of emancipatory reflection 151
Constructing 152
Deconstructing 153
Confronting 154
Reconstructing 154
An example of emancipatory reflection 156
Constructing 157
Deconstructing 157
Confronting 158
Reconstructing 161
Summary 161
Key points 162

8 Reflective practice in research and scholarship 164
Introduction 164
Incorporating reflective practice into research methodologies 165
Types of research 165
Possible applications of reflection in research 167
The reflective research approach 167
Summary 174

Reflective processes in other research approaches   175
Research involving reflection and action research   177
Combining reflection and action research   178
  Facilitating an action research and reflection group   179
  Nursing research projects using reflection and action research   184
  Summary   185
Fostering scholarship   186
  Presenting your reflective research at a professional conference   186
  Writing a journal article   191
Summary   194
Key points   194

9 Reflection as a lifelong process   196
Introduction   196
Maintaining reflective practice   196
  Affirming yourself as a reflective practitioner   196
  Responding to the critiques   197
  Creating a daily habit   198
  Seeing things freshly   199
  Staying alert to practice   200
  Finding support systems   201
  Sharing reflection   201
  Getting involved in research   202
  Embodying reflective practice   202

10 Conclusion   205
  Key points   210

References   212
Index   221

Introduction

I have really enjoyed writing the second edition of this book, because it gave me a chance to make it even better than the first edition. Life does not give us many chances to go back and do it again, so I was pleased to revisit this book and do some things a little differently this time. For example, readers tell me how much they love reading the practice stories, so there are many more of them in this edition. In addition, I have included more critical friend responses to the practice stories to demonstrate reflective discussions. The literature has been extended to include recent trends and research in reflective practice. Critiques and debates of reflective practice are described in this book and these are welcomed, as any practice innovation worth its positive reputation must be open to constructive criticism. Other important inclusions in this book are the reflectors, which invite you to reflect on your life and work.

For example, in Chapter 2 I invite you to reflect on some of your child-hood memories to locate some rules for living that may now influence the way you work. As a teacher, I usually try to undertake the tasks I construct for students, so I am happy to share with you how I have responded to this reflector.

I was born in Burnie, Tasmania, on Sunday, in the very early morning on the ninth day of September 1951. I was the fourth child of my father Leonard and my mother Johanna. One of my first recollections is as a 3-year-old child. I was standing near a sunny wall at my home at Round Hill near Burnie, and someone holding a box Brownie camera, said: 'Watch the birdie!' I kept looking and looking, but I did not see a birdie. I'll come back to this story later. The second memory is when I was older, around 7 years old, when I remember contemplating infinity, imagining space beyond space beyond space.

From the time I was 5 years of age, my family lived in a working-class housing estate in Burnie, called Acton Estate. It was the kind of neighbour-hood where kids walked along the top railing of fences, played cricket on the road and ran everywhere they had to go. As a child I was physically healthy and most of my free time was spent at the beach, because I loved swimming. The people who were important to me were my mum, dad, grandmother Eva, brothers Kenny, Bobby and Allan, and my only sister Di. These people were important to me because they loved me, I loved them, and I knew I could trust them for basic things, like loyalty and protection.

Our home seemed large to my child's eyes, but I have been back to Grenville Street since as an adult and I have realized how small our housing commission home really was! I remember the unpretentious manner with which we related to one another; kids roaming relatively freely in bare feet and hand-me-down clothes, wrangling with and sticking up for one another, within a straight-talking yet mostly benevolent autocracy ruled over firmly by my father, and by my mother when dad was away working in the bush as an axeman. I have not regained that sense of carefree belonging and familiarity since those days at Grenville Street, where I knew that I belonged to my family and that my father, mother and grandmother were there to love, care for and protect me.

Other important influences in my childhood were my cat 'Tom', who rode patiently around in my pram and taught me about caring for someone beyond myself. The Hobbs kids next door, who enjoyed even less childhood luxuries than we Bugg kids, taught me about being happy with next to nothing of a material nature, and of speaking up for myself to win a share of whatever good things were on offer, such as freshly baked biscuits or who batted next in the backyard game of rounders. I was also influenced by the local Baptist church, of which I was a serious member. It was at Sunday School that I learned to 'do unto others as you would have them do unto you'. Other rules of living I learned around then were related to 'being a good girl'. I remember winning a competition at Sunday School for the person who could remain most silent for the longest time. I won it hands down, because I found it very simple to do as I was told.

I wanted to become a nurse so that I could 'evangelize' India. I had this arrogant notion that people in India needed me and I was filled with an altruistic zeal to save their souls, while I nursed their wounds. I imagined myself as an all-encompassing helper. By the time I decided to do nursing, I had lost these ideas and settled instead for doing nursing for the joys of the practice itself, plus the kudos of acquiring certificates and having a full-time, reliable job. My personal approach to practice was conscientious. I won the hospital medal for the 'best bedside manner', and even though I know I was worthy of that prize, I suspect that the award was really for being a very hard-working nurse. In the second year of my general training I stopped running around at full speed and with immense anxiety, and actually noticed that the people in the beds were humans, with all the hopes and fears I possessed.

There were many childhood ways of seeing the world that I brought with me into adulthood, but I'll focus on two I mentioned before – the memories of the little girl standing in front of the sunny wall and the infinity-imagining 7-year-old, who won the 'best child' award in Sunday School. The little girl waiting for the birdie is the optimistic adult in me now, who waits patiently for something lovely to happen. Sometimes I'm disappointed, and sometimes I'm thrilled by what transpires, but I retain a sense of anticipation and, to some extent, trust and patience. The little girl in Sunday School still knows how to stay quiet when it matters, and she works hard at doing things correctly and on time. She organizes herself well and puts a lot of time into pleasing other people, while imagining deep and mysterious concepts, often of a metaphysical nature.

Some 'rules for living' formed in my childhood have been transferred into my adult work life. I'm not in clinical practice now, but when I was, I always tried to treat people well, in the hope that they would treat me well in return. This rule did not always work, as the people I was 'doing unto' did not necessarily live by the same rule. This meant that I spent a lot of years in selfless service, giving so much of myself to patients, and not expecting anything back. After many years I became a reflective practitioner and, among many huge insights, I realized that I was so busy giving of myself that I did not leave enough space for people to give anything back to me. This came to a head one day when a woman in a postnatal ward gave me a hug for some simple words I offered her. I stayed still and silent and she was able to give me a hug. In my journaling later, I was able to see that my rule for living had been applied so conscientiously that it had kept me from receiving the very thing I hoped for most from my work – the love of the people for whom I cared. This insight was important for learning about myself and my relationships with other people, and it has been applied in many different ways in my life and work since that initial reflection.

This edition brings all of the best aspects of the first book and offers you a lot more, to assist you in becoming a reflective practitioner. For example, in Chapter 1 I describe the nature of reflection and practice. I support Donald Schön's emphasis that reflection is a way in which professionals can bridge the theory-practice gap, based on the potential of reflection to uncover knowledge in and on action. I introduce some reflective practice literature relating to practice, clinical supervision and research, and I introduce technical, practical and emancipatory reflection and describe work constraints that affect the way nurses and midwives work.

In Chapter 2 I suggest ways of preparing for reflection, because it takes time, effort, determination, courage and humour to initiate and maintain effective reflection. There are many strategies you can use when engaging in systematic reflection, such as writing, audiotaping, creating music, dancing, drawing, montage, painting, poetry, pottery, quilting, singing and videotaping. I share hints for reflecting, such being spontaneous, expressing yourself freely, remaining open to ideas, choosing a time and place to suit you, being prepared personally, and choosing suitable reflective methods. In addition, I discuss the role of a critical friend, who can offer external perspectives to extend your reflective capacity, by asking important questions and making tentative suggestions to unseat your previous perceptions, to find other possibilities and insights.

In Chapter 3 I introduce the 'Taylor model of reflection' as a systematic flow approach to successful reflection. The model uses a mnemonic device of the word REFLECT, to represent Readiness, Exercising thought, Following systematic processes, Leaving oneself open to answers, Enfolding insights, Changing awareness, and Tenacity in maintaining reflection, in and through practice, within the context of self in relation to other people, within the ground of internal historical, cultural, economic, social and political constraints, orbited by and in the contact with external forces and influences.

In Chapter 4 I introduce three main types of reflection: technical, practical and emancipatory. Empirical knowledge comes from technical reflection, interpretive knowledge comes from practical reflection and critical knowledge comes from emancipatory reflection. It is important to consider these categories as ways of creating temporary frameworks on which to hang certain broad principles, because knowledge and reflection defy absolute categorization.

In Chapter 5 I describe technical reflection. I base technical reflection on Bandman and Bandman's (1995) view of scientific reasoning and the functions of critical thinkers, the features of critical thinking and thinkers described by van Hooft *et al.* (1995), and the problem-solving steps of the nursing process (Wilkinson 1996).

In Chapter 6 I describe practical reflection, which is derived from the work of Smyth (1986a, 1986b) and Street (1991), with an adaptation to emphasize the communicative nature of this type of reflection, within the process of experiencing, interpreting and learning.

In Chapter 7 I describe emancipatory reflection, as a process that provides you with a systematic means of critiquing the status quo in the power relationships in your workplace and which offers you raised awareness and a new sense of informed consciousness, to bring about positive social and political change. The emancipatory reflective process constructs, confronts, deconstructs and reconstructs your practice.

In Chapter 8 I describe reflective practice in research and scholarship. I suggest that reflective processes may be used solely as the research approach, or they may be integrated into other research approaches. I describe the main modes of scholarship development in nursing and midwifery, by giving you a step-by-step guide in how to prepare professional conference presentations and publications.

In Chapter 9 I suggest that you maintain your reflective practice by affirming yourself as a reflective practitioner, responding to the critiques, creating a daily habit, seeing things freshly, staying alert to practice, finding support systems, sharing reflection, getting involved in research and embodying reflective practice.

Enjoy your life, your work and this book.

1 The nature of reflection and practice

Introduction

Humans have the potential to think, and to think about thinking, because we are endowed with the gifts of memory and reflection. When we take time to reflect, we allow ourselves to attune to deeper levels of awareness, even if only in momentary flashes, as we raise thoughts to consciousness. That is not to say that we always turn our reflection towards useful or noble pursuits, such as to improve our lives or someone else's, because we have the power of choice and we can live life as we choose, even if it means our reasoned choices are at someone else's expense.

Thinking can be a gift and a curse, depending on how we employ it in our daily lives. For example, we can orientate our thinking towards our own peacefulness, or towards the perpetuation of anxiety. At times we can reflect for the sheer joy of thinking, to fill an empty moment, to create new ideas, to imagine, to hope, to reminisce, and to consider possibilities and purposeful actions. At other times, we may use thinking to plot revenge, to open old emotional wounds, to churn over old anxieties, and to create unrest within ourselves and other people. Therefore, intentions and outcomes of reflection differ, according to why they are employed and by whom, so a personal philosophy of reflection is implicit in human experiences. This book assumes that nurses and midwives will orientate towards useful and positive thinking, that has the potential to improve their lives as people and clinicians, and therefore has an ongoing beneficial effect on themselves and the people with whom they interact.

This chapter introduces you to the nature of reflection and practice, by covering definitions and sources of reflection, and recent and relevant literature pertaining to reflective practice in nursing and midwifery internationally. The nature of nursing and midwifery practice is explored, to demonstrate why reflective processes are necessary for quality care.

Definitions and perspectives of reflection

In the physical world, reflection means throwing back from a surface, such as that creating heat, sound or light. In connection with human reflection, I extend the definition to the throwing back of thoughts and memories, in cognitive acts such as thinking, contemplation, meditation and any other form of attentive consideration, in order to make sense of them, and to make contextually appropriate changes if they are required (Taylor 2000: 3). This comprehensive definition allows for a wide variety of thinking as the basis for reflection, but it is similar to many other explanations (Mezirow 1981; Boyd and Fales 1983; Boud *et al.* 1985; Street 1992) due to the inclusion of the two main aspects of thinking as a rational and intuitive process, which allows the potential for change.

The most notable name in the general reflective practice literature is Donald Schön, who emphasized the idea that reflection is a way in which professionals can bridge the theory-practice gap, based on the potential of reflection to uncover knowledge in and on action (Schön 1983). He acknowledged the working intelligence of practitioners, and their potential to make sense of their work in a theoretical way, even though they might tend to underestimate their practical knowledge. He referred to tacit knowledge, or knowing in action, as the kind of knowledge of which they may not be entirely aware.

When clinicians, such as nurses and midwives, are coached to make their knowing in action explicit, they can inevitably use this awareness to enliven and change their practice (Schön 1987). Interestingly, this assumes that reflection is not a natural state, known without introduction, to all people who engage in practice. Schön realized that systematic processes need to be guided experiences, so that practitioners can derive the best possible outcomes from them.

Reflector

Do you think you have tacit knowledge about your practice? If it is tacit, how will you get to know what it is?

Argyris and Schön (1974) and Argyris *et al.* (1985) suggested that practitioners often practise at less than effective levels, because they follow routine. Furthermore, their actual practice does not necessarily coincide with their 'better knowledge' or espoused theories about good practice. In fact, as Kim (1999) suggests, they may not even be aware of this divergence. Praxis is different practice as a result of reflection, which encompasses a change in the status quo of nursing and midwifery practice (Taylor 2000). As Kim (1999: 4) states:

through the researcher's questioning and probing, practitioners can engage in self-dialogue and argumentation with themselves in order to clarify validity claims embedded in their actions, bringing forth the hidden meanings and disguises that systematically result in self-oriented and unilateral actions or ineffective habitual forms of practice.

Nursing and midwifery have applied reflective practice ideas to many of their disciplinary areas. In particular, nursing has used reflective processes for some time, for example, to improve practice and practice development (Taylor 2000, 2002a, 2002b; Thorpe and Barsky 2001; Stickley and Freshwater 2002; Johns 2003), clinical supervision (Todd and Freshwater 1999; Heath and Freshwater 2000; Gilbert 2001), and education (Cruickshank 1996; Freshwater 1999a, 1999b; Kim 1999; Anderson and Branch 2000; Clegg 2000; Platzer *et al.* 2000a, 2000b).

Practice and practice development

Much of the literature focuses on the work of nursing, as practised in clinical contexts (e.g. Freshwater 1998, 2002a, 2002b; Heath 1998a, 1998b; Glaze 1999; C. Johns 2000, 2003; B.J. Taylor 2002a, 2002b, 2003, 2004; Wilkin 2002). Freshwater (1998) provided a meta-analysis of reflection and caring using the analogy of the acorn becoming an oak tree. To emphasize the role of reflection in nurses' personal and professional development, Freshwater used an awakening and growth analogy, when she claimed:

> Reflective practice can be viewed as the call to awake. It is also a process of becoming, being with the unfolding moment . . . Reflective practice helps us to explore what is just beyond the line of vision, it encourages us not to stare straight ahead, but to turn around . . . In the context of acorn theory, reflective practice can be seen as a way of viewing the unfolding drama of the nurse becoming . . .
>
> (Freshwater 1998: 16)

Heath (1998a) described the experiences of clinicians in keeping reflective journals of their practice. Based on the experiences of continuing education students, Heath was able to offer practical guidance in writing reflectively, to gain deeper levels of reflective awareness in learning, practice implications, relevance and applicability, conclusions and wider context constraints and action.

Heath (1998b) also extended Carper's (1978) patterns of knowing, already integrated into Johns' (1994) model of guided reflection, to include two further patterns of unknowing and sociopolitical knowing. Heath (1998b) suggested that nurses may have difficulty applying knowledge forms to their practice and see it is an academic exercise, not immediately urgent in their busy work settings. Hence, the extension of knowledge into the unknown and sociopolitical categories creates room for movement in practice that captures clinical concerns.

Glaze (1999: 30) described reflection, clinical judgement and staff development 'to encourage perioperative nurses to reflect on their practice'. She used exemplars of expert practice 'to illustrate how knowledge is used and developed in the practice setting'. The outcomes of reflection include practical advice and insights into how perioperative nurses may improve their practice.

C. Johns (2000: 199) reflected on his own practice of 'working with Alice', which assisted him to draw 'out key issues of practice and reflection that enabled [him] to gain insight and apply to future practice within a reflexive learning spiral'. Through clear and thoughtful writing, Johns describes Alice's appearance, their conversation, and his part it in, reflecting in action on his words and their affect on Alice. Through this encounter he was able to raise reflective questions for himself and other nurses in the unit in relation to Alice's care.

Freshwater (2002a) connects a nurse's deeper sense of self to healing outcomes of a therapeutic nature for patients, and contends that the 'practice of reflection is a central skill in developing an awareness of self' (p. 5). In creating possibilities for therapeutic nursing, nurses examine self as workers, learners and researchers, to transform self-awareness into a process through which patients feel cared for and acknowledged within 'the context of a therapeutic alliance' (p. 10).

Reflector

Do you agree with Dawn Freshwater that a deeper sense of self is important in providing therapeutic practice? Why? What areas of your sense of self need further exploration?

Freshwater (2002a: 225) describes the importance of 'guided reflection in the context of post-modern practice'. Freshwater asserts that self-awareness 'is deemed to be central to the process of successful reflection, with the "self" being the main instrument of both the practice and guidance of reflection'. In a postmodern description of the process of guided reflection, Freshwater explores 'some of the reflections that took place in the pauses between the lines of the text in the act of looking up from the reading' in order to 'bring light to bear in certain elements of the text, whilst recognizing that this casts a shadow on other expects of the dialogue' (p. 225). In this chapter Freshwater deftly captures the postmodern conundrum of partialities, gaps, silences and shifts in meaning, while resting on the assurance that an exploration of self is a reflective exercise that offers some insights into local truths.

Wilkin (2002) explored expert practice through reflection, by focusing on a clinical experience of caring for a 12-year-old boy diagnosed with brain death, and her experience of remaining on duty in the unit to facilitate the parents' wishes concerning his care. Wilkin (p. 88) used 'the unusual experience . . . to enable self-criticism and expansion of personal knowledge', in order to explore the complexity of expert practice and to facilitate holistic care.

B.J. Taylor's writing centres on reflection in nursing practice, for example, in giving advice for technical, practical and emancipatory reflection for practising holistically (2004), describing emancipatory reflective practice for overcoming complexities and constraints in holistic health care (2003), giving guidance in technical reflection for improving nursing procedures using critical thinking in evidence-based practice (2002a), and on becoming a reflective nurse or midwife, using complementary therapies while practising holistically (2000).

Clinical supervision

Reflective practice has been applied effectively to clinical supervision (Todd and Freshwater 1999; Heath and Freshwater 2000). Todd and Freshwater (1999: 1383) examined the 'parallels and processes of a model of reflection in an individual clinical supervision session, and the use of guided discovery'. The authors advocate reflective practice as a model for clinical supervision 'because it provides safe space that facilitates a collaborative and empowering relationship which enables the practitioner to experience a journey of discovery in examining his/her everyday practice' (p. 1388).

Heath and Freshwater (2000: 1298) used 'Johns' (1996) intent-emphasis axis to explore how a technical interest, misunderstanding of expert practice and confusion of self awareness with counselling can detract from the supervisory process'. They examined the nature of clinical supervision and reflective practice and how the two can combine effectively, especially when supervisors are reflective about their roles, and the clinical supervision experience is a guided reflection that enables deeper insights for the supervisee and supervisor.

Gilbert (2001: 199) focused on the 'meticulous rituals of the confessional' and the potential for reflective practice and clinical supervision to act as 'modes of surveillance disciplining the action of professionals'. Using Foucault's (1982) concept of governmentality, Gilbert argued that, like governments, health settings act as 'forms of moral regulation' in which professionals exercise power through 'the complex web of discourses and social practices that characterize their work' (2001: 199). In critiquing the discourses of empowerment that underlie the emancipatory intent of reflective practice and clinical supervision, he identifies the tendency of empowerment discourses to assume 'the existence of a damaged subject-traditional and rule bound [who] requires remedial work ... to achieve forms of subjectivity consistent with modern forms of rule' (p. 205).

Reflector

Imagine that you are responding to Gilbert's criticism that reflection may act as a source of surveillance and confession. In what ways might this criticism be valid? In what ways might it be invalid?

Clouder and Sellars (2004: 262) wrote from the perspective of a physiotherapist, using research conducted with undergraduate occupational therapy and physiotherapy students, to 'contribute to the debate about the functions of clinical supervision and reflective practice in nursing and other health care professions'. The authors responded to Gilbert's (2001) criticism of the sterility of debates about reflection and clinical supervision, and the potential for moral regulation and surveillance. They concluded that although both strategies make individuals more visible within the gaze of the workplace, Gilbert 'overlooked the possibility of resistance and the scope for personal agency within systems of surveillance, that create tensions between personal and professional accountability'.

Education

Reflective practice in nurse education is integral to effective outcomes (Cruickshank 1996; Freshwater 1999a, 1999b; Kim 1999; Anderson and Branch 2000; Clegg 2000; Platzer *et al.* 2000a, 2000b; Lian 2001; Kenny 2003).

Cruickshank (1996: 127) used the medium of drawing to 'allow students to express learning that occurred on their clinical placement'. The nursing students were enrolled in an undergraduate programme based on the philosophy of critical social theory, underpinned by notions of emancipation, empowerment and raised consciousness. The students were divided into small groups of six to eight people, and asked to draw their learning on a large sheet of cardboard. The themes that emerged from one hour of the process were representative of the technical, practical and emancipatory forms of knowledge they observed within nursing practice and experienced within their curriculum.

Kim (1999: 1205) presented 'a method of inquiry which uses nurses' situated, individual instances of nursing practice as the basis for developing knowledge for nursing and improving practice'. Using ideas from action science, critical philosophy and reflective practice, she described a critical reflective inquiry method and process that allows nurses to raise their awareness of their work constraints to free themselves towards more informed and liberating insights about their work.

Freshwater (1999b: 28) undertook a research project to explore 'the lived experience of student nurses during a three year Diploma of Nursing program'. The students and tutor (researcher) examined 'how their own personal stories interfaced with those of the patient'. The students and tutor kept a reflective journal pertaining to their experiences of moving from perceived levels of novice to expert nurse. The project demonstrated how self-awareness through reflective practice and other strategies, such as clinical supervision and experiential learning, enhances personal and professional development in the clinical area.

Anderson and Branch (2000: 1) endorsed the use of storytelling to promote critical reflection in RN students, as 'a mechanism for one to talk about past actions as well as the results to these actions', for giving voice to experiences, and 'revisiting the past for the purpose of shaping the future'. She concluded that 'adult educators can benefit tremendously from further research' that involves creative methodologies, such as storytelling and reflection.

Reflector

In what ways can storytelling be useful for you as a clinician? How does story-telling relate to reflective processes?

Clegg (2000: 451) explored 'the use of reflective practice statements as sources of data' to provide insight into 'the underlying mechanisms at work in organisations', especially in light of 'reflective practice taking on the veneer of educational orthodoxy'. Underlying the exploration was a suspicion that its proponents in nursing, social work and teacher training may have inflated the positive claims of reflective practice. Nevertheless, Clegg (p. 467) suggested that 'reflective practice in higher education can provide a useful and insightful tool for knowledge production'.

Platzer et al. (2000a: 689) set up reflective practice groups in a post-registration nursing course 'to enable students to reflect on and learn from their experience'. The learning was evaluated through in-depth interviews and although students identified barriers to their learning, 'some students made significant developments in their critical thinking ability and underwent perspective transformations that led to changes in attitudes and behaviours'.

Kenny (2003: 105) described 'the use of a creative thinking game to stimulate critical thinking and reflection with qualified health professionals undertaking palliative care education'. The idea to use Edward de Bono's six hats game came about because she was concerned that many reflective practice models were 'either too simple or too complex to be valuable in practice'. The six hats game stimulated students to use a variety of thinking techniques and thereby unleashed their creative and critical thinking processes to be more effective in reflection.

The value of reflection in nurse education has been debated for some time (Driscoll 1994; James and Clarke 1994; Newell 1994; Palmer *et al.* 1994; Burrows 1995; Hulatt 1995), but the conclusion is that it is important for teaching and learning (e.g., Posner 1989; Atkins 1995; Johns 1995a, 1995b; Smith 1998; Hannigan 2001; Noveletsky-Rosenthal and Solomon 2001; Freshwater 2002a, 2002b; Lau 2002; Evans 2003; Kuiper 2004).

Criticisms of reflective practice

Even though it has proved successful, critics have perceived limitations in reflective practice. For example, there has been criticism of how the nursing profession seized on the idea of reflection (Jarvis 1992). Greenwood (1993) took issue with the underpinning of Schön's idea of reflection that proposed that theories, which underpin reflective activity, are difficult to articulate, as they are embedded in activity itself.

Other concerns and criticisms have been that there may be a high degree of personal investment required by midwives for successful practice outcomes (Taylor 1997), barriers to learning must be overcome before midwives and nurses reflect effectively (Platzer *et al.* 2000b), there may be cultural barriers to empowerment through reflection (Johns 1999), negative consequences may ensue when practitioners are pressured to reflect (Hulatt 1995), reflection is a fundamentally flawed strategy (Mackintosh 1998), there are potential dangers in promoting 'private thoughts in public spheres' (Cotton 2001), reflective processes have failed to 'address the postmodern, cultural contexts of reflection' (Pryce 2002), and there is a lack of research evidence to support the mandate to reflect (Burton 2000).

Ghaye and Lillyman (2000) critically reviewed the foundations and criticisms of reflective practice to question whether reflective practitioners were really 'fashion victims', and having explored the limitations of it, concluded that reflective practice has a place in the postmodern world, because of its ability to explore micro levels of human interaction and personal knowledge. Contrastingly, C. Taylor (2003: 244) argued that 'reflective practice tends to adopt a naïve or romantic realist position and fails to acknowledge the ways in which reflective accounts construct the world of practice'.

Reflector

C. Taylor argues that reflective accounts 'construct the world of practice'. What does she mean by this? Look at Chapter 9 in the section on responding to critiques, if you are having difficulty thinking of what this might mean.

Nurses have responded directly to critics (e.g., Sargent 2001; Markham 2002; Rolfe 2003) and in spite of the concerns and critiques, clinicians, educators and researchers tend to agree that although reflective practice has its limitations, and requires time, effort and ongoing commitment, it is nevertheless worth the effort to bring about deeper insights and changes in practice, leadership, clinical supervision and education.

Types of reflection

In this book I reiterate my previously stated position that it simplifies the enormous task of thinking about reflection if we imagine that there are three main types of reflection useful for people engaged in any kind of practice – technical, practical and emancipatory reflection.

Technical reflection, based on the scientific method and rational, deductive thinking, will allow you to generate and validate empirical knowledge through rigorous means, so that you can be assured that work procedures are based on scientific reasoning. This means that you will develop an objective method for working out how to make policies and procedures better, by exposing your technical work issues to systematic questioning and coherent argumentation and revision. For example, you may want to update a procedure, or argue whether a policy is still appropriate. Technical reflection gives you the knowledge and skills of critical thinking and provides a framework for questioning, which results in an objective, well argued position to support any adaptations and improvements needed.

Practical reflection leads to interpretation for description and explanation of human interaction in social existence. This simply means that you can use this type of reflection to improve the way you communicate with other people at work, thereby improving your practice enjoyment and outcomes. For example, you may identify a dysfunctional communication pattern with other staff, such as peers, doctors and allied staff. Practical reflection provides a systematic questioning process that encourages you to reflect deeply on role relationships, to locate their dynamics and habitual issues, so that changes can be made to improve communication.

Emancipatory reflection leads to 'transformative action', which seeks to free you from taken-for-granted assumptions and oppressive forces, which limit you and your practice. In other words, this type of reflection lets you see what subtle and not so subtle powerful forces and circumstances are holding you back from achieving your goals. When you have an increased awareness, you have taken the first step in making some changes in the ways you think about and overcome these constraints. For example, you may identify powerlessness at work in relation to making clinical decisions in your work. Emancipatory reflection provides a systematic questioning process to help you to locate the bases of the problem, identify the constraints and begin to address the issues, either alone or through collaborative action with other nurses or midwives.

Work and life issues and challenges do not fit easily into regular compartments, so I make the point now, and reiterate later, that the types of reflection can be used alone or in any combination you choose, to address the work issues in your practice. All kinds of knowledge can be generated through reflection and nurses and midwives can benefit from a range of reflective processes.

Sources of reflection

Life is a source of reflection, because it is an energized process through which humans are embodied to live daily as individuals and act in relation to other people and contexts. Taking an active interest in life through reflection turns one's existence into something more than the mere passing of time. When life and all of its expressions, such as events, circumstances, symbols and relationships with other people and our environments come into clearer and finer focus, life has the potential to be more meaningful. Plato was so convinced with the power of reflection that he declared 'The unreflected life is not worth living'. While death seems a severe alternative to thoughtlessness, reflection can turn an unconsidered life into an existence, which is consciously aware, self-potentiating and purposeful.

Within human existence, traditions and rituals become sustained over time, such as work and leisure, philosophies, disciplines, art and religious beliefs. These form rich sources of reflection and they can in turn facilitate further reflection. Unpaid and paid work hours may take up significant time in the overall time apportioned to a human life, so if reflective attention is focused on work rituals, habits and routines, the drudgery and obligation to pay the bills or fill in idle time can be transformed into life and work insights and changes. Leisure time can be given over to thoughtfulness, as time and space is taken to reflect outside the recurrent demands of work responsibilities.

Philosophies share the love of knowledge and philosophers ask the perennial question: what is existence and what is knowledge? This question and associated enquiries is asked over and over in new circles, in the light of previously reflected and debated positions, to create new paradigms. Through reflection, disciplines such philosophy and sociology continually generate ever-increasing and refined knowledge. Practice disciplines, such as nursing, midwifery and education, use reflection to identify and refine their practice bases and to find meaning in the work.

Through the inspiration of creativity and reflection artists of all kinds create novel representations of life, such as paintings, pottery, ceramics, music, sculpture, literature and poetry. Art comes from a creative and thoughtful source and we respond to it through a similar process, as it 'speaks' to us. Novel images, textures, sounds and forms are assimilated into the repertoire of 'givens' in our lives in that very moment we experience them through our senses, making the unfamiliar familiar through an instantaneous reflective awareness. Just as we find every human face familiar as we take our first fleeting glimpse, so we have the capacity to 'take on board' newness, strangeness and difference in the flash of a thought.

Through religious and spiritual practices, humans reflect on the nature of human life and its potential connections with higher consciousness. World religions of all faiths and denominations differ in their definitions of a supreme entity, although they agree that a sense of daily closeness to that entity comes through some form of reflection and supplication. Because humans have the capacity for thought, they also have the potential to imagine something or someone greater than themselves.

Reflector

Do you agree with Plato that the 'unreflected life is not worth living'. Take some time to discuss this question with a friend. Try taking opposite positions in answering it and see which one best approximates your approach to being reflective at this time in your life.

There is value in reflection, even if it does not achieve the importance in your life ascribed to it by Plato. The value comes from the process of thinking itself and the possibilities that engagement offers. Imagine a world in which all actions towards people and the environment are unconsidered and the outcomes of those actions are unreflected. What happens to social order and welfare in an unreflected human existence? Even when people have strong moral bases and nations appear to have well-developed social consciences, inequalities, prejudice, greed, famine, genocide, wars and other crimes against humanity still occur. At this worldwide level, reflection becomes the basis for history, the present, and the future. If people do not consider the events of their past, they are unable to take advantage of the present and powerless to shape their future, because they will remain oblivious to patterns, habits, trends and forces that shape their lives and those of the wider human community.

In this book I place a strongly positive light on the value of reflection, because it has the potential for making sense of the past and present, to project you forward into a more considered future as a person and as a worker. Nurses and midwives are busy people, who work hard in their daily work. I am of the opinion that if you become convinced of the value of reflection in your life and work, and that if you take time to practise reflective thinking as an everyday habit, you will experience personal and professional benefits. Reflection is not magical; it is a daily commitment to thinking systematically and purpose-fully, to raise your awareness and potentiate positive changes.

The nature of nursing and midwifery

The complexity of nursing and midwifery means that it is not a simple job to be effective in your work. With so many tasks, roles, relationships, expect-ations and unforeseen aspects to negotiate, it is no wonder that practice has a tendency to become chaotic and unpredictable, and that nurses and midwives leave their professions to secure less demanding work. In the relative madness that makes up a 'good' work day, the least you might hope for is that your work will be safe and polite, and at the very best that it will be therapeutic and genuine. This book envisages helping you move towards therapeutic and genuine practice, by helping you to identify and act on those factors that prevent you from being as effective as you might ideally hope to be on a regular basis at work.

Nursing

Nursing has been described from Nightingale to the present day and many of the definitions vary according to perceptions of the roles, responsibilities and relationships of nurses with patients (Marriner-Tomey and Alligood 2002). Refer to Table 1.1 to see how definitions of nursing have changed over time.

Reflector

If you have had nursing experience, how do you define nursing? If you have not had nursing experience, what definition(s) of nursing do you prefer in Table 1.1? In answering this question, reflect on why you have chosen this definition against other possibilities.

Midwifery

The term 'midwife' means 'a woman who is with the mother at birth' (Oakley and Houd 1990: 17). Women have been attending other women in birthing since time began. Midwifery is a growing practice discipline, having struggled in the twentieth century to regain its power and autonomy and to resituate the experiences of women and babies back into a health model of women-centred care. For this reason, there is to date not much theory which is midwifery-exclusive, but midwifery enjoys a very proud history, which dates back to well before the time of the 'wise women' who were also suspected of being witches.

Midwives work with mothers and their partners and families throughout the various phases of the pregnancy, birth and postnatal periods. With their

Table 1.1 A chronology of definitions of nursing

Nightingale (1893 in Seymer 1955: 33)	'[Nursing puts] us in the best possible conditions for Nature to restore or to preserve health – to prevent or to cure disease or injury'.
Frederick and Northam (1938: 3)	'Nursing requires the application of scientific knowledge and nursing skills and affords the opportunities for constructive work in the care and relief of patients and their families'.
Peplau (1952: 16)	Nursing is 'a significant, therapeutic, interpersonal process'.
Henderson (1955: 4)	'Nursing is primarily assisting the individual (sick or well) in the performance of those activities contributing to health, or its recovery (or to a peaceful death) that he would perform unaided if he had the necessary strength, will, or knowledge'.
Orem (1959) and Kinlein (1977)	Nursing involves self-care, putting the responsibility back into the hands of the person receiving care, with the nurse giving assistance only as required.
Abdellah et al. (1960: 24)	'Nursing is a service to individuals and to families; therefore, to society. It is based upon an art and science which mold the attitudes, intellectual competencies, and technical skills of the individual nurse into the desire and ability to help people, sick or well, cope with their health needs, and may be carried out under general or specific medical direction'.
Orlando (1961), Rogers (1961), Wiedenbach (1964)	These authors agree with the supportive role of the nurse depicted by Nightingale, Henderson, Orem, Kinlein and Abdellah et al.
Travelbee (1971: 7)	Nursing is 'an interpersonal process whereby the professional nurse practitioner assists an individual, family, or community to prevent or cope with the experience of illness and suffering and, if necessary, to find meaning in these experiences'.
King (1971: 22)	Nursing is supportive in 'a process of action, reaction, interaction, and transaction'.
Roy (1976: 18)	Nursing is about supporting people's adaptation.
Paterson and Zderad (1976: 51)	Nursing is 'the act of nursing, the intersubjective transactional relation, the dialogue experience, lived in concert between persons where comfort and nurturance prod mutual unfolding'.
Watson (1981), Benner (1984), Leininger (1985), Pearson (1988), Benner and Wrubel (1989)	Nursing is holistic caring, involving transcultural sensitivity and practice expertise, encompassing the therapeutic effect of the nurse-patient relationship.
Kermode and Brown (1996), Keleher and McInerney (1998), Taylor (2000)	Nursing is part of a postmodern world, in which ideas are left open to question and there can be no absolute definition of nursing.

knowledge and skills, midwives facilitate the processes surrounding birth for the general well-being of all the people concerned. Experienced midwives work in seemingly effortless ways to bring together all components of the pregnancy, birth and postnatal periods into a process which is perceived as a continuous human event by women, their partners, family and friends. The work of midwifery has great value in creating those conditions in which mothers and others feel 'cared for' by midwives. Midwives are key people for women facing birth and child care afterwards and, sometimes, for facing lost hopes and dreams of a new child and family. Midwifery practice is valued for its ability to make a difference in the lives of women and the people with whom they relate.

Even though midwifery has been keen to divorce itself from biomedical influences, midwives may be willing to align with some of nursing's theoretical content, especially those parts which emphasize holism and client-centred care. The relationship between nursing and midwifery has been affected by male-dominated medicine. The controlling influence of nurses by doctors was established by the time of Florence Nightingale, and the bio-medical view of illness became entrenched, favouring the reduction of people to their smallest and most manageable parts. Midwifery has been keen to rid itself of the biomedical view of people, and the perspective that pregnancy, labour and delivery are disease states requiring active medical monitoring and intervention. Successive research and reviews of midwifery practice (World Health Organization 1985; Cunningham 1993; Brown and Lumley 1994; Rothwell 1996; Sullivan and Weitz 1998) have emphasized women's dissatisfaction with maternity services and have called for women-centred birth processes (Couves 1995).

Midwives have been using action research, a collaborative inquiry approach using reflective processes, to assist them in improving their practice (Deery and Kirkham 2000; Barrett 2001; Munroe et al. 2002) and education systems (Fraser 2000; McMorland and Piggott-Irvine 2000).

Barrett (2001) used participatory action research processes to work with mothers in their early mothering period, to improve midwifery practice, by facilitating mothers' satisfaction with their care and experience of early motherhood, while maximizing their informed choices. Barrett met with the new mothers weekly in a mothers' group and by using company, talk and tea in a supportive social milieu, mothers were able to voice their delights, concerns and fears, and they were thereby helpful in assisting midwives to create optimal caring conditions for enhancing early mothering experiences. Deery and Kirkham (2000) used an action research approach to assist midwives to move from hierarchical to collaborative midwifery care, and Munroe et al. (2002) used action research to identify their concerns about the overuse of electronic foetal monitoring in labour and to explore different midwife-led care methods.

Fraser (2000) explored the use of action research to bring about curriculum improvements in a local pre-registration midwifery programme and to influence national policy and guidelines for similar programmes. The action research group found that the action research process of problem identification and collaborative solution finding was an important component of curriculum design to prepare midwives to become competent practitioners. McMorland and Piggott-Irvine (2000: 121) facilitated action research/learning groups in various contexts to 'confront the challenge of assisting people to work and learn together in authentically collaborative ways'. They likened the process to midwifery, in that action research has a 'colaboring' function of 'facilitating the birth of a whole and healthy group process in which honest and bilateral interactions of action and reflection occur'.

Summary

Nursing and midwifery are person-focused helping professions requiring hard work and a strong knowledge and skill base from which to face the daily challenges of practice. Much has been written about the nature and effect of nursing and midwifery in books, journal articles, conference presentations and research projects and the words often present these professions in their most altruistic light, as noble work intended to help others. Reflection reveals the other side of helping that shows itself in sore feet and lost idealism. Interestingly, the rhetoric of ideal practice may unwittingly contribute to the disenchantment nurses and midwives experience when their dreams to help others fade against the daily struggle to manage work responsibilities with diminishing resources. For every dream to help may come the waking reality that there is too much to do, with too little money and staff, for too many people. The contradiction of the 'downsizing' decades is that nurses and midwives are expected to work 'smarter, not harder', while hospitals and health care agencies are run as businesses that must 'break even' or attempt to turn a profit. Where does this leave nurses and midwives intent on staying in their professions and working within the constraints to give the best possible care? Systematic approaches to reflection and action are needed to strengthen your resolve to be effective and happy in your work, because lack of planning and back-up may result in a failure to sustain your work enjoyment and effectiveness.

Reflector

What are your hopes and dreams for becoming a nurse or midwife? Have your hopes and dreams for becoming a nurse or midwife always been realized? What has constrained you from realizing your hopes and dreams for your profession?

The nature of work constraints

When you go to work for an employer you step into a context outside the relative comfort and predictability of your own home. Work is a complex situation where you experience the intersection of different people, and their motives, agendas, and ways of working and interacting, so that routine and unexpected events result in a seemingly endless array of cascading outcomes. With so much happening and with so much at stake in terms of people's health and well-being, it is no wonder that 'things go wrong' in nursing and midwifery.

After years of working with nurses and midwives I realize that they find it relatively easy to blame themselves when 'things go wrong' at work. There are many reasons why nurses and midwives are 'hard on themselves' and we will go into some of these later. The realization that you are not the only thing that can go wrong in your practice may free you from bitter self-recriminations and raise your awareness to be able to transform some or all of the conditions that constrain you. If you recognize your tendency to blame yourself when things go wrong at work, you may be relieved to know that a careful appraisal of the possible constraints on your work practices can show you that many variables interact to construct a complex situation, and that they can be acknowledged and worked on intentionally and systematically, to improve your work satisfaction and effectiveness. It may help you to think of work constraints as being cultural, economic, historical, political, social and personal, and that they may affect the ways in which you are able to interpret and act at any given moment at work.

Cultural constraints

Cultural constraints refer to the determinants that hold people in patterns of interaction within groups, based on the interpretation of shared symbols, rituals and practices. Symbols of nursing and midwifery may include any of the artefacts that comprise practice, such as specific medical language, discourses and 'tools of the trade'. Rituals and practices may include assisting generally with specific patient and mother/baby care, drug rounds, writing clinical notes, doing postnatal checks, and any of the habitual interactions that occur during these practices.

Examples of specific medical language are: 'Mr Jones has circumoral cyanosis and dyspnoea', and 'Ms Smith's contractions are two minutely and strong, and her cervix is seven centimetres dilated and fully effaced'. Discourses are conversations and ways of speaking that convey the relative roles, intentions, status and authority of the speakers. Examples of discourses are:

Nurse: Mr Jones has circumoral cyanosis and dyspnoea.
Doctor: Mr Jones has respiratory distress, sit him upright, give oxygen intranasally, and I'll be there stat.

(The nurse already knew the diagnosis, but did not state it, as that would be to assume a diagnostic role. She also had Mr Jones sitting upright, had made sure he was not alone, and had checked to the orders to ensure oxygen prn was ordered and had begun therapy.)

An example using the midwifery context is:

Midwife: Ms Smith's contractions are two minutely and strong, and her cervix is seven centimetres dilated and fully effaced.
Obstetrician: I'll be there in five minutes.

(The unspoken assumptions of this discourse are that both know Ms Smith is a multigravida – many times pregnant, the final dilatation of the cervix to 10 centimetres is likely to be rapid, and that the baby will be born very soon.)

'Tools of the trade' include all of the equipment and technologies used in practice, how they are used and by whom, to denote cultural norms. Tools of the trade come in all sizes and include infusion pumps, CAT scanners, dialysis machines, fob watches, suture scissors, uniforms, work shoes and identification tags. The public knows who works the equipment and technologies and assigns respect and deference according to the relative importance of these cultural symbols, rituals and practices. For example, greater deference is usually paid to the person operating the CAT scanner than it is to the person taking the patient's temperature.

Rituals and practices form the fabric and culture of daily work and they are plentiful. For example, it is part of health care agency nursing and midwifery cultures to wear a uniform at work. A uniform serves many purposes and maintains a predictable pattern of interpersonal relating. It is a symbol of service and servitude and lets everyone know where nurses and midwives fit in the order of the organization. Doctors do not generally wear uniforms; usually they wear a white coat and they drape a stethoscope around their necks, even if they are not in the vicinity of patients. The symbolic representation of doctors' dress and the draped stethoscope tells people about their role and status in the health care organization. When nurses and midwives in hospitals started draping stethoscopes around their necks, it violated the cultural norm of 'white coat and stethoscope equals doctor'. Similarly, when nurses stopped wearing veils, bonnets, aprons and stripes on their lapels, patients and medical and allied staff bemoaned the lack of identification and hinted at possible drops in standards as the cultural fabric of the organization unravelled.

Over time, cultural expectations are shifting to accommodate changes, not only in nurses' and midwives' dress, but also in their role relationships with medical and allied staff. In some organizations, nurses and midwives do not rush to greet doctors, nor carry their files, nor set up for minor surgical procedures in units, nor rush after them to request written orders, nor accede to an unwritten cultural convention that doctors are 'godlike' and beyond question and reproof. However, in other organizations, and at individual level, cultural conventions of subservience and deference beyond the reasonable bounds of adult–adult communication still control the ways in which nurses and midwives relate to one another, doctors and other staff. Even though cultural constraints may seem to be relatively insignificant in themselves, they are nevertheless very powerful, because they represent shared symbols, rituals and practices that have endured over time as unquestioned assumptions of authority, status and ways of communicating. Nurses and midwives who choose to operate outside the unwritten rules of cultural constraints may find themselves censored and chastised by individuals and the organization to varying degrees.

Reflector

What other examples of cultural constraints can you imagine? If you are having trouble getting started, think about the kind of symbols, rituals, habits and practices that are unquestioned in your workplace, that do not seem to have any reasonable basis, other than that they have endured for some time and define the ways people relate to one another.

Economic constraints

Economic constraints refer to a lack of money and the resources money can provide. If you have been practising for some time as a nurse or a midwife, you are most probably conversant with this constraint and have plenty of examples of it. Money, or lack of it, drives contemporary health care. Each year the 'bad news' about health organization budgets is circulated: financial belts are tightened further, resources are cut, organizations are closed down or downsized, experienced people are offered voluntary redundancy packages, staff-patient ratios suffer or are rationalized by budgetary constraints, and profits are favoured over people – or so it seems for many workplaces.

No constraint exists alone. For example, economic constraints flow out of and into other constraints. A scenario reads like this:

> Statement: The budget looks bleak for next year. Positions must be cut. A new education role had been projected for next year, but it will need to go 'on hold'.
> Question: Who would have occupied that education role?
> Answer: An experienced midwife.

Question: But how does this decision sit with the acquisition of new antenatal diagnostic equipment next year worth the salary of three midwife positions?

In this scenario, cultural and economic constraints combine to work against forward-thinking midwifery practice.

Reflector

What group of people generally win in the competition for economic resources in hospitals? Why?

Not all economic constraints operate at large levels. Even so, they may start at local levels with familiar places and faces and eventually balloon out into far bigger, faceless forums. For example, consider an everyday issue as simple as the allocation of nursing and midwifery staff by their peers to wards and units to cover shifts adequately. In this scenario, nurses and midwives 'control' the allocation of resources within their budget, and they have the responsibility to ensure that health care contexts are staffed adequately. However, the nurse/midwife managers are given finite resources, and they are in turn constrained by bosses up the line in the hierarchy, who in turn may ultimately place the blame for poor staff ratios on the government's health budget. In this manner we perpetuate the blame shifting exercise of: 'it is not my fault, it is someone else's fault'. So when nurses and midwives leave their careers to become shopkeepers or drug reps and care agencies and national governments bemoan the lack of qualified nurses and midwives, who stands up to exposes economic constraints and poor staff ratios, which caused overworked, underpaid nurses and midwives to fall out of enchantment with their practice, because they could bear the constraints no longer?

Reflective practice uncovers the nature and effects of economic constraints and attempts to locate associated constraints, which may or may not be conducive to change. This is not to claim that the reflection alone will fix a budgetary cut, or convince a health minister to leave open a cost-ineffective hospital. No grand claims such as these can be made for reflection, but it can throw a light on economic tendencies and patterns and identify reactions of organizations to financial strictures in the system. Having located these, concerted reflection and strategies can put into place a means by which economic constraints can be challenged through individual and collective political action at local, state and federal levels. The type of reflection in this book best suited to tackle such an overt political agenda is emancipatory reflection, because it identifies and challenges all of the constraints that work against effective nursing and midwifery care.

Historical constraints

Historical constraints are those factors that have been inherited in a setting, which remain unquestioned because of the precedence of time and convention. History creates the present and hints as to the possible nature of the future. This is not to suggest that history is immutable and that once set in place, historical events cannot be diverted, adapted or ceased from their original trajectories. Rather, it has been said often that if we are ignorant of our past, we are helpless to identify our present and to shape our future. History is important, because it helps us to see what has been, in order to decide on what can be.

In nursing and midwifery practice, historical precedents align themselves closely with cultural and social determinants. In other words, the cultural norms created by symbols, rituals and practices combine easily with the interpersonal relationships defined by social contexts, to become relatively enduring events and behaviours, because of the influence of strong historical antecedents. Even so, trends can be disrupted, stalled and/or reversed depending on what forces win in the powerful stakes of creating history.

For example, historical records inform us that the first officially recognized midwives were wise women, who cared for women giving birth. The practice of midwifery continued unaffected until the Middle Ages, when it received negative attention from the male-dominated state and the Church, at the time of the witch hunts in Europe, which lasted from the fourteenth to the seventeenth centuries (McCool and McCool 1989). The midwives of that time worked with herbs and other healing modalities. The first regulation of their practice came about because of fear of their powers as lay healers and their supposed identity as witches, together with the political and religious threat they posed to the dominant forces, by virtue of being self-directed and influential women (Ehrenreich and English 1973; Kitzinger 1991). It is not surprising to find that the extermination of midwives as witches came at a time when medicine was reaching its peak.

Midwifery history does not provide a clear description of the connections between midwives and witchcraft (Oakley and Houd 1990). While there is no proof that midwives were also witches, many women were sacrificed to the ideals of the Church and the state, which combined forces to eradicate the 'evil' of the time. However, it has been deduced that the terms 'woman', 'witch', 'midwife' and 'wisewoman' were used interchangeably, and that these people all fell within the category of 'a great multitude of ignorant persons' (Oakley and Houd 1990: 25–6).

The witch hunts and the rise of medicine are considered to be the two main reasons why midwives' practice became more and more regulated. From a beginning of autonomous practice in the care of mothers and babies, midwives became subordinated to the medical model as 'obstetric nurses'. It is interesting, however, that the first men involved in the care of women giving birth were barber surgeons, who were called in by the midwives to perform destructive surgery on obstructed dead foetuses. It was not until the seventeenth century, when forceps were developed, that barber surgeons were present to assist in live births (Kitzinger 1991). As women were excluded from education, the barber surgeons and the physicians were men, and thus the male domination of midwifery was set into train.

This small slice of midwifery history informs us about some of the present-day struggles in which midwives find themselves. While being advocates of birth as a natural process, they nevertheless are aware of the problems that can occur in complicated cases, and they know they must accede to the knowledge and skills of staff better qualified to intervene when things go wrong. However, in remaining mothers' and families' advocates, midwives struggle to ensure that pregnancy and birth are natural processes in a culture that has historically looked at medical and surgical intervention to eradicate delays, discomfort, pain and unusual and potentially life-threatening circumstances. The problem for midwives is that biomedical arguments for intervention win out against 'being with' women in a natural process of waiting and supporting. Midwives know that it is historically, culturally and socially imprudent to question such arguments, so the intervention rates continue to rise in a well-intentioned, fear-based society.

Much has been written of the history of nursing (Marriner-Tomey and Alligood 2002) and authors have debated whether the historical influences of Florence Nightingale have been positive or negative for present-day nurses. Some writers point to the influence Florence had with the powerbrokers of her day in male-dominated English society and how she prevailed against those men's agendas to set nursing up as a thinking, autonomous profession. Other authors emphasize her attention to detail, order and control and place the blame squarely on Florence for the subservience of nurses to doctors and to the biomedical model of care and research. History can be read from various perspectives and this has been the case with nursing history. Regardless of the position we take, we can look at nursing history and suggest causes for our present nursing dilemmas and victories. The dilemmas include the relative powerlessness of a predominantly female occupation still struggling to attain all the features of a profession, beset with problems of subservience and overwork, being paid less for their work than many other occupations with less education and responsibility. The victories are the existence of nursing as a distinct practice discipline even in the era of technicians and specialties, and the increasing status and influence in health care through high tertiary education standards, undying public respect and representation of nurses in political arenas and national committees.

History influences the present and shapes the future, but different people can perceive it differently and it can be rewritten according to the dominant values and voices of the time. Reflective practice allows nurses and midwives to examine the events of the past to better understand present-day practice and envision the kind of future they want for themselves and the people in their care. This is not to underestimate the powerfulness of historical constraints, as they are a force with which to reckon. Nevertheless, change is possible. Change can only come with awareness and action, so reflection is integral to practice improvements, as historical constraints are recognized and worked on systematically, through reflective processes oriented to action and change.

Political constraints

Political constraints are about the power, competition and contention in relationships in day-to-day life. Politics is everywhere, not just in parliaments and courthouses. The early feminist movement had a catch-cry: 'The personal is political'. This statement brought home the message that power and power-plays are inherent to everyday human life and that oppression and dominance are ever-possible states of human existence; they happen wherever and whenever people struggle for ascendancy and power. A nurse may use power against another nurse; a midwife may attempt to dominate the wishes and intentions of another midwife. Political issues do not have to be about big things, such as who wins an election, or sits on a powerful committee; political issues may be about who goes to lunch first and who influences the senior management in the dispensation of rewards and incentives.

Reflector

Reflect on the sources of political constraints in your work. To do this, think about who constrains you from being the nurse or midwife you might ideally choose to be, when, how and why, with their power and influence.

Power is potent in organizations, because their structures and functions are conducive to the distribution of power through everyday practices, acted out through the authority of seniority and expertise in the 'pecking order' of the hierarchy. Proponents of organizational theory claim that organizations have changed over time. Organizational structures and processes have moved 'from the centralised control of bureaucracies' in the 1950s and 1960s 'to shared decision-making through consultation and participative management' in the 1970s and 1980s, to the 1990s focus on 'best practice, customer-focused action and outcomes; and the manager's role as a researcher, teacher and enabler of creativity' (Anderson 1996: 30). Even so, nurses and midwives relate practice stories with themes of powerful domination and control by political forces and people in hospitals and health care agencies.

Power does not have to be a 'bad thing' – it can be a force for potentiating positive outcomes. The difficulty arises in the definition of positive and negative, as the question can be rightly asked: 'Positive or negative for whom, and why? Power becomes one-sided and iniquitous when this question is not asked and the game of politics is played for the game itself. When politics constrain the ways in which people interact, it is not the reasonable, well-argued position that is heard and acted on, but rather the betraying voice whispered behind closed doors, or the powerful voice spoken loudly with the most authority and aggression. The nature of politics is power and contestation and that is how the game is played, but the game has rules and conventions to which appeals can be made for transparency and reasonableness.

Politics is alive and well in health care. The structure of health care organizations ensures the vivacity of politics and defines the ways in which interactions occur between individuals and groups competing for power, status and resources in the organization. Individuals engage in power-plays in clinical discourse and 'us and them' mentalities thrive where lack of understanding and respect for roles sets staff up against one another in a culture too busy and/or indifferent to explore anything other than their own practice realities. Doctors may not know or respect the roles of nurses; nurses may not know or respect the roles of occupational therapists, and so on. It takes time, effort and courage to break down political constraints. Reflective practice offers a means by which perceptions can be challenged, politics can be exposed and there can be some negotiation of political differences in the light of new information and a spirit of cooperation. This is not to underestimate the power of political constraints, because the powerful benefit from their powerful positions and are unlikely to give up the benefits of their power easily. In some cases, political constraints hold strongly against all attempts to appeal to them, but at the very least, reflective practice assists you expose and to find a voice to speak against political injustices at work.

Social constraints

Social constraints are the habitual features of a setting and the ways in which people define themselves through interactions in that setting. They relate to interpersonal interactions and are connected closely to cultural and historical constraints, which are also seated in human interaction through shared meanings over time. The social norms of a setting vary – for example, the way you behave in the social setting of work is different to how your behave in the privacy of your own home. The way a midwife behaves in a birthing room may be different from the way they behave when receiving a baby from a Caesarean section. A nurse may act in a certain way in a rehabilitative unit to how they act in an emergency department. The point is that the social setting in some way determines the way we act and how we relate to other people within that setting.

Nurses may be most comfortable interacting with other nurses; midwives may be most comfortable interacting with other midwives. The reasons are not difficult to speculate – individuals belonging to the same group are aware of the social conventions that govern their behaviour and they can embody them well and with relative ease. When we relate socially outside our preferred groups, we need to be aware of acceptable ways of relating, so effective communication is maximized and misadventures are minimized. Confusion, misunderstanding and varying degrees of miscommunication are possible if we do not know how to relate to relatively unfamiliar individuals and groups. In nursing and midwifery practice, we overcome social blunders and consequent negative outcomes by learning how to fit within the social setting of the work-place, and to interact appropriately with the people working there. On the whole we may feel comfortable and that we understand how to relate to patients/mothers and families, as these people are the focus of our work; they are why we have learned the knowledge and skills of our practice discipline. Even so, social relationships with patients/mothers and families become defined by the role relationships and we learn how to act appropriately towards them.

Social constraints define relationships at work and assist us in acting appropriately, but they may also inhibit and limit our responses to a point where we hide behind appropriateness to save ourselves from closeness. For example, Jourard (1971) wrote about 'professional armour' and how nurses can put on protective behaviours to shield themselves from the relative tragedies and uncertainties of daily practice. Midwives may also choose to limit the ways in which they show their thoughts and feelings to people in their care, so that they remained detached and aloof, risking little in social engagement with others at work. Reflective practice allows you to explore the ways you relate to others and to examine the reasons why and how social constraints may have developed your patterns of behaving that are sometimes non-productive.

Personal constraints

Personal constraints have to do with unique features about you as a person, shaped by influences in your life, into which you may or may not have insights. That is to say, you are as you are, but you may not know who and how you are. I have put this constraint last, because it is usually the first one nurses and midwives think of when they are reflecting on their practice. In other words, I do not want to give it the same importance in this list of constraints, because I contend that we are not the main or sole reason things can 'go wrong' at work. While accepting that we may be in part responsible for some things some of the time, we nevertheless need to recognize the other constraints that operate at work and elsewhere in our lives.

Personal constraints come about because of identified or unidentified obstacles inherent in the way we present ourself to the world and lead our own inner life with ourself. Self-work is personal work and it takes time, effort and courage to face yourself honestly, to identify strengths and weaknesses. One of the saddest songs I know is: 'I've Been to Everywhere, but I've Never Been to Me'. My interpretation of the song is that the singer is disclosing that she has had a full and very interesting life, but she has not done any work on herself and explored her own thoughts and feelings. She does not know herself, so how can she begin to love and accept herself or look at what may be changed about herself, when, how and why. How can she feel 'at home' in herself and feel comfortable in interacting outwards from herself to others?

In my opinion (Taylor 2000), and in the writing of other authors (Freshwater 2002a, 2002b; Johns 2002) nurses and midwives are all the more effective when they are actively and constantly working on reaching deeper levels of self-knowledge through self-developing processes, such as reflection, contemplation, meditation, visualization, prayer and thoughtful engagement in the arts, such as music, painting and poetry, and with other people in authentic communication.

Another way of looking at personal constraints in nursing and midwifery is to consider the deficits that you may be carrying in practice knowledge and skills. In other words, we have to face up to the fact that some nurses and midwives may have inadequate, outdated or incorrect knowledge and skills and these deficits could be constraining them personally from effective practice. Sometimes we are aware of what we do not know and we can take steps to amend this problem. Other times we may go along quite happily not knowing we have knowledge and skill deficits, until 'a near miss' happens and someone suffers at our hands. Everyone can make mistakes, and mistakes happen to the best people, but there is a big difference in mistakes and misadventures in practice, when the latter are brought about from knowledge and skill deficits. In this book, the type of reflection best suited to attending to this form of personal constraint is technical reflection, because it asks what is wrong or lacking and sets up a systematic means of questioning to arrive at solutions to clinical issues.

Summary

This section described cultural, economic, historical, political, social and personal constraints at work and the ways in which they may affect your practice. Looking at your own practice in order to raise your awareness about your own values and actions encourages you to shift your focus outwards towards the context in which you work and how you interact there. When you shift the focus away from blaming yourself exclusively, to reflect on cultural, economic, historical, political and social constraints issues that may be affecting your practice, you begin to see that that your work is complex and there are many reasons why things go wrong, and ways in which constraints may be identified, explored and changed. This book will help you to work through this reflective process with the aim of enlivening and enhancing your practice. Reflective practice is not a panacea for all the ills of nursing and midwifery, but it provides a systematic process through which constraints can be identified and issues can be examined.

Issues nurses and midwives often face

After years of working with nurses and midwives to assist them in becoming reflective practitioners, I have noticed trends in the issues they face. I present the main issues now and exemplify them with practice stories, so you can see how they are part of everyday work and how they are rich sources for reflection and potential for changed practice.

Engaging in self-blaming

When something goes wrong at work and you are at the centre of it, by making direct and simple connections between causes and effects, you may decide that it is your fault and resort to self-blaming, guilt and self-recrimination. While there may be some occasions in which circumstances show that you have acted inappropriately or that you could have acted more wisely, there may also be occasions in which you have been too ready to blame yourself, by not being mindful of all the other constraints that were operating in the situation at that time. Reflective processes can alert you to ponder the determinants of situations and give you the means of working through them systematically so they can be managed now and prevented in the future. The following practice story exemplifies this issue.

> ## Practice story
>
> *Meg, aged 55 years was looking forward to retirement, having worked in busy, acute-care settings for most of her career. Two weeks before she was due to go on her last lot of holidays before retirement it was a very busy day at work in the 25-bed ward, with four new admissions, seven discharges and six operations. Although she was allocated six patients, she was aware of newer members of staff who were not managing their caseloads well, and that many observations and essential parts of routine body care were not being done. Even she struggled to keep up with the demands of the day and could only stay at lunch for 15 of the*

allotted 30 minutes. She returned after lunch to find that one of the people for whom she was caring had fallen out of bed, even though she had put the side rails in place and notified another staff member that the person was confused and anxious. Meg blamed herself for the patient's fall and felt personally responsible for all the bruises that appeared on the patient as the day wore on.

Reflector

When we look closely at this practice story we can see that Meg had many constraints influencing her work. Why do you think she resorted so readily to self-blame? It may help you to look at the description of constraints in the previous section of this chapter.

Wanting to be perfect and invincible

Nursing and midwifery education give the definite message to students that they are morally and legally responsible for competent and safe practice. To enforce the expectation, undergraduate programmes use examinations and essays to test knowledge acquisition and competency assessments for clinical skills. Students of nursing and midwifery also learn, from the clinical areas in which they are placed for experience, that the work demands high standards because people's health and welfare are at stake. We are not taught mediocrity in care, because we have to aim for the highest standards. Even so, mistakes happen because practice can be chaotic and complex and we do not always work carefully or effectively for various reasons. Mistakes in nursing and midwifery practice can be costly, especially if they are related to certain risky aspects of care, such as the administration of drugs or the management of life-support systems.

Safe practice involves up-to-date knowledge and checks and measures for ensuring that mistakes are prevented, and it is part of responsible practice to pay due attention to these strategies. For fear of making mistakes, however, some nurses and midwives may develop ritualistic modes of behaviour, in which they act from a base of chronic anxiety to prevent mistakes from happening. In other words, a nurse or midwife may think: 'If I always do this procedure, in this way, nothing bad will happen'. While this approach may produce safety standardization, it does not necessarily take account of other unexpected variables, such as how the patient is responding.

Issues such as power, control and blaming other people may be manifestations of wanting to be perfect and invincible in all aspects of work. Versatility is needed in nursing and midwifery practice to deal with whatever comes up in the course of daily work. However, versatility can be mistaken for invincibility, and sometimes nurses and midwives may expect to 'walk on water', never being in trouble for making mistakes and never being unable to cope magnificently in every situation.

Practice story

John, aged 35 years, had been a homebirth midwife for two years, having left the hospital system to engage in independent practice. He loved his work, revelled in the ways he facilitated natural birth and enjoyed being present with families to assist the process. He was attentive to all of the aspects of antenatal care, monitoring the progress of pregnancy, getting to know the woman and her significant others and preparing them all as a cohesive group for the birth of the baby. John worked long hours to maintain a supportive presence during the birthing process and did not leave to go home until all aspects of care had been completed. He literally 'turned himself inside out' to do everything possible to be the best midwife he could possibly be. At 1 a.m. one morning he was called to the home of Susan, a 30-year-old multigravida he had known and cared for throughout her entire pregnancy. When he arrived at 1.30 Susan's membranes had ruptured some five minutes before and she said she noticed a soft feeling between her legs. When John looked he noticed a prolapsed umbilical cord and immediately lifted Susan's hips onto two pillows to relieve pressure on the cord. John ascertained that Susan was in early labour and needed transfer to the local hospital, where he was well known and respected and had adjunct arrangements for emergency care of homebirthing mothers. Due to his quick thinking and action, Susan's baby survived and had good Apgar scores at one and five minutes after birth. Even so, John was terrified of the possible consequences for the baby had he not arrived sooner and he seriously considered giving up homebirth midwifery and returning to the hospital system.

John's practice story is of a midwife with two years' experience in homebirths, who excels in all aspects of practice, but who is unable to stop potentially awful things from happening to himself and to the people in his care. Sometimes, even with the hardest, most conscientious work and the best possible care, emergencies happen. This emergency was not due to work faults or constraints. A prolapsed cord may occur in any birth when the presenting part is high and the cord is flushed with the amniotic fluid out of the partially or fully dilated cervix. Even though this is a fact of midwifery and it cannot always be averted, midwives know how to manage the situation and act quickly to assist the safe birth of the baby. In John's case, he acted well and rapidly, but his anxiety after the event for future emergencies created a doubting in himself that he could cope in the future in homebirth settings.

This is a complex dilemma, because John may have to face the fact that deep down he wants to be perfect and invincible in all things in his practice, and in the often messy world of human interactions and processes that may not always be possible.

If you have a need to be perfect in your work and to 'be all things to all people', you may need to look at the issue of your ideal need for perfection and invincibility. Reflective processes encourage you to examine the reasons behind your need to be perfect and invincible, by asking yourself questions, such as how you came to feel that way, the purposes it serves, and why you continue to need to feel that way, even when it is not always possible or reasonable to reconcile that need to your work.

Examining daily habits and routines

Often, the most difficult things to change are those things that lie just in front of our noses, and are so commonplace that we cease to notice them, or to question their place in our lives. Work can be so commonplace that we take it for granted and never ask why we do what we do. Even though some work is anxiety-provoking, upbeat and high turnover, other aspects of work can be repetitive and tedious. In nursing and midwifery, repetitive tasks can result in entrenched routines and habits that serve their purposes of getting the routine, essential work done, but can also become a source of practical and emotional boredom; as a result they become counterproductive as unexamined practices.

Daily habits and routines are a rich area for reflection, because they show you why you are practising in taken-for-granted ways and how you might be able to make some changes, given the constraints under which you work. Consider the following practice story.

Practice story

Jocelyn, aged 38 years, had been working in an aged care facility as an RN for ten years. She had built up a lot of friendships with the staff and residents, and on the whole she enjoyed going to work. One morning she was getting each resident out of bed at 7 a.m. when a newly-admitted male of 77 years, George, refused to comply. Her insistence that he would be able to eat his breakfast better and get much-needed exercise fell on deaf ears and George steadfastly refused to budge. Being busy, she moved on to the next residents and continued the habit of getting them out of bed. At morning tea she was telling the story of the new resident's refusal to get out of bed and another nurse asked: 'Why do we get them all out of bed at 7 a.m.? Who really benefits – them or us?'

Reflector

You might like to discuss this practice story with a colleague and answer the question asked by the nurse: Who really benefits – them or us? Then go on to discuss a further question of: How could this be different?

The issue of unexamined routines and habits extends to many examples in nursing and midwifery practice. One of the problems in dealing with this issue is recognizing the commonplace aspects of your work as they may be relatively invisible to you, even though you engage in them daily. Pretend you are a visitor to the ward or unit in which you work, or better still that you come from another planet, and that you know nothing of the habits and routines there. Pay careful attention to the mundane aspects of your workplace, such as who comes and goes, why, when and how. You may begin to see many issues that could benefit from reflection, such as traffic flow, how many times people in your care are disturbed from their rest, mealtimes, the timing of procedures, how staff and visitors relate to one another, who talks the most in interactions, why, with whom, with what authority, and with what outcomes, and so on. The possibilities are as bountiful as your willingness to observe and identify them.

Struggling to be assertive

There are many people interacting in health care settings, doing important work, most probably in a hurry, and with too few resources, so it is unsurprising that communication can become difficult. Add to this the cultural, social and historical constraints and the complexity increases. Then imagine particular circumstances when power is involved, such as when a person with greater power and authority is communicating with a person with perceived lesser status in the organization, and you have the right mix of constraints and conditions for one-way communication in which some people's voices are never or seldom heard. If the situation is to be challenged, someone has to find the courage to speak up and be assertive. A practice story exemplifies the point.

Practice story

Julia, aged 24 years, had recently completed her undergraduate mid-wifery programme and had been practising at a local hospital for five months. In the early weeks of her practice Julia had been tentative, getting to know the routines and 'fitting into' the unit. She was quiet and respectful in the presence of the other, more experienced midwives, as she knew they had a great deal of expertise and they could teach her well in the art and science of midwifery. A very senior midwife, Sheila, who had 'trained' in the former hospital-based system, was dismissive of Julia, often criticizing the tertiary system of midwifery education, muttering comments just out of Julia's hearing, and finding fault in her work as often as she could. Julia was afraid of Sheila, not only because she was senior to her, but also because she felt she did not have the courage to speak up against her frequent taunts.

Reflector

Reflect on Julia's dilemma and possible reasons why Sheila is actively creating it. Why does Julia lack courage to speak up? What causes Sheila to act this way towards her? In thinking of possible reasons for this situation, refer to the constraints discussed previously and remember that these can influence Julia *and* Sheila.

Nurses and midwives need to be assertive in their communication, in order to be effective as clinicians, and to put forward the interests of their patients and their discipline in the multidisciplinary health team. If you are struggling to be assertive, you may be experiencing the effects of not 'finding your voice' at work, leading to feelings of frustration, or even powerlessness and apathy. The remedy may not be as simple as assertiveness training. You may also need to explore whether your lack of assertion is due to being silenced at work by powerful constraints that could make 'the world's best communicator' mute. Reflective processes assist you to identify constraints that have acted as silencing factors and you can begin to take steps to lessen, and eventually be freed from, them.

Struggling to be an advocate

Advocacy means speaking up on someone else's behalf. Nurses and midwives need to speak up on behalf of people in their care and sometimes for themselves, especially when power relationships are at play – for example, in patient-medical practitioner interactions. Hospital and clinic work situations may provide scant opportunities for patients to feel they can speak up for themselves, especially if other people with higher status seem to be too busy, unapproachable, too difficult to understand or unwilling to communicate at the level and rate the other person needs.

Practice story

Bill, aged 40 years, had been practising for 15 years in a busy cardiology unit, and he had seen many new 'budding' cardiologists come and go in that time. He noticed that when the novice doctors first arrived in the unit they were quiet and considerate towards the experienced nurses, but as time went on, some of them became increasingly dismissive and arrogant. While he understood that doctors have their own unique set of socializing factors into the culture and practice of cardiology, Bill also lived by a personal code of respect towards all people and he would not tolerate blatant rudeness from anyone. On many occasions during patient-doctor consultations, Bill acted as an advocate for patients, calmly asking doctors to repeat what they had just said, but this time in words the person could understand. He also intervened when he noticed dismissive and arrogant behaviour by doctors towards nurses, and counselled nurses in ways in which they could use advocacy for themselves and other people. Bill had not always enjoyed this level of confidence in acting as an advocate. His clinical and communicative knowledge and skills had been developed after years of reflective practice.

Reflective processes can help you understand why advocacy is difficult for you in relation to the constraints within which you are working. You may find that being an advocate has deeper foundations than you first imagined. Speaking up for someone else takes communicative skill, which is nurtured through experience and practised through confidence, both of which take time, effort and courage to develop. Although becoming an effective advocate is not a simple undertaking, it is possible through focused reflective processes.

Differentiating between ideal and real practice expectations

Nurses and midwives need to be aware of the difference between ideal and real practice, because they are different, and the distinction can be the basis of recognizing issues in practice. We develop ideals through forming a value system. Values are what we hold as good, true and dear in our lives. For example, I value telling the truth, respect for others and being kind to other people. My values come from various sources, such as my family, friends, school, church, education and so on. My practice as an academic shows some or all of my values, because these form, and to some extent dictate, who I am and how I represent myself in the world. I can maintain my value system in most human interactions and in that sense I am 'true to myself'. However, sometimes I act outside my value system and the ideals I espouse may need to be altered or dropped to fit a given situation. For example, when I am trying to save someone else's feelings I do not always tell the whole truth, I do not respect people who abuse other people and sometimes I am too dammed angry to be kind to some people! In making these alterations to my espoused value system I have found instances in which my ideals do not always hold for me and I am clear in my own mind why I have made these value adjustments. In clinical practice, differentiating between ideal and real practice is exemplified in the following practice story.

> ## Practice story
>
> *Christina, aged 43 years, had been practising as a hospital-based mid-wife for 23 years and she was respected by all of her colleagues for being the 'best midwife' in the unit. Christina was aware of the respect with which she was held and she worked hard to maintain the standards she set herself from the very beginning of her career. The other midwives could always rely on Christina to be at work, to never 'fake a sickie', to do her work on time, to help them when she had finished her own work and to be an 'all-round' expert in all respects. Christina's values of working hard, treating people kindly and respectfully, and giving her time and efforts for others, showed clearly in her practice. One morning Christina noticed a first-time mother, Hazel, crying, so she went over to her, sat on the bed and listened while Hazel poured out her despair that she could ever be 'a good mother'. Fifteen minutes later, and after much reassurance punctuated by quiet listening, Christina stood up to go, feeling fairly sure that for the time being at least, Hazel felt comforted. To Christina's surprise, Hazel leapt out of bed and hugged her warmly, thanking Christina for taking time to talk with her. Christina was surprised by the hug because it was the first one she had ever received from a mother at work. She wondered why it was the first hug and why it surprised her so much and began to reflect on the situation to make sense of it.*

To all intents and purposes, this practice story reads well – Christina *is* an expert midwife and she helped Hazel. To find the issue here, we have to look deeper. One of Christina's values is 'to give her time and efforts for others'. Few people would argue that this value is ignoble, or that giving to others is an issue. However, in Christina's case, the level of her surprise at receiving the hug led her to wonder beyond the act itself to the trends and patterns in her practice and how they defined her at work. She realized that she had been so caught up in the value of giving to others in selfless service that she had very little experience of receiving something *back* from people in her care, and that realization in turn contradicted her espoused theory of midwifery, that practice is about adult-adult reciprocity. This does not mean that Christina will stop giving her time and attention generously to the people in her work, but she will be more aware now about leaving herself open to the possibilities of receiving what other people may be wanting to give her, in terms of their appreciation and so on.

Reflective practice can assist you to see what parts of your work are based on ideals, and whether they are realizable in the face of work constraints. You may discover that your daily practice falls short of your ideals, and that this is not always a 'bad thing'. For example, if you think that, ideally, 'all people are good', you may be challenged when you are involved in nursing and midwifery interactions with people such as patients, families and other health care workers who have motives that do not fit your definition of 'good'. Even in the face of blatant contradictions of your ideals, you may try to hang on to them, to preserve some sense of personal integrity. When personal ideals are shattered in practice you may experience emotions such as loss, anger, confusion, helplessness, lack of self-esteem, loss of sense of purpose and so on. Therefore, by reflecting on the issue of ideal versus real practice, you may be able to identify the origins of your firmly-held values and explore whether they still serve you in every case in your work. You may need to reconcile the absoluteness of some of your ideals at work with relative considerations, while maintaining basic principles that guide your daily interactions with other people.

Playing the nurse/midwife-doctor game

There is a well-recognized phenomenon in nursing and midwifery practice called the nurse/midwife-doctor game (Stein 1967). In this game nurses or midwives pretend they will not tell doctors what to think or do, while giving them subtle hints devoid of any patronizing tone and intentions, to direct them towards appropriate diagnosis and/or management of the patient. The nurse-doctor game goes like this:

> Nurse: Could you come to see Ms White please doctor?
> Doctor: Yes, what's the trouble?
> Nurse: Since admission, she has been nauseated, her BP is 100 over 60, her pulse is 110, she has pain in her right iliac fossa, and there is some rebound tenderness.
> Doctor: I'll be in. It sounds like appendicitis.

Even though the nurse making the phone call knew the possible diagnosis, he did not deign to tell the doctor his business, because he knows that nurses do not diagnose. Even so, the nurse knows that the well-described clinical picture will bring the doctor to the bedside quickly, which is in Ms White's best interests.

Although Stein referred to the nurse-doctor game, it could be equally well applied to midwifery practice, as the midwife-obstetrician game. In this case, the game would be played like this:

Midwife: Could you come to see Ms Green please doctor?

Obstetrician: Yes, what's happening?

Midwife: Her contractions are coming every two minutes, she is approaching full dilatation, and she is getting the urge to bear down.

Obstetrician: She's ready to deliver. I'll be right there.

Some nurses and midwives do not play the game; rather they make the statement of what they think may be happening and deal with the consequences later if they happen to offend the doctor. Take the case of the midwife and imminent birth for instance; most experienced midwives would start the conversation with: 'Ms Green is ready to deliver!' and then go on to give the details.

The nurse-doctor and the midwife-obstetrician games become issues when they constrain nurses and midwives from effective care and/or create moral and practical dilemmas in the way they work. Such games are an issue for rich reflection, as they inform you about the pressures under which you work that cause you to conform to set expectations and rituals in relation to doctors. You may also get to the point where you ask yourself why you continue to promote the status quo and if, how, when and why interactions could be managed differently. This book guides you in reflecting on this and related issues.

Managing collegial relations

Relations between colleagues in nursing and midwifery can lack joy and friendship, and reasonably happy relations can sour and deteriorate due to all kinds of unexamined issues, such as lack of acknowledgement, jealousy, lack of sharing of knowledge and expertise, and that old-time 'evergreen', horizontal violence. Many collegial issues are self-evident, as some colleagues may be only too willing to let you know, in no uncertain terms, just what irks them about you. At other times, you may get the sinking feeling that all is not well – there is less eye contact, less congeniality, unspoken rivalry and non-verbal messages, the meaning of which you can't quite discern.

Bullying can occur wherever people congregate and work in large numbers together, such as in schools, factories, businesses and organizations. Bullying, described specifically as horizontal violence (Duffy 1995; Glass 1997), means a lashing outward, laterally against one's own group, and it is often associated with the need to overpower and subordinate others. It is often seen where people are working upwards through a hierarchical system and instead of remembering their early experiences and being empathetic towards others coming 'upwards', they use their increased seniority to 'give as good as they have been given' and perpetuate the culture of retribution and violence. The following practice story exemplifies the issue.

> ### Practice story
>
> *Rachael, aged 28 years, was feeling pleased that she had been accepted into a postgraduate research programme to study towards her Ph.D. and she mentioned this to a group of nurses after handover report at work the next day. Many of her nursing friends congratulated her and asked what it meant to be doing a Ph.D. and how it might help her in the future. However, one nurse in a senior management role overheard Rachael telling her friends, and she remarked loudly as she walked down the corridor away from the group: 'What a load of crap! Why in the hell would you want to do a Ph.D.? Are you going to work in uni and turn out more of those useless tertiary nurses!'*

Reflector

As you can see, the issue of bullying and abuse is evident in this scenario, but do you think it is easy to rectify? The senior manager is older, more experienced and influential. What does it take to tackle this situation? Will reflection help here?

Reflective processes can help in any difficult situation, because its first requirement is that you take time to think. Reflection does not promise to make your workplace a nirvana so everyone works together in harmony, or to alter anyone else's behaviour, but it can give you insights into why people behave as they do, and help you to reflect on ways to manage that behaviour. For example, the bullying behaviour in the previous practice story did not happen in that instant; it had been systematically and densely built up over years of unexamined intentions and unchallenged abusive acts. The perpetrator developed abusive behaviour in a culture that allows horizontal violence to happen, and in a setting in which constraints cause nurses to act in dysfunctional ways towards one another. This insight does not condone the behaviour, rather it tries to deconstruct the context in which bullying is tolerated, to seek ways in which it can be challenged and possibly eradicated. This kind of reflective practice takes a great deal of thoughtfulness and courage, but nothing changes if we do not make it our business to change it.

Dealing with organizational and health care system problems

Organizational problems and changes in the health care system, such as staffing shortages, bed and ward closures, communication breakdowns, lack of acknowledgement and support from administration, downsizing and rationalization of services, and the introduction of new monitoring and management systems, such as case mix, diagnosis-related groups, quality assurance and competency standards, are just a few examples of the many and varied changes in health care organizations that are the result of shifts in the health care system at large. Most often, political and economic motives drive the changes.

As a nurse or midwife, you may find that these problems impact on you and your work life directly in the form of increased workloads with reduced resources, and higher expectations that you will scale the career ladder, extend your qualifications, and enlarge your administrative and research output. While you are trying to adjust to these pressures, you may be receiving minimal support from other people, who may also be scrambling to keep their jobs and fulfil the sets of expectations imposed on them. All of these pressures and changes do not create cordial work relations, and communication within the organization can become distorted and exceedingly difficult to maintain at an effective level. This 'hotbed of discontent' is the very place in which reflective processes find their place, as they provide a systematic approach for making sense of how things came to be and how they could be different. The following practice story exemplifies the point.

Practice story

Mary, aged 33 years, had been the midwife managing the antenatal unit for six years, and in that time she had witnessed the arrival and depart-ure of three new hospital directors and two new directors of midwifery services. In her experience, Mary noticed that each new director enforced their ideas at hospital and midwifery practice levels, caused a lot of stress among staff, and then left to go to a higher paying job elsewhere in the health care system. When the most recent director of midwifery services took up her position, she informed the unit managers in a meet-ing that all of the procedures and policy manuals needed revision and there would be no added resource to complete this task by the end of the month, when she would personally inspect them all. As the midwifery managers were leaving, the director added: 'Oh, by the way, the mid-wifery services budget has been cut and there will be no professional development money for projects next year!'

You will have no difficulty in seeing the issues here for Mary and of realizing that her practice dilemma is a rich source for reflection. There are many issues inherent in this story and there are no easy answers. It is an example of complex organizational problems passed down to care delivery levels, and it will take some time to examine critically for possible solutions. This book will show you how to approach such issues in a systematic reflective process.

Managing self-esteem and worthiness problems

Self-esteem and a sense of worthiness may seem strange inclusions in a book about reflective practice for nurses and midwives, but I have found these very personal issues lie at the heart of many clinicians' concerns about themselves and their practice. Nurses and midwives are people and they, like other people, need to feel positive self-esteem and worthiness. Even though you may have been educated and prepared carefully for practice, you nevertheless remain human, first and foremost, with all the foibles of humanness. Your humanness is at the same time your strength and vulnerability. The most qualified nurse or midwife may seem self-sufficient and confident at work, but does that mean they do not seek approval from others, or need to be thanked for a job well done?

Your feelings of low self-esteem and unworthiness may spring from many causes and you will be the best person to identify what these are. Possibly, you may be feeling low self-esteem and unworthiness because no one has ever taken the time to thank you, to point out your strengths or to acknowledge you in any way at work. You may already know that you do not know everything, you cannot be everywhere, you cannot fix everything and it is not possible to be loved by everyone, but these realizations do not stop you from trying to be 'super nurse' or 'super midwife'. The problems of low self-esteem and a sense of unworthiness are so large that they lie at the basis of a happy life generally, not just work life. Sensing the immensity of these issues, I have made them the first step on the pathway to becoming a reflective practitioner. You will find that the first reflective task is to think about yourself and your rules for life, to gain a richer sense of who you are and what motivates you to be a nurse or midwife. Although this first step may not solve all your feelings of low self-esteem and unworthiness, it will alert you to their presence and assist you in getting started on the process of building a positive sense of personal and professional worth.

Ensuring quality practice through reflective processes

Quality care in nursing and midwifery is usually counted in numerical terms, such as in collating and analysing clinical indicators of excellence that are observable and measurable. Quality care is in turn connected to evidence-based practice, in which it can be demonstrated that practice is being directed by the latest and best research findings. Evidence-based practice encourages observable and measurable assessment of quality care through quantitative means. Quantification relates to numerical assessment methods that give clinicians, managers and researchers statistical certainty that the best care outcomes are known, reliable and predictable, given standard, stable conditions in the clinical setting and adherence to proven procedures.

Most clinical indicators in which we have placed our faith to date have been verified as successful by quantifiable means, such as reduced infection rates, reduced length of stay in hospital, reduced readmission rates, high patient satisfaction scores and so on. These means have relied mainly on numbers. Reflective practice requires linguistic processes, in the form of words, sentences, conversations, discourses and stories. How can reflective processes fit into a number-oriented system of quality assurance and evidence-based practice?

It requires a reconfiguration of what health care systems count as valuable, to incorporate into organizational policies and procedures clinicians' own insights, through in-depth analyses of their own practice. Reflective practice constitutes research capable of generating local theories of action that inform practice. Local theories are knowledge statements about practice that have been developed through focused attention on issues and problems, and the solutions thus generated have the capacity to be transferred to other like situations, given that the insights and findings resonate with people working in those situations.

If reflective processes are to be valued as counting towards the assurance of quality care and best practice, they must be of a quality themselves as to assure effective outcomes. Another way of explaining this is that if you want to use reflective processes to make contributions to quality care where you work, make sure you are using them well yourself, so they have the best possible chance of being successful in guiding quality care that counts as best practice. This book coaches you in how to be effective in reflective processes. Once understood and practised, these processes have the potential to create a daily vigilance in you that keeps you alert to what is happening around you, and increases the likelihood that you will be able to be active and enthusiastic about developing and maintaining quality care in your practice.

Summary

This chapter introduced you to the nature of reflection and practice by covering definitions and sources of reflection, and recent and relevant literature pertaining to reflective practice in nursing and midwifery internationally. The nature of nursing and midwifery practice was explored to demonstrate why reflective processes are necessary for quality care. Welcome to reflection! I hope that it will be life-changing in a positive sense, even when it becomes challenging and you wonder why you decided to live a reflective life.

Key points

- Reflection is the throwing back of thoughts and memories, in cognitive acts such as thinking, contemplation, meditation and any other form of attentive consideration, in order to make sense of them, and to make contextually appropriate changes if they are required.
- Donald Schön emphasized the idea that reflection is a way in which professionals can bridge the theory-practice gap, based on the potential of reflection to uncover knowledge in and on action.
- Nursing and midwifery have used reflective processes for some time to improve practice, clinical supervision and research.
- Technical reflection, based on the scientific method and rational, deductive thinking, allows you to generate and validate empirical knowledge through rigorous means, so that you can be assured that work procedures are based on scientific reasoning.
- Practical reflection leads to interpretation for description and explanation of human interaction in social existence, and improves the way you communicate with other people at work, thereby improving your practice enjoyment and outcomes.
- Emancipatory reflection provides a systematic questioning process to help you to locate the bases of the problem, identify the political constraints and begin to address the issues, either alone or through collaborative action with other nurses or midwives.
- Nursing and midwifery are person-focused helping professions requiring hard work and a strong knowledge and skill base from which to face the daily challenges of practice; therefore, systematic approaches to reflection and action are needed.
- Cultural, economic, historical, political, social and personal constraints may affect the ways in which you are able to interpret and act at any given moment at work.
- Cultural constraints refer to the determinants that hold people in patterns of interaction within groups, based on the interpretation of shared symbols, rituals and practices.
- Economic constraints refer to workplace issues caused by a lack of money and the resources money can provide.
- Historical constraints are those factors that have been inherited in a setting, which remain unquestioned because of the precedents of time and convention.
- Political constraints are about the power, competition and contention in relationships in day-to-day life and work.
- Social constraints are the habitual features of a setting and the ways in which people define themselves through interactions in that setting.

- Personal constraints have to do with unique features about you as a person, shaped by influences in your life, into which you may or may not have insights.
- When you shift the focus away from blaming yourself exclusively to reflect on cultural, economic, historical, political and social constraints issues that may be affecting your practice, you begin to see that your work is complex and there are many reasons why things go wrong, and ways in which constraints may be identified, explored and changed.
- Issues faced by nurses and midwives that may benefit from reflection include engaging in self-blaming, wanting to be perfect and invincible, examining daily habits and routines, struggling to be assertive, struggling to be an advocate, differentiating between ideal and real practice expectations, playing the nurse/midwife-doctor game, managing collegial relations, dealing with organizational and health care system problems, and managing self-esteem and worthiness problems.
- Understood and practised, reflective processes have the potential to create a daily vigilance that keeps you alert to what is happening around you, and increases the likelihood that you will be able to be active and enthusiastic about developing and maintaining quality care in your practice.

2   Preparing for reflection

Introduction

In this chapter I describe qualities and hints for reflecting, and guide you through your first systematic reflective task, so that you can experience reflective processes first hand. I also describe the role of a critical friend, who helps you to reflect at deeper levels, and I explain that this is a role you can adopt in helping others to become more effective in their reflective practice.

Qualities for reflecting

After years of practising, teaching and researching reflection, I have come to the conclusion it takes considerable time, effort, determination, courage and humour to initiate and maintain effective reflection.

Taking and making the time

Reflection requires time and that is one of the main reasons why nurses and midwives do not make a commitment to creating a reflective work life. I imagine that you are a busy person already, most probably working shifts, managing home life to keep up to family responsibilities, and trying to fit in some personal fun, leisure and relaxation when you can. This means that you may be hesitant to squeeze in any more activities, such as taking or making time to reflect on your practice. Therefore, the first quality you need to have as a successful reflective practitioner is the willingness to take and make time in your life to make a commitment to the process. Only you can take and make the time for reflecting. When you experience the benefits of reflective practice, you may be keen to continue, so when you *do* take and make the time to reflect, give it your full attention to do it well, to maximize the potential for its success.

Making the effort

Life is full of activities, few of which happen if you do not make an effort, which you *will* make when you suspect that something is of value, reasonably easy and of benefit to you personally. Reflective practice is all of these things – worthwhile, easy and beneficial. However, if you are new to reflective practice, you require some fundamental skills which will take some effort to acquire. This book guides you through all of the skills you need, but you have to make the effort to read the words, assimilate the information and maintain the practice. As your work life is inextricably connected to your personal life, by association, reflective practice means a commitment to yourself, which requires effort in creating and maintaining a healthy lifestyle, such as getting regular rest and exercise, healthy nutrition, stress management, and maintaining satisfying relationships with your family and friends. It is entirely up to you to make the effort to be involved in your work and life and I commend regular reflection as an integral part of it, because it is really worth the effort.

Reflector

Do you have trouble making an effort to be involved in potentially useful activities? Why? In what ways can you ensure you make the effort to reflect?

Being determined

Determination is needed for reflection, because it is easy not to begin, or to stop regular reflective processes, due to tougher pressures that compete for your time and attention. It takes determination to get started and to keep going on reflection, because lack of resolve can easily result in inactivity, as reflection surrenders to other demands. The multifaceted demands of life will not cease, but you have the right to choose how and when you will respond to them. Determination will give you the power to propel your intentions forward into actions. Determination will also ensure that you keep on reflecting. Be determined!

Having courage

You need courage to look at yourself and your practice, because it takes honesty and frankness to move outside your comfort zones. It also takes courage to invest yourself in the depth of reflection needed to change dysfunctional procedures, interpersonal interactions and power relations at work. Work issues and problems become identified as such because they present dilemmas and are inherently difficult to face and solve. However, issue-identifiers and problem-solvers are not faint-hearted people; they are people prepared to muster and develop the courage needed to face up to and tackle difficulties directly. When you reflect intently on your work problems and issues, you need courage to identify constraints within your practice and workplace, and begin to make changes. You may find opposition from other people, who have political motives for maintaining the status quo, so they may try to betray you or display open aggression to change, and/or block any progress you may be making. Added to facing other people's reactions, is the courage you require to face yourself. Reflective processes identify your own patterns of thinking and reacting, which may need adaptation. This is not to infer that all reflective practitioners have immense courage to always be pro-active and assertive at work, because this is not necessarily the case. On the contrary, they are people who muster the courage to face the next step in the process, and having achieved that, move onto the next step. If you think of this as 'sequential courage', you may see that you are also capable of it.

Practice story

Peter, aged 43 years, has been a home midwife for ten years, after five unhappy years in the hospital system. In order to support women in their choice to have homebirths, Peter has learned how to become an advocate, and that role takes courage. When it comes to reflecting on his own practice, however, he owns up to his tendency to be afraid to write and reflect. When questioned about it by a critical friend, he realized that his lack of courage was in opening up his thoughts to himself and in sharing these disclosures with other midwives.

Reflector

Think about your preparedness to reflect on your practice issues, in relation to the courage you might have to face them squarely. It might help to imagine any people or situations you find intimidating in some way, and ask yourself why they have power over you. When you have some tentative answers to those questions, imagine ways you could build your courage sequentially to reflect systematically on practice issues concerning the intimidation you are feeling.

Using humour

At this point, you may think that reflection is sounding very serious, complex and difficult, because it takes time, effort, determination and courage. Even though reflection needs to be approached seriously, and it has the potential to be complex and difficult, it is not always onerous and without some degree of fun. Nurses and midwives have a propensity for seeing the funny side of life and work, because humour is an effective way of lightening our workloads by making the day appear to go faster and easier. It also helps us to look less seriously at ourselves and other people. Reflection can incorporate humour by putting the memories of even the most gruelling challenges into perspective, and by naming the curious aspects of our work culture that have their absurdly funny side when viewed through that lens. Developing a mature sense of humour is an effective repellant for anxiety and it forms strong bonds with colleagues, who resonate with subtle messages within shared jokes or funny clinical stories. Reflection using humour provides an alternate source of insights into the nature of work constraints, because when they are 'turned on their heads' to intentionally look silly, cultural, economic, historical, political, social and personal constraints can lose some of their sting. Effective reflective practitioners demonstrate a sense of humour in the way they tackle their work and lead their lives, so be assured that reflection is not all serious; it can have its funny side.

Reflector

Imagine a practice situation in which you were feeling overwhelmed in some way and you wanted the 'floor to open up and swallow you'. Now stand back and look at yourself in that situation. Was there anything laughable about it? In hindsight, is there a lighter side that you can now see?

Summary

When you are ready to reflect and to maintain a reflective attitude to your life and work, you will most probably already possess many of the requisite qualities of taking and making time, making the effort, being determined, having courage and knowing how to use humour. These qualities will serve you well as you develop reflective knowledge and skills. Even if your levels of these qualities are low and almost imperceptible, they can be nurtured through reflective practice.

A kitbag of strategies

There are many strategies you can use when engaging in systematic reflection. Some inspire reflection, others guide, and some may inspire and guide you simultaneously. The following kitbag of strategies contains approaches that are like ingredients for a recipe and you should feel free to use and adapt them in any combinations and quantities you prefer. The kitbag suggests using reflective strategies such as writing, audiotaping, creating music, dancing, drawing, montage, painting, poetry, pottery, quilting, singing and videotaping. While this is not a finite list of reflective strategies, it is designed to help you get started and to have fun in experimenting with a variety of methods.

Writing

When reflective processes are taught to people in practice, the impression is often given that keeping a journal or log of some sort is a fundamental requirement. Even though writing *is* an important means of recording your thoughts and feelings, it is not the only way of aiding and recording your reflection. This news may come as a pleasant surprise if you are someone who has trouble writing things down, or prefers other means of thinking systematically. Writing *can* be easy and effective and this section guides you in writing reflectively and creatively.

Reflector

If you have trouble writing, spend some time thinking about the possible reasons why. Do you associate writing with assessment of some kind? Do you imagine your writing may not compare well with other people's efforts? Write the reasons why you might be having trouble writing, but write the ideas quickly in whatever form it takes to get them down on paper or on the computer screen. Keep a copy of this and continue reading this section.

To prepare for writing, you need an exercise writing book or a computer or typewriter. Starting with handwriting materials, I suggest that you buy a fixed-page exercise book, so that you will be less likely to tear out pages when you are tempted to edit your writing. This may mean that your journal becomes 'messy', but it will be complete, 'warts and all'. Completeness is necessary so that you have a complete record of all your thoughts, especially if they change direction or move through unexpected areas. The pen, pencil or biro you use should handle well with minimal drag, so you can write quickly and easily. You might prefer to buy a special set of writing materials that encourage you to write and that you keep especially for reflection.

When you write don't be concerned about stylistic aspects, such as neatness, grammar, spelling and punctuation. The journal is yours, shared only as you choose, so there is no need to edit the writing for other people. The structure you use will be according to your growing expertise and confidence, and in the early part of your reflective experience this book guides you by posing questions and exercises to get you accustomed to what to write, when, how and why. When you reflect through writing, a particular mental approach is useful, such as spontaneity, openness and honesty, and these qualities are discussed later in this chapter.

If you are using a computer, you will most probably be aware of the usual tips for computing, such as making files, using good quality floppy disks, CDs or memory sticks, and saving your document often if you do not have an automatic save function. The best hints I can give you are what to avoid. Just type; don't edit your writing by cutting out sentences and paragraphs. Unlike word processing for formal tasks such as assignments, it is a good idea to type spontaneously as you think, without much, if any, planning. Thoughts may come in random order and themes may not be connected. This is the way some thinking happens privately, so don't try to change it or put it into a 'sanitized' form to suit a wider audience. Don't shift chunks of writing to other parts of the document to make it look better, or for it to be more grammatical or ordered.

If you are using a typewriter, it is also important for you not to try to order or edit your writing, so it looks nice or reads well. You need to let your typing flow with your thoughts and 'learn to live with' any disordered typing mess which may arise. You also need to keep anything you write in a self-holding folder, which keeps all the pages in the order in which they were typed.

Audiotaping

Not everyone is blessed with a love of writing and an ability to do it easily, and if you are such a person it may be good for you to learn that you can reflect without a lot of writing. If you are really systematic in how you use other methods I'm suggesting here, you may be able to avoid writing altogether. Do you enjoy telling stories? If you do, you could tell your stories into a tape recorder so you have a record of what you say. Once you get over the awkwardness of sitting alone and chattering away to yourself and a machine, you will get accustomed to reflecting through talking. If you feel a bit silly at first, say it out aloud, experience the feeling completely, and then choose to 'get over it'. Value the silent gaps which may also occur when you are drawing breaths or thinking quietly to yourself. Let the words come easily and effortlessly. Also, leave your words unedited by speaking unself-consciously and by resisting the temptation to rewind and tape over certain sections.

If you are intending to use the tape recordings without any written notes to yourself, you need to develop the habit of reviewing what you said previously to record verbal remarks on successive recordings. In this way you will be able to keep a progressive record of the insights you have gained, so that you can make connections to what is yet to become apparent through the reflective process. This may mean that you accumulate a lot of audiotapes, so be sure to date and label them carefully, so you know which ones to replay as the need arises. The reflective processes described in this book work just as well by audiotaping as they do by writing, so long as you review the audiotapes frequently and carefully to identify and work on connections in what you have said about your practice. Alternatively, you may choose to make summary notes in a journal to complement your audiotapes, thereby tracking your reflective progress.

Reflector

Locate a cassette recorder and a blank audiotape. Record yourself talking about a happy childhood memory. After this, record yourself talking about why it was a happy occasion and why it still means so much to you. This exercise will give you some idea of whether taping your reflections will be useful for you.

Creative music

Have you noticed how music evokes emotions and memories? For example, music can make you sing, cry, laugh and open up to reminiscence. Playing personally significant music can heighten your awareness and put you into a reflective space. If this is the case for you, play music when you reflect and allow it to enhance your thinking processes.

Alternatively, you can 'make your own kind of music'. You do not have to be a musician to make music, if you simply let the instrument express how you are feeling and thinking. For example, you could beat out a rhythm on a drum or the back of a lid, shake a tambourine or a bag full of marbles, or strike randomly on a musical keyboard such as a piano, organ or xylophone. While you might make a fairly awful noise, that few musicians might call music, it is nevertheless important to make the sound. Let the volume and tempo of the notes express your feelings, loudly and quickly for anger, quietly and regularly for peacefulness, and so on. The creation of the music will help you to vent your feelings and to get in touch with your emotions and this is helpful to get you into the mood for effective reflection.

If you have formal training and musical skills, you can create a more harmonious sound to inspire your reflection or to help you create sounds which represent what you are thinking. Thoughts and feelings are components of reflection and they can become locked in if they cannot find expression.

Play your music, or make your noise, and reflect on what is happening. You may find creative expression for feelings you are having about clinical issues and, as you are experiencing them, tune in to reflective insights. Once the stories start to flow through the release of music, you will have some substance on which to reflect and you can use music at any stage of the reflective process thereafter.

Dancing

You may claim that you are not a dancer, but if you have some means of mobility, you can dance. You do not have to be upright and bipedal to dance. People in wheelchairs and on walking aids can dance. Even if you feel like a baby elephant, or that you have two left feet when you try to dance, move your body anyway. It's easy if you just let go and dance, with or without music. Move by whatever means you have and let your body show you how you feel about work issues. At the same time, as with any other creative expression, you can also notice yourself as an interested observer. The feelings and thoughts evoked by dance will be useful for reflective processes. Having been evoked, thoughts and feelings can be channelled into the systematic reflective processes which are described in this book.

Record your reflections evoked or played out through dance. You could audio- or videotape the thoughts as partial or complete stories. A videotape would be especially helpful, as it could capture the dance and your reflections during or after. The recording needs to be available for reviewing, so you can make progressive reflections as new issues emerge from your practice. If dancing inspires reflection or represents what you are thinking and feeling, it may be a creative reflection possibility for you.

Reflector

Dancing as release is an interesting way of preparing yourself for reflection. Try dancing to a familiar tune. Does the music and the movement take you to another time and place? What memories and sensations does it conjure up for you?

Drawing

You may have the ability to draw what is in your head and 'heart', but if you do not, don't worry. Simply think of drawing as systematic doodling and you might feel a bit more confident about using it as a means of reflecting. Remember also that drawings are whatever you say they represent, so they do not need to be realistic or accurate, or to fulfil other artistic criteria. Whether the drawings happen spontaneously as an expression of what you are thinking and feeling, or whether they happen intentionally as a result of these processes, they can be useful with interpretations of your clinical experiences.

When you have drawn or doodled, record your responses to, or reasons for, the drawings you have made in relation to issues you are experiencing at work. Record your insights systematically in a lasting form so they can be revisited. For example, you could compile them in a book with space in between each for interpretations and insights, or you could record your reflections by speaking into a tape recorder. If you are keeping a journal they could be incorporated into what you are writing. Do whatever feels right for you.

Montage

A montage is a collection of images, often created from pictures, words and symbols cut out from old magazines and newspapers. If you have the time and interest in making a montage this may be an excellent way of assisting your reflective processes. As you search for images to express what you are thinking and feeling about clinical issues, you might find that you begin to reflect more fully, so that the emergent montage is a comprehensive representation of the sense you are making of certain practice events. On the other hand, the montage may provide you with a glimpse of where further reflection may take you, and you may not make connections until later when you take previous montages out of storage to review them.

Regardless of the way in which you organize your montage-assisted reflections, you need to record successive interpretations, so that the processes described in this book can be applied to them. The assimilated ideas and themes may be represented in other montages as you progress as a reflective practitioner and form a pictorial account of your personal and work insights.

Reflector

Collect some old magazines, scissors, glue and paper. Create a montage that depicts you as you see yourself now. When it is complete, take it to a friend and tell them about your montage, pointing out what the symbols and pictures mean to you. When you are ready, create a montage that depicts you as a practitioner and use a similar process to tell someone about your professional self. Invite that person to reciprocate and offer to listen to their account.

Painting

Watercolours, oils or acrylic paints can be used to paint a picture of your practice. By painting, you can represent a situation, a thought, an outcome, or whatever it is that needs depiction for further thought. It does not matter if it turns out to be a mess, because you are the painter and your painting is what you say it is. Let's face it – your painting may not be up to gallery standard, but it will be valuable for you as it can depict your responses to issues in your practice. As you are painting, notice the colours you choose and how you apply the paint. Tune in to what you are thinking and feeling as you paint each stroke. You can paint spontaneously in response to your emotions and thoughts, or you can make deliberate strokes to create a painting to slow down and structure your thinking.

Keep all your paintings and a commentary about them on tape or in a journal. Issues change over time, and you may notice that your painting style changes with them. It is important that you make sense of your paintings and incorporate your interpretations into the systematic reflective processes described in this book. Use this method for as long as it is helpful, in combination with other methods, which provide some written or spoken words about the meaning of the paintings, where they fit and why in your reflective practitioner experiences.

Poetry

While making no claims to be Shakespeare, everyone can write poetry, which has personal style and meaning. If you know the rules of poetry, by all means apply them, but even if you don't have the slightest idea of the structure of a poem, you could write one anyway. I write poetry from time to time and I imitate the rhythm and flow of other poems I have read, or I simply put as many words along one line as I fancy. My poems may never be published, but every time I take my own poetry book off the shelf and read it, my words bring back all the thoughts and feelings I had at the time of writing. This is why I think poetry could help you as you engage in systematic reflection on your practice.

When I write poetry I just let the words come. Sometimes the words repeat in my head until I can write them down. The slightest inspiration can be the basis of a poem. If you have had a hectic day at work, which has stirred up a lot of emotions and thoughts, try putting them into words. Your poem might be one line, or develop into proportions that would make Shakespeare envious. It does not matter, just let the poem flow as long as it needs to, so that you can express the issues on your mind.

As with all creative expressions for assisting reflection, you need to record your responses to your poetry, explaining when and how you wrote it, why and for whom, and what it means in relation to your practice reflections. Keep all your poems and commentaries and incorporate them into any other methods you are using for reflection.

Reflector

Imagine an event of any kind that happened to you within the last week or so. Write a short poem that begins with the first line: 'Last week I . . .' There is no limit to the words and lines in the poem – just let it flow.

Pottery

Based on the idea that anything is accessible to you if you can imagine it, pottery is another creative possibility to inspire and represent reflection. Not only is clay a wonderful medium for venting your emotions, it can form into many shapes, forms and symbols, which can represent clinical issues. If you have had a particularly terrible day at work why not throw the clay literally, for example, at the wall? Alternatively, you can play with clay or make works of art. It is up to you. If you create a clay form spontaneously or intentionally, notice how you are feeling and the thoughts you are having in relation to work. You might create a series of pots or pieces, and give them a name according to their evolution. Keep all the dried clay pieces, or take a photograph and record your insights successively to weave them into future reflections.

Quilting

Quilting is a deliberate act of sewing to represent selected themes of life. The symbols are selected carefully to contribute to the whole story depicted in the quilt. As you sit and sew, you can reflect on each symbol, and how it relates to the whole. In between quilting you can record your reflections using other methods for reflecting you may be using, such as writing or audiotaping.

Singing

You can sing by creating melodies and words that come spontaneously from a creative space inside yourself. As with many creative tasks, this can be difficult if you are overly self-conscious. To get started, sing a song you know. This will help you get used to the sound of your own singing voice. As you will be singing in private it does not matter if you sing off key or if your lyrics are less than poetic. Just open your mouth, breathe in, and sing out spontaneously!

As this is singing with reflective practice intentions, you need some form of recording, such as audiotaping or videotaping. You can decide on your level of comfort and skill in using either of these two recording methods. Also, you need to write successive interpretations of, and insights into, your songs and singing, noticing the words you used, the volume, pitch and mood of your singing, and your thoughts and feelings as you sang. These ideas and any more you develop along the way can be orchestrated into the other methods of reflection you are using, so that you can gain maximal effects from your reflective practice.

Videotaping

If you have ready access to video equipment, you might like to consider videotaping as the primary medium by which to enhance your reflection. One of the obvious benefits of using this medium is that you will be able to review yourself in terms of what you say and how you say it. Your own non-verbal cues may also be interesting for you to observe. For example, in telling some of your clinical stories, you may find that there is a substantial emotional component of which you were not fully aware. Your posture or pitch of voice may have something to tell you about yourself and the way a practice issue is affecting you. When you use the reflective processes described in this book, you will discover that they require you to be as honest and frank with yourself and your work as you can. Seeing yourself respond to these questions may enhance your reflections as you ask yourself about your non-verbal and verbal representation as portrayed on video.

As you need to make sense of your reflections, you need to develop a method for amassing progressive insights, questions and connections in your practice. You may choose to record these impressions directly on the video or into some other form of semi-permanent record, such as a journal or audiotape.

Reflector

Locate a video recorder and set it up so you can record yourself. Read the reflective exercise in this chapter (see pp. 62–3). When you are ready, respond spontaneously to the questions on video.

Summary

Reflective processes include more than writing, which is good news for nurses and midwives who have difficulty maintaining a journal. Reflection can also be inspired and maintained by creative strategies such as audiotaping, creating music, dancing, drawing, montage, painting, poetry, pottery, quilting, singing and videotaping, used in any combination you prefer. In all of these cases, it is important to record reflections over time, so they can be analysed carefully for awareness and insights, and form a sequential account of your progress as a reflective practitioner.

Hints for reflecting

Before your first reflective practice exercise, there are some hints for reflecting that might also help relate to any strategies you might use to enhance reflection, such as writing, audiotaping, videotaping or some form of creative representation such as painting, montage, drawing, quilting, pottery, poetry, singing, dancing and/or creative music. In this section, I suggest that when you are reflecting, remember to be spontaneous, to express yourself freely, to remain open to ideas, to choose a time and place to suit you, be prepared personally, and choose suitable reflective methods.

Be spontaneous

Be as spontaneous as possible in representing and recording your thoughts and feelings. It is from your frank and honest self that important insights come, from the depths of your emotions, where the meaning of motives and responses resides. Be spontaneous in your thinking, writing and other creative expressions, so that you create rich descriptions of your practice and your responses to issues and problems within it. If you are spontaneous you may uncover ideas and thoughts that have lain dormant for some time, or that you have kept locked away until 'some other time'. Be spontaneous in expressing all that you are now ready to express, and use the reflective guidelines in this book to help you make sense of it.

Express yourself freely

As your reflections are for yourself primarily, feel free to express them as directly and honestly as you can. These are your reflections, which you will only share with other people as you see fit, so be as explicit as you possibly can. This might mean that you swear sometimes, or use language in ways that you might not otherwise do in public. Sometimes a 'profanity' says all there is to say or write at that moment, and you can go back to it later to unpack what you actually meant when you said or wrote it. Admit to and face emotions and thoughts which emerge as you work through the reflective frameworks in this book. When you are expressing yourself freely, don't be slowed down and inhibited by trying to adhere to rules of grammar, spelling and punctuation. Just think, write and speak and so on, as freely as you can, so it pours out as directly and honestly as it can at that time.

Remain open to ideas

Reflection brings insights and partial 'truths' that may have some relevance for your practice. However, the first insight may not always be the best or the only flash of awareness that can enhance your work, so remain open to ideas so that they have a chance to grow, change or even disappear. Jumping to early conclusions may inhibit further insights and solutions, so be prepared for twists and turns in your thinking. Some questions may remain puzzles to which you always seek some answers, and that is OK, because sometimes what you learn in the search is more beneficial than what you find in the discovery. Enjoy the puzzles in reflective practice and realize that your answers will not be absolutes, but tentative responses to present problems and issues, that may need revisiting later.

Choose a time and place to suit you

Recognize the times of day when you feel alert and when you feel tired. Choose a time of day to reflect when you feel fresh and ready to give some quality time to thinking about your practice. Good planning will also mean that you set time aside in your busy life for reflecting; if it is not left to chance, it may mean that you are more likely to develop regular reflective habits. In this way, you create a time in which you can reflect, where no other pressures intervene for a while. Also, find a place to reflect that is conducive to thinking and creativity. If you are using creative strategies such as videotaping, creating music, dancing, drawing, montage, painting, poetry, pottery and quilting, these activities will to some extent determine the place in which you reflect. Even so, you can be creative in choosing places to reflect, such as parks, the beach, pool patios, aeroplanes, cruise ships and so on. The main requirement is that the place is conducive. Choose carefully a time and place in which to reflect and your reflections will be enjoyable and beneficial, while you also reward yourself by creating a space outside the confines and responsibilities of everyday work and life.

Be prepared personally

Identify the aspects of your lifestyle that put you in the best sense of freshness and preparedness. I have linked the two aspects because they relate to one another; if I feel fresh, I feel prepared for the activities of life, such as work, home duties, relationships and so on. Getting ready for reflection requires some personal preparation. What you do will be entirely up to you, but I suggest that to feel as fresh and alert as possible, you might like to do some favoured activities, such as walking, swimming, gym exercises, meditation, visualization or any other form of stimulation or relaxation which puts you into an attentive, imaginative mood.

Choose suitable reflective methods

Any of the methods/strategies in the kitbag discussed earlier, or whatever you imagine beyond the kitbag, may be used alone or in combination to enhance and maintain your reflective practice. All you have to do is decide what you want to do and set it into action. Choose your most favoured activities and experiment after that. For example, you may start by writing in a journal and then become more adventurous with video and dance. If you don't take it too seriously and have fun in the process, who knows what strategies you will use! The idea is to reflect as freely, spontaneously, deeply and honestly as possible, so experiment until you find the combination of methods which suit you best. Regardless of the reflective strategies you choose, you need to keep a record of your practice stories for reviewing, so be sure to build recorded summaries and insights into your chosen strategies.

Summary

When you reflect, by whatever method(s), it is important to consider how you prepare yourself and undertake the process. Remember to be spontaneous, to express yourself freely, to remain open to ideas, to choose a time and place to suit you, to be prepared personally, and to choose suitable reflective methods: the rest will be fun and of benefit to you.

A reflective exercise

In this section I suggest how you can recall and record your childhood memories in relation to who you are now as an adult and a clinician. I guide you through a reflective exercise, in which you respond to structured questions. This exercise is to demonstrate reflective questions and responses. This is not to suggest that you are not already reflective, because you have managed your life to this point and much of that success has come about through your reflective ability. However, for some readers, this reflective exercise marks the beginning of their intentional and systematic reflection as a clinician. If this is the case for you, welcome to reflective practice and may it make you a happier and more effective person and clinician.

I invite you to use whatever method of reflecting you choose, such as writing, audiotaping or other creative ways of enhancing reflection as described in this chapter, to think about this exercise. You may find that the answers to some questions come quickly, while others need more time. Life is not always about happy memories either, and you may find that these questions bring up memories which may be tinged with sadness or some other emotion you have not faced before.

This is a good point in the process to make a comment about the *depth* of reflection. It is a good idea to reflect only to the level at which you are relatively comfortable. This does not mean that you avoid challenges surrounding unfinished issues, but that you choose to look at them at the rate and depth at which you feel able to cope with them. This is not a process of deep psychoanalysis, because you need a skilled person to guide you in deep personal exploration. What is being encouraged here is your willingness to be open to the questions and to respond to them as directly and honestly as you can.

Reflector

Think on the person you were as a child. Find a time in your childhood in which you felt you had a good sense of who you were. Record in writing, verbally or by some other creative representation, some spontaneous responses to the questions posed below.

What were you like as a child, physically, mentally, emotionally and spiritually?
Where did you live and what was it like?
Who were the important people in your life?
Why were these people important to you?
What other influences were important in your childhood, such as other people, places and events?
What were some of the 'rules for living' you learned from these people, places and events?

Now that you have created a cameo of yourself as a child, make some connections to your adult work life as a nurse or midwife, by responding freely to these questions:

Why did you want to become nurse/midwife?
Who were some of the important people in your life during your professional education?
What is important now in your practice and the ways you choose to work?
What, if any, childhood 'rules for living' have been transferred into your adult work life as a nurse/midwife?

From your responses to these questions you may be able to see a little more clearly who you are as a person and a nurse, and how you think nursing or midwifery should be practised according to your personal values and ideals. Your responses may tell you a little or a lot about how you think your life and work should be conducted according to some of your personal ideals. The responses may also serve to show you how values, beliefs and actions can operate between the ideal expectations of childhood and the real experiences of adulthood. Keep your responses to this reflective exercise, so that you can identify connections in the stories you are yet to record. It is amazing how ideas fall into place when you take time to review them and put them into perspective. If you would like to take this exercise further, share your responses with a trusted friend, or offer some of it as a story to colleagues during a work break. You will find that you keep thinking about these questions and that other possible responses come to mind from time to time. Record all future responses to these questions and reflect on the additions, changes and extensions to your original thoughts. There is no end to reflection; it keeps on changing and moving forward.

The role of a critical friend

Sometimes external perspectives can spark interest and involvement in reflection, to move personal responses to questions beyond your present field of vision. A critical friend can offer external perspectives to extend your reflective capacity. 'Critical' in this sense does not mean criticizing, but being prepared to ask important questions and make tentative suggestions to unseat previous perceptions, to find other possibilities and insights.

A critical friend is chosen by you as someone you trust and respect, to assist you with your reflection. In this way the relationship is akin to mentorship, although with time and trust a delegated clinical supervisor could also fill this role. Because it requires professional respect and confidentiality, a critical friendship is initiated ideally by the person requiring guidance, and not as a delegated responsibility to a relative stranger working in the organization.

The role of a critical friend is to listen and respond to your reflections about clinical incidents and to assist you in making some sense of them. A critical friend realizes that they are not meant to be the person with answers to every dilemma that you might raise; rather, the role is to encourage you to find the answers yourself. By a well-timed question or a spontaneous supportive comment, a critical friend provides the necessary support and stimulation for you to be the main 'sense-maker' of your reflections.

On the whole, reflective practice centres on the work of the reflecting clinician, that is, it does not make judgements about other people's practices. This means that reflective practice requires deep thought on an individual level and the danger of that is in not being able to see the practice constraints operating in the whole situation. A critical friend can help you see the 'wider picture' and broaden your possibilities for awareness and change.

Sharing practice stories requires courage, especially when less than best practice is revealed. It takes courage and a fair measure of maturity to admit that you are not invincible, that you make mistakes sometimes, or that you could have acted better in a situation. A critical friend hears what you have to say, and lets you talk it out as fully as you can, while being non-judgemental about you as a person.

Critical friends listen more than they talk, and they avoid making early foreclosures on what they think might be the issues at hand. A critical friend allows you to talk as much as you need to, in order to give a full description of the incident that occurred, so that there will be more substance to reflect on together. By encouraging you to talk, they will allow you to come to your own awareness. They may ask a question here or there to clarify what you have said, and to point out inconsistencies in your account if they become apparent.

One of the most important parts of a reflective story is its emotional content, because if you can identify your feelings you can begin to reflect on why they are as they are, and what you can learn from them. A critical friend can encourage you to express how you really felt about something that you have identified as problematic, and contained within that disclosure may be some clues as to the nature and the effects of the problem itself and how it relates to you and your practice.

Sometimes a critical friend jots down notes of what seem to be the salient points as you speak, rather than interrupt your flow of your ideas. The critical friend may also take special interest in the specific words you use, which suggest the emotional content of the story and the sense you have made of your experiences. If your story is very brief, or it lacks sufficient details on which to reflect, your critical friend may encourage you to elaborate further.

A critical friend is willing to help you in a supportive way, to challenge you to improve your reflective practice. To do this well, there must be a sense of trust, respect, rapport and enough time and space to allow you to come to your own awareness.

Practice story

Virginia and Thea are midwives who have been practising at a local birthing centre since it opened five years previously. In that time, they have seen some changes in the way midwifery is practised, because they had both come from a hospital-based background to midwifery, where intervention rates were relatively high and natural birth was not always evidenced. They enjoyed embodying woman-centred care in their work at the birthing centre, and loved facilitating natural childbirth. Even so, at times they noticed tendencies towards interventions in labour at the birthing centre, usually when new staff such as undergraduate doctors and midwives became anxious and reactionary during labour and birth. Sensing that these practice issues would be ongoing with each influx of new staff, Virginia and Thea decided to set up a critical friendship in their reflective practice, to work through issues together.

One of the ways in which you can be encouraged to go beyond your initial interpretation of your work issues is to explore the answers to questions which trigger reflection. Some reflective questions are suggested in the next section.

Encouraging reflective questioning

In Chapters 5, 6 and 7 of this book, relating to technical, practical and emancipatory reflection respectively, you will find lists of questions that you can pose about the procedural, interpersonal relationships and power aspects of your work. They are specific questions to guide you in uncovering insights into your work and to make you a happier and more effective clinician.

Some questions are not listed easily, because they come up as a conversation continues, but the chances are that they will emerge appropriately if your critical friend is attentive to the content and flow of what you are saying. Remember that not all questions have answers and some are worth asking for their rhetorical value. One of the benefits of asking questions in this process may be the realization that it is OK to leave discussions open-ended and that quick-fix solutions are not always necessary or appropriate.

Whereas the reflective questions that follow are not 'the definitive list', they may be useful cues for you or your prospective critical friend to get you started on cycles of deeper reflection.

The reflection begins with a practice story, which describes the 'who, when, what, where, why and how' of a particular clinical situation. If the person telling the story is having difficulty in maintaining the flow of the account, some prompts may be given, such as:

What happened then?
Who was involved?
What was your part in the situation?
How did that make you feel?

If there is a departure from the main theme of the conversation and it is time to refocus, prompts can be given, such as:

You were saying before . . .
Let's go back to where you were talking about . . .

The questions used thereafter depend entirely on the content and flow of the story and these are best exemplified in the following practice story.

Practice story

Cheryle, aged 43 years, has been practising as a palliative care nurse for ten years and previous to that she worked in acute care settings in busy metropolitan hospitals. She has been committed to reflective processes for a year, since she was introduced to the ideas as a research participant in an action research project. During the project, facilitated by a nurse academic from the local university, Cheryle learned the value of reflecting on her practice. Her favoured reflective methods are writing in a journal and doing drawing and paintings occasionally to complement her writing. She also enlists the help of a trusted colleague, Jilly, who meets with Cheryle regularly and they act as critical friends for each other. On this occasion, Cheryle describes a recent experience at work and Jilly assumes the role of critical friend.

Cheryle: *I was working a morning shift in the palliative unit. I had been assigned a patient named Tom, who had carcinoma of the lung with cerebral metastases. I knew Tom reasonably well, as I had cared for him before and we got on well, sharing a joke now and then when he felt well enough. Even though most of Tom's symptoms were being controlled well, he was getting occasional breakthrough pain. He had Fentanyl patches, but he sometimes needed morphine mixture as well, to fix his breakthrough pain. He was in the unit because of a recent chest infection, so he was on antibiotics, and we were encouraging him to cough and breathe deeply, as much as he could, but we did not pressurize him too much. Anyway, I went in to see Tom and John, the other patient sharing the room with Tom, and I could tell as I walked in that Tom had been incontinent of faeces. The smell was strong and I was concerned for John. I knew Tom was due to have his daily shower, so I pulled Tom's screens and asked him quietly if he was ready for his shower. To my dismay he refused to let me help him get out of bed and said he wanted to leave his shower until the next day. My next suggestion was that he allow me to help him clean himself up and I offered to bring him in a washbowl and fresh bed linen. I was completely 'gobsmacked' when he refused to be cleaned up also!*

Jilly: *Why 'gobsmacked'?*

Cheryle: *It put me in an awful position, because he was incontinent and needed to be cleaned up, but at the same time, I did not want to push my good intentions on him by forcing him to have a wash and a linen change. To make it worse, when I tried to reason with him, he became angry and defiant, telling me to 'piss off' and leave him alone.*

Jilly: *Was that usual for Tom – to get angry?*

Cheryle: *Sometimes he reacted with anger to other nurses, but we put that down to the cerebral metastases.*

Jilly: *What was the problem in this situation for you?*

Cheryle: *What do you mean? I just said, he was incontinent and needed to be cleaned up . . .*

Jilly: *I was wondering more why it created a major response in you. What is it about the situation that made you feel 'gobsmacked'? It sounds like you also felt anxious.*

Cheryle: *Anxious, yes, definitely.*

Jilly: *Why?*

Cheryle: *Well, I haven't really thought that one through before. Yes, I was very anxious, and I think it was because I was expected to give Tom a shower, to keep him clean and to make him smell OK for John and anyone else who came in the room.*

Jilly: *Expected?*

Cheryle: *Other nurses expect you to do your job. You have to do whatever work is expected on your shift. A good nurse does the work well and on time. I did not want to look like a lazy nurse, or to look bad in some way.*

Jilly: *So, what was happening?*

Cheryle: *I can see that I was torn between Tom's need to just be left alone and my own need to be a good nurse; you know, attend to the hygiene, prevent bedsores, keep the air smelling sweetly, think of John . . . But I can see that I really felt caught up in doing what was expected of me and what I expected of myself . . .*

Conclusion

This chapter suggested that reflective practitioners need to nurture the qualities of taking and making time, making the effort, being determined, having courage and of knowing how to use humour. A kitbag of strategies for reflecting was described, including writing, audiotaping, creating music, dancing, drawing, montage, painting, poetry, pottery, quilting, singing and videotaping, used in any combination you prefer. When you reflect I encouraged you to remember to be spontaneous, to express yourself freely, to remain open to ideas, to choose a time and place to suit you, to be prepared personally and to choose suitable reflective methods. The role of a critical friend was described as a trusted and respected colleague, who assists you in reaching deeper levels of reflection by asking questions and encouraging you to challenge some of your assumptions and intentions. Reflective questioning was exemplified in a practice story. Reflective practice can take you to deeper levels of knowledge about yourself and your practice and the introductory ideas in this chapter can get you started on your way. I wish you well as you engage in reflective processes within your practice and I trust that this book will be of great benefit to you in that endeavour.

Key points

- It takes time, effort, determination, courage and humour to initiate and maintain effective reflection.
- Reflection requires time and that is one of the main reasons why nurses and midwives do not make a commitment to creating a reflective work life.
- Life is full of activities, few of which happen if you do not make an effort, which you *will* make when you suspect that something is of value, reasonably easy and of benefit to you personally.
- Determination is needed for reflection, because it is easy not to begin or to give up regular reflective processes, due to tougher pressures that compete for your time and attention.
- You need courage to look at yourself and your practice, because it takes honesty and frankness to move outside your comfort zones and invest yourself in the depth of reflection needed to change dysfunctional procedures, interpersonal interactions and power relations at work.
- Even though reflection needs to be approached seriously, and has the potential to be complex and difficult, it is not always onerous and without some degree of fun.
- There are many strategies you can use when engaging in systematic reflection.
- When you write, don't be concerned about stylistic aspects, such as neatness, grammar, spelling and punctuation, rather use spontaneity, openness and honesty.
- If you are intending to use the tape recordings without any written notes to yourself, you need to develop the habit of reviewing what you said previously to record verbal remarks on successive recordings, to keep a progressive record of the insights you have gained, so that you can make connections to what is yet to become apparent through the reflective process.
- Playing or creating music may help you to find creative expression for feelings you are having about clinical issues and to tune in to reflective insights.
- The feelings and thoughts evoked by dance can be channeled into systematic reflective processes.
- When you have drawn or doodled, record your responses to, or reasons for, the drawings you have made in relation to issues you are experiencing at work. Record your insights systematically in a lasting form so they can be revisited.
- As you search for images to express what you are thinking and feeling about clinical issues, the emergent montage becomes a

comprehensive representation of the sense you are making of certain practice events.

- By painting, you can represent a situation, a thought, an outcome or whatever it is that needs depiction for further thought.
- Your reflective poem might be one line, or develop into impressive proportions – it does not matter, just let the poem flow as long as it needs to, so that you can express the issues on your mind.
- Pottery is another creative possibility to inspire and represent reflection, so you might decide to form clay spontaneously or intentionally, noticing how you are feeling, and record your insights successively to weave them into future reflections.
- Quilting is a deliberate act of sewing to depict selected themes of life, using symbols to carefully represent the whole story depicted in the quilt.
- You can sing reflectively by creating melodies and words that come spontaneously from a creative space inside yourself.
- If you have ready access to video equipment, you might like to consider videotaping as the primary medium by which to enhance your reflection, to review yourself in terms of what you say and how say it.
- When you are reflecting, remember to be spontaneous, to express yourself freely, to remain open to ideas, to choose a time and place to suit you, to be prepared personally and to choose suitable reflective methods.
- A good exercise to get you started on reflecting is to recall and record your childhood memories in relation to who you are now as an adult and a clinician, to discover some of the values and rules for living that influence your practice.
- A critical friend can offer external perspectives to extend your reflective capacity, by asking important questions and making tentative suggestions to unseat your previous perceptions, to find other possibilities and insights.
- A critical friend realises that they are not meant to be the person with answers to every dilemma that you might raise, but rather the role is to encourage you to find the answers yourself.
- A critical friend hears what you have to say, and lets you talk it out as fully as you can, while being non-judgemental about you as a person.
- One of the most important parts of a reflective story is its emotional content, because if you can identify your feelings, you can begin to reflect on why they are as they are, and what you can learn from them.
- One of the ways in which you can be encouraged to go beyond your initial interpretation of your work issues is to explore the answers to questions, which trigger reflection.

3 The Taylor model of reflection

Introduction

As an easy guide, in a systematic flow approach to successful reflection, this chapter offers the 'Taylor model of reflection', elaborated for the first time in this book. The chapter begins with a diagrammatical representation of the model (see Figure 3.1), followed by a detailed explanation of each part of the flow. A mnemonic device using the word REFLECT is used, to represent Readiness, Exercising thought, Following systematic processes, Leaving oneself open to answers, Enfolding insights, Changing awareness and Tenacity in maintaining reflection.

Explanation of the diagrammatic representation

Diagrams of models always present a problem – of how to represent inter-related concepts in two-dimensional form and somehow achieve a sense of movement, flow and dynamism. This diagram attempts to demonstrate the systematic flow of reflection, in and through practice, within the context of self in relation to other people, within the ground of internal historical, cultural, economic, social and political constraints, orbited by and in contact with external forces and influences.

The systematic flow of reflection is within the dynamic context and tension of the workplace. Reflection is represented as a flow, rather than as steps, to show the ongoing and seamless connections between the reflective processes that permeate and flow in and through the human and material matrix of the sphere of practice. The flow may be rapid or slow, elongated or truncated, shallow or deep, bursting through the sphere of practice in unexpected places, or being directed purposefully through the matrix, depending on the clinical issues within the context and the internal and external constraints operating at any given time.

Figure 3.1 The Taylor model of reflection

Reflective processes go within, through, around and across the sphere of practice, taking reflexive turns as they dive into and out of clinical issues and phenomena. The sphere of practice is moving constantly, turning up, down and around, changing shape within itself due its own internal context and constraints, and evolving, distorting and indenting, due to pressures and influences from the external constraints, pressures and influences that constantly orbit, touch and sometimes collide with the sphere of practice.

The internal context of the sphere is made up of the complex and relatively unpredictable matrix of human and material entities, as people relate to self and to other people, within the determinants of internal historical, cultural, economic, social, political and personal constraints. The constraints act as obstructions, retardants and challenges to practice, that are negotiated by reflective processes as they flow in, around or through the constraints depending on the degree of opposition.

External constraints, pressures and influences are historical, cultural, economic, social, political and personal forces that have a bearing on work. These constraints are potentiated by other external constraints, pressures and influences, such as environmental factors, politics, consumer and professional communities, and health patterns and initiatives, from general and distal global and international levels to focused and proximal national, regional and local levels. All of the external constraints are complex and interrelated, always present, sometimes unpredictably, in an unstable and often chaotic external environment.

The closest analogy to draw from the diagrammatic representation of this model is that the sphere of practice is like a palpable and organic, yet mysterious, entity under challenge and attack from within itself and from external forces. The seamless flow of reflective processes are like the proactive, interactive and reactive means by which the sources and effects of the unpredictable and inevitable obstructions, attacks and challenges are identified and worked through to restore, maintain and possibly improve the overall integrity of the entity. Due to the ongoing severity of the insults and challenges on and in the sphere of practice, other means are also necessary to bolster the integrity of the entity, so reflective processes do not claim to be the panacea for all of the ills and challenges of practice. Rather, reflective processes provide one of many ways through which the sphere of practice can be restored, maintained and improved. Given the enormity of the task, the sphere can be assisted by people willing to engage actively in reflective processes, represented in this model by the mnemonic device REFLECT.

Reflector

Study Figure 3.1 and the explanation above and respond to the concepts the model represents, by answering the following questions:
What is your sphere of practice like?
What pressures and constraints are within your practice world?
What external pressures and constraints act on your practice world?
Do you imagine that reflection in and on your practice will assist you? If not, why not? If yes, how?

Readiness

Readiness to reflect comes from silence from within oneself, even if it is only for a moment. Being ready by being silent, even in a microsecond, prepares the person to centre from an inner place of quietness, and from there to move outwards through thought to action. The intention to be ready through momentary silence assumes an orientation towards reflective processes and acknowledges that they are potentially valuable enough to spend some time in engaging actively with them on and in practice.

Readiness for reflection also comes from some knowledge of concepts and a willingness to practise skills, shown already by other reflective practitioners to be useful. The accumulation of some knowledge and skills in readiness for reflection is akin to starting out on a journey with some idea of the itinerary and knowing in general how to get where you are going, but not necessarily with a detailed memory of the landscape, and or even a sense of the eventualities along the way.

Getting ready to reflect and to maintain a reflective attitude to your life and work requires the qualities of taking and making time, making the effort, being determined, having courage and knowing how to use humour. These qualities will serve you well as you develop reflective knowledge and skills. Even if your levels of these qualities are low and almost imperceptible, they can be nurtured through reflective practice.

Practice story

John, aged 38 years, was well known as an aged care expert. He had practised and researched aged care nursing for 16 years, and was often called on by the local university to give guest lectures and act as a clinical supervisor for nursing undergraduates gaining aged care experience in the clinical area. Even so, he had only just embarked on systematic approaches to his own practice and was aware of how much he had to learn in the area. To enhance his learning, John decided to enrol in a postgraduate course in reflective practice offered by the university. As part of that learning experience, he commenced a critical friendship with a senior lecturer at the university, skilled in assisting his reflective practice experiences. We will follow John's experience of working through a clinical issue with his critical friend, Rachael, in this section, to demonstrate the systematic flow of the REFLECT model.

John reflected on a clinical situation. He had been caring for a woman, Elsie, aged 92 years of age. Elsie had often expressed the wish to die, as she was very frail and succumbed to frequent chest infections, needing treatment at the aged care unit where John works. John became very close emotionally to Elsie over her successive admissions, and they often enjoyed conversations when Elsie was recovering. On this admission, however, Elsie was not recovering as usual after antibiotic therapy, and John was concerned that this might be her final admission. He shared his concerns with Rachael in a one-to-one meeting at the aged care centre.

Critical friend response

John: *So, where do I start with reflection?*
Rachael: *Well, when going on a journey of discovery, you need some preparation, by getting ready.*
John: *What do I do?*
Rachael: *Nothing.*
John: *Nothing? What do you mean?*
Rachael: *Just be silent for a while. Sit in quietness for a few moments and then we'll begin.*

Exercising thought

Reflection is mediated through thought on and in experience. Turning on to and tuning into thought is essential for reflective practice, because reflection is the 'throwing back of thoughts and memories, in cognitive acts such as thinking, contemplation, meditation and any other form of attentive consideration, in order to make sense of them, and to make contextually appropriate changes if they are required' (Taylor 2000: 3). Tacit knowledge, or knowing in action, which is the kind of knowledge of which clinicians may not be entirely aware, can be made explicit through exercising thought in reflection during or after practice (Schön 1987).

There are many strategies that can be used when exercising thought in systematic reflection. Some inspire reflection, others guide, and some inspire and guide simultaneously. A variety of strategies can be used and adapted in any combination and quantity to suit the situation (see Chapter 2).

When you are exercising thought in reflection, remember to be spontaneous, to express yourself freely, to remain open to ideas, to choose a time and place to suit you, to be prepared personally, and to choose suitable reflective methods.

Practice story

After a few moments of silence, John's practice story continued. He explained to Rachael that until this point in his career he had not given much thought to regular reflection. It was not as though he did not practise thoughtfully – he did – but his thinking had been mostly reactive and ad hoc, with a tendency to jump to quick and easy answers. He asked Rachael about the kind of thinking that was necessary for successful reflection.

> ### Critical friend response
>
> Rachael: *When you think, what do you do?*
> John: *I don't get what you mean.*
> Rachael: *Imagine you are watching yourself think. What are you doing?*
> John: *Nothing much. It's not as if I can see my thinking processes, but when I try to imagine it, I can see that my thoughts are often all over the place, without a lot of order and intention.*
> Rachael: *Often we are unaware of thinking, so we tend to think randomly, in reaction to situations. When we exercise thought intentionally in reflection, we direct our attention to thought and make it purposeful.*

Following systematic processes

When concepts and ideas are complex it is useful to break them down into smaller parts to make them more manageable. Reflection has the potential to be very complex, especially when practice issues and problems are in focus. For this reason, this model imagines three types of reflection – technical, practical and emancipatory, based on ways of knowing and Habermas's 'knowledge-constitutive interests', described in Chapter 4.

Technical reflection helps you to improve your instrumental action through technical control and manipulation in devising and improving procedural approaches to your work. Practical reflection helps you to understand the interpersonal basis of human experiences and offers you the potential for creating knowledge, by interpreting the meaning of lived experience, context and subjectivity, and the potential for change, based on raised awareness of the nature of a wide range of communicative matters pertaining to nursing and midwifery. Emancipatory reflection leads to 'transformative action', which seeks to free you from taken-for-granted assumptions and oppressive forces, which limit you and your practice, by critiquing the power relationships in your workplace and offering you raised awareness and a new sense of informed consciousness to bring about positive social and political change. No type of reflection is better than another; each has its own value for different purposes, and each type can be used alone or in combination with the other types.

Systematic questioning is the basis of all the reflective processes. For example, technical reflection encourages scientific reasoning, using questions within the steps of assessing and planning, implementing and evaluating. In 'assessing and planning' you set up the premises for rational thinking by making an initial assessment of the problem and planning for the development of an argument. 'Implementing' is the part of the technical reflection process in which you develop an argument by analysing the issues and assumptions operating in the situation. In 'evaluating' you review the problem in the light of all the information gained through the process of technical reflection. The outcomes of technical reflection can be immediate, if the process has been shared with, and the findings endorsed by, the key people who are in a position to influence and ratify health care practice. Technical reflection has the potential for allowing you to think critically and to reason scientifically, so that you can critique and adapt procedures and policies. You may also be able to predict likely outcomes for similar procedures and improve many work practices through objective and systematic lines of enquiry.

Through systematic questioning processes in practical reflection you will be assisted to understand the interpersonal basis of human experiences and the potential for creating new knowledge, in your lived experience, context and subjectivity. Practical reflection is a process of experiencing, interpreting and learning. Experiencing involves retelling a practice story so that you experience it again in as much detail as possible. Interpreting involves clarifying and explaining the meaning of a communicative action situation. Learning involves creating new insights and integrating them into your existing awareness and knowledge. Change is possible in practical reflection through new insights from raised awareness.

The systematic processes of emancipatory reflection will assist you to analyse critically personal, political, sociocultural, historical or economic contextual features, and constraints that may have a bearing on your practice. Emancipatory reflection provides you with a means of critiquing the status quo in the workplace and offers you a new sense of informed consciousness to bring about positive change. The process of emancipatory reflection for change is praxis, which offers you the means for change through collaborative processes that analyse and challenge existing forces and distortions brought about by the dominating effects of power in human interaction. Emancipatory reflection provides a process to construct, confront, deconstruct and reconstruct your practice. Construction of practice incidents allows you to describe, in words and other creative images and representations, a work scene played out previously, bringing to mind all of the aspects and constraints of the situation.

Deconstruction involves asking analytical questions regarding the situation, which are aimed at locating and critiquing all the aspects of that situation. Confrontation occurs when you focus on your part in the scenario with the intention of seeing and describing it as clearly as possible. Reconstruction puts the scenario together again with transformative strategies for managing change in the light of the new insights.

All kinds of knowledge can be generated through reflection, and nurses and midwives can benefit from a range of reflective processes. The first set of questions you should ask yourself in choosing a specific type or combination of types of reflection consists of: 'What do I want to know through reflection?' 'Why do I want to know it?' 'What questions will stimulate and guide my reflections and lead me to the answers I am seeking?' 'Is my primary focus on work procedures, human interaction or power relationships, or a combination of these interests?'

Finding a balance for using types of knowledge and reflection is important, because knowledge exists for all sorts of purposes and the reflective means nurses and midwives use will depend on what they need to achieve. The division of reflection into technical, practical and emancipatory is artificial and contrived for convenience – each type does not exist in isolation from another and they are not mutually exclusive. If you can develop a reflective consciousness based on balance and context, it will serve you well in deciding how to reflect on any issues which present themselves in your practice.

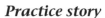

Practice story

John followed a systematic reflective process (see Chapter 6) to share his story about Elsie with Rachael. John responded to the questions raised in the process. He recounted:

It was about 4 p.m. I had been in charge on the afternoon shift for a few hours and everything was fairly quiet. We had enough staff for our shift and the patients were settled and many of them were enjoying visits from their relatives. I could smell the aroma of the evening soup coming up from the kitchen below, there was a low hum of conversation in many of the rooms, and all seemed to be well with the world.

Elsie was in a room near the nurses' desk, because she was having IV antibiotics and we needed to keep a close eye on her, because she was especially dyspnoeic this admission. I knew Elsie very well. We became friends over the years, as she was admitted often for treatment for recurrent chest infections. I had also got to know Elsie's family, especially her grandson, Keith, who was a man in his 50s. Keith always accompanied Elsie into hospital, and he was most faithful in visiting her daily. Keith's parents lived 100 kilometres south and visited Elsie as often as they could, but Keith was Elsie's mainstay.

I went into Elsie's room and Keith was sitting lovingly beside her bed. Elsie was having intranasal low flow oxygen and the IV was running on time. Elsie raised her arm weakly and beckoned me to her side, and whispered: 'Johnny, I am out of puff. I can't go on like this. I'm an old lady Johnny. Let me die.' I was so overcome with emotion that tears flowed down my face. I have never cried in front of a patient or relative before.

Critical friend's response

As John told the story his eyes glistened. He went on to say that Elsie died peacefully the next day, with Keith and her son and daughter-in-law at the bedside. He cared for Elsie's body after death and attended the funeral a week later. Rachael asked John some questions to help him interpret his own experience of caring for Elsie.

Rachael: *What were your hopes for Elsie?*
John: *I hoped she would get well and go home, as she always did.*
Rachael: *How were your hopes for Elsie related to your ideals of 'good' nursing practice?*
John: *Good nursing helps people to get better. Ideally, Elsie would get well and go home again.*
Rachael: *But Elsie did not go home. Does that make you a 'bad' nurse?*
John: *Oh no, no, of course not. I think what gets me is my reaction. I have never cried at work before in all this time!*
Rachael: *So, are your tears the issue here?*
John: *Well, yes, why did I cry? I have cared for so many other people who are dying and they never got to me like Elsie did.*
Rachael: *What are the sources in your life and work for your ideas and values about crying at work?*
John: *I come from the whole 'boys don't cry' tradition. My father always shook my hand when he greeted me, and even though my mother always encouraged me to show my feelings, I could never really get away from dad's influence. It's not that I don't feel emotion; it's just that I don't usually show it.*

Leaving oneself open to answers

Reflective processes do not necessarily provide you with indisputable 'truth' or correct answers to specific clinical issues and problems. Even so, reflection may bring insights and partial 'truths' that may have some relevance for your practice. However, the first insight may not always be the best or the only flash of awareness that can enhance your work, so remain open to ideas so that they have a chance to grow, change or even disappear. Jumping to early conclusions may inhibit further insights and solutions, so be prepared for twists and turns in your thinking.

Some questions may remain puzzles to which you will always be seeking some insights, and that is OK, because sometimes what you learn in the search is more beneficial than what you find in the discovery. Enjoy the puzzles in reflective practice and realize that your answers will not be absolutes, but consider them as tentative answers to problems and issues that may need revisiting later. Be prepared to live with uncertainty and let go of your need to know indisputably. A sense of openness and preparedness for what comes puts you in a state of readiness to entertain multiple possible answers to issues and problems encountered in rapidly changing clinical contexts.

Practice story

John and Rachael continued their conversation about John's tearful reaction to Elsie's impending death. Rachael assisted John to learn from his practice story by asking him some questions to prompt reflection.

Critical friend response

Rachael: *John, what does this story about Elsie tell you about your expectations of yourself?*

John: *I expect myself to act professionally at all times at work.*

Rachael: *And that means?*

John: *Not showing my emotions, I guess.*

Rachael: *And now?*

John: *Now it's not so 'cut and dried'. I don't regret crying for Elsie. I loved her so much and I felt genuine sadness for her. Keith was in tears too, because he heard what Elsie said to me. Even though he didn't want to face it, he knew his beloved grandmother was dying.*

Enfolding insights

As you remain open to ideas, enfold insights from multiple sources and mix new insights into present understandings, you may decide to use a variety of reflective processes and strategies as an individual or within a group and you may enlist critical friendships to assist in enfolding insights.

A critical friend can offer external perspectives to extend your reflective capacity, by asking important questions and making tentative suggestions to unseat your previous perceptions, to find other possibilities and insights. A critical friend realizes that they are not meant to be the person with answers to every dilemma that you might raise. The role is to encourage you to find the answers *yourself*. A critical friend hears what you have to say, and lets you talk it out as fully as you can.

Enfold insights and let them rest a while. What arises out of the insights will be all the richer if you allow them to gather, coalesce and merge into deeper and more meaningful possibilities for your life and practice.

> ## Practice story
>
> *John and Rachael met one week later and in the meantime John had time to think over their conversation and to enfold other insights into his experience of caring for Elsie.*

> ## Critical friend response
>
> John: *This reflective practice sure gets you in, doesn't it!*
> Rachael: *Yes, what's been happening for you John?*
> John: *I've been thinking of what we talked about – not all the time – just every now and then.*
> Rachael: *And what have you come up with? What have you learned from this situation?*
> John: *I was so surprised by my own tears. I didn't know where they came from. Previously, I lived my work life by the thought that a good nurse is a good man, and a good man does not cry. Now, I am not so sure.*

Changing awareness

Insights raise awareness and raised awareness in turn raises the possibility of change. Sometimes change is small, at local levels and sometimes it is large, within wider contexts – it does not matter, as change is change and it shifts the status quo, if only in fractional amounts. Make small, manageable changes in preference to no changes at all.

Changing awareness through reflective practice often comes through examining the emotional content of your practice stories, because if you can identify your feelings, you can begin to reflect on why they are as they are, and what you can learn from them. Express how you really felt about something that you have identified as problematic, and contained within that disclosure may be some clues as to the nature and the effects of the problem itself and how it relates to you and your practice.

Practice story

John shared his insights into himself and his practice. Rachael listened intently, nodding her head in assent most of the time, saying nothing. John had come to his own insights and all Rachael did, as his critical friend, was to listen quietly and ask a question here and there.

Critical friend response

Rachael: *So John, do you think that your story about Elsie changes your awareness about the ways you communicate at work?*

John: *Definitely. I'm not about to start crying all over the place, because that is not what it is about for me. I'm coming to understand that I can be a professional and still be able to show my emotions now and then, when they are genuinely from the heart. Maybe that's the best thing I ever did for Elsie – to show her how much I cared for her, had grown to love her, in fact. Getting close to Elsie made me vulnerable, because when she died I felt I had lost a grandmother. But, if I had it all to do over again, I'd still get to know Elsie and risk closeness, in favour of being detached and never really to get to know her as a friend.*

Tenacity in maintaining reflection

Demonstrate tenacity in your resolve to maintain reflection, so that you become a reflective practitioner for life. Some ways of maintaining reflective practice are by affirming yourself as a reflective practitioner, responding to the critiques, creating a daily habit, seeing things freshly, staying alert to practice, finding support systems, sharing reflection, getting involved in research and embodying reflective practice.

Affirm your worth as a reflective practitioner, by acknowledging your insights and how far you have come from whom and how you were when you began, to whom and how you are now. To be assured of the worth of reflection, you may need to respond to the critics, so that your investment in maintaining reflection does not suffer. To affirm your experience of reflection, it will be important to maintain the everydayness of your reflective practice, by using opportunities to take time out from the busyness of life to spend time in silence. Adopting a new way of seeing the events of everyday life can assist in maintaining reflective practice, by trying actively to keep a fresh perspective on ordinary aspects of life that you would otherwise have taken for granted. You can affirm your status as a reflective practitioner by staying alert to your practice, noticing the details that can keep you entrenched in unexamined clinical procedures, patterns of human relating and power-plays. Ascertain whether there are other clinicians engaged in reflective practice to encourage one another to maintain reflection. Share reflective experiences in your ward, department or organization, by organizing a professional development seminar or conference. There is wide scope for research incorporating reflective processes or centred on experiences of reflective practice. As a daily routine of life, begin to embody reflective practice, so that it becomes an integral part of who and how you are.

Reflector

When you engage in reflection, try using this REFLECT model, augmented by details in this book. To what extent is the model helpful/unhelpful? In what ways can you adapt it to make it more useful for your practice? When you have answers to these questions, write a journal article using the information in Chapter 8 of this book. In this way, the knowledge of reflective practice is developed with newer and deeper insights.

Summary

This chapter described a systematic flow approach to successful reflection, in the Taylor model of reflection. The chapter began with a diagrammatical representation of the model, followed by a detailed explanation of each part of the flow. A mnemonic device using the word REFLECT was used.

Key points

- The Taylor model of reflection is a systematic flow approach to successful reflection.
- The model uses a mnemonic device of the word REFLECT, to represent Readiness, Exercising thought, Following systematic processes, Leaving oneself open to answers, Enfolding insights, Changing awareness and Tenacity in maintaining reflection.
- The model represents the systematic flow of reflection, in and through practice, within the context of self in relation to other people, within the ground of internal historical, cultural, economic, social and political constraints, orbited by and in the contact with external forces and influences.

- Reflection is represented as systematic flow, to show the ongoing and seamless connections between the reflective processes that permeate and flow in and through the human and material matrix of the sphere of practice.
- Reflective processes go within, through, around and across the sphere of practice, taking reflexive turns as they dive into and out of clinical issues and phenomena.
- The sphere of practice is moving constantly, due its own internal context and constraints, and evolving, distorting and indenting, due to pressures and influences from the external constraints, pressures and influences.
- The internal context of the sphere is made up of the complex and relatively unpredictable matrix of human and material entities, as people relate to self and to other people, within the determinants of internal historical, cultural, economic, social, political and personal constraints.
- The constraints act as obstructions and challenges to practice, that are negotiated by reflective processes.
- External constraints, pressures and influences are historical, cultural, economic, social, political and personal forces that have a bearing on work.
- External constraints are potentiated by environmental factors, politics, consumer and professional communities, and health patterns and initiatives, from general global and international levels to focused and proximal national, regional and local levels.
- All of the external constraints are complex and interrelated, always present, sometimes unpredictably, in an unstable and often chaotic external environment.
- Due to the ongoing severity of the insults and challenges on and in the sphere of practice, other means of help are necessary, so reflective processes do not claim to be a panacea for all of the ills and challenges of practice.
- **R**eadiness to reflect comes from silence from within oneself, some knowledge of concepts and a willingness to practise skills, and the qualities of taking and making time, making the effort, being determined, having courage and knowing how to use humour.
- Exercising thought comes in the use of strategies, such as writing, audiotaping, creating music, videotaping etc. When exercising thought in reflection, remember to be spontaneous, to express yourself freely, to remain open to ideas, to choose a time and place to suit you, to be prepared personally, and to choose suitable reflective methods.

- Following the systematic questioning processes of technical, practical and emancipatory reflection assists you in making sense of your practice and allows for the possibility of raised awareness and change.
- Leaving oneself open to answers allows you to be prepared to live with uncertainty and let go of your need to know indisputably. That sense of openness and preparedness for what comes puts you in a state of readiness to entertain multiple possible answers to issues and problems.
- Enfold insights from multiple sources as you remain open to ideas, and mix new insights into present understandings.
- Changing awareness through reflective practice often comes through examining the emotional content of your practice stories, because if you can identify your feelings, you can begin to reflect on why they are as they are, and what you can learn from them.
- Tenacity in maintaining reflection can be achieved by affirming yourself as a reflective practitioner, responding to the critiques, creating a daily habit, seeing things freshly, staying alert to practice, finding support systems, sharing reflection, getting involved in research and embodying reflective practice.

4   Types of reflection

Introduction

This chapter sounds a note of caution about the use of categories, before introducing three types of reflection you can use in your work, and adapt to your personal life if you wish. Ways of knowing in nursing and midwifery are described as the basis for understanding how knowledge is related to reflection. Empirical, interpretive and critical knowledge are connected to Habermas's 'knowledge-constitutive interests' to create technical, practical and emancipatory reflection. The relative merits and shortcomings of the types of reflection are described, to assist you in choosing the types to use for your practice.

Caution about categories

When concepts and ideas are complex it is useful to break them down into subsections to make them more manageable. Reflection has the potential to be very complex, especially when practice issues and problems are in focus. For this reason, I have imagined three types of reflection, based on ways of knowing and Habermas's 'knowledge-constitutive interests', which are described in this chapter. Before moving to these ideas, it is important to discuss why I have chosen different types of reflection, rather than referring to one type, encompassing all the foci of reflection.

It is a tricky business to put ideas into neat, fixed categories, because concepts do not necessarily fit in 'boxes'. The complexity of knowledge has been recognized by postmodern thinkers (Baudrillard 1988; Giroux 1990; Rosenau 1992), who warn against accepting 'grand narratives' to explain human behaviour and natural phenomena. In other words, postmodernists argue that 'big' theories and categories of knowledge do not necessarily represent what we can rely on as 'truth'. Even so, in the absence of experience and prior knowledge, we need to start somewhere from a point of reference when things are relatively new and strange for us. While it is all very well for post-modernists to critique all-encompassing explanations of human life as being too generalized to matter on a personal level, sometimes we need guideposts and markers to channel our thinking. When potentially complex phenomena are in focus, structures for thinking, such as theories, models and categories can be used gainfully.

Reflector

Think about a complex issue in your life, for which you have generated simplified explanations and generalizations. If you are having difficulty finding an example, think of the ways in which your family members relate to one another. What categories do you form in your mind to explain different relatives' personalities and their ways of responding to other members of your family? When family issues come to the surface, how do you negotiate potentially difficult situations, based on your expectations of your family members' anticipated behaviours? In answering these questions, you will be relying on categorizations of family member types. From this reflection, what do you suspect are the benefits and limitations of categories and personal theories?

In this chapter, I suggest that empirical knowledge comes from technical reflection, interpretive knowledge comes from practical reflection, and critical knowledge comes from emancipatory reflection. This is not saying anything novel, as these categories have been written about previously in relation to education (Mezirow 1981) and research (Carr and Kemmis 1984). That these categories have been used successfully elsewhere suggests that they are useful, even though caution is needed in trying to fit ideas into categories.

It is important to consider these categories as ways of creating a temporary framework on which to hang certain broad principles. The tendency to create a structure fits the assumption that there are major paradigms, or world-views of knowledge, which can account for particular ways of thinking. It would be shortsighted to have an absolute conviction that there are only three forms of knowledge and reflection. I do not intend to give that message to you. The categories I am suggesting here are ways of structuring your thinking until you have the confidence you need to disregard the conceptual boxes, so that you can roam freely in open fields of uncategorized knowledge and reflection.

The three forms of knowledge and reflection described in this chapter are complementary to one another, because they share common features and at times they merge into one another. All three approaches use similar ways of thinking, even though in some cases it seems a fairly 'clean cut' decision as to the specific type of thinking to use in particular instances. For example, the tasks involved in technical reflection are best served by a high degree of rationality of a 'scientific model' kind. Also, emancipatory reflection might include some aspects of scientific rationality – say, for example, if part of the process involves changing outmoded clinical procedures to those that can be shown to demonstrate better practice. Therefore, even though I differentiate three forms of reflection connected to three knowledge types, feel free to mix and match them according to your own needs, based on the assumption that all knowledge is integrated and everything that adds something to a solution or insight is equally important. In the future, when you become more adept at being a reflective practitioner, you may choose to reflect using a specific type, or to take a 'mixed bag' approach, because you will have gained expertise in knowing how to reflect according to the demands of a particular situation.

Knowledge in nursing and midwifery

People are curious by nature, wanting to find answers to questions, and even to ask questions that have no answers. Because of this natural curiosity, human knowledge has developed over time into massive archives of particular information. Ancient cave paintings chronicle the earliest forms of knowledge, as humans thought about their place in the natural world and made sense of their existence. From the first recorded thoughts of philosophers, the history of knowledge has been structured under the broad classifications of the humanities and sciences. Knowledge specializations have developed into finer and finer distinctions within humanities and sciences, responding to two implicit concerns of human knowledge and existence, explored through epistemology and ontology. *Epistemology* concerns itself with knowledge generation and validation, meaning that it tries to ascertain how to make new knowledge and how to judge whether it is trustworthy and 'true'. *Ontology* is the meaning of the human existence. These two main foci of human interest are related to one another if you accept the argument that knowing about human existence is the basis for knowing the answers to any questions humans might pose (Heidegger 1962; Gadamer 1975).

There are many ways of thinking about knowledge and existence. Historically, in nursing and midwifery, several approaches have been suggested (Carper 1978; Parse 1985; Allen *et al.* 1986; Chinn and Kramer 1991). Carper (1978) suggested four fundamental patterns of knowing in nursing: empirics, the science of nursing; aesthetics, the art of nursing; the component of personal knowledge in nursing; and ethics, the moral component. Chinn and Kramer (1991: 15) supported Carper, but warned nurses and midwives that if these categories were removed from the context of the whole of knowing, they could lead to 'patterns gone wild'. By this they meant that each form has the potential for unbalanced applications – for example, empirics can result in control and manipulation; ethics can produce rigid doctrine and insensitivity to the rights of others; personal knowing can produce isolation and self-distortion; and aesthetics has the potential for producing prejudice, bigotry and lack of appreciation for meaning.

Practice story

Stewart is an RN with a strong fundamentalist Christian background. He has been working in community nursing areas since graduating from his university school three years ago. His community practice includes caring for people of all ages, with a wide variety of work ranging from wound management to palliative care. Stewart is conscientious in his work, never takes a sick day, and can always be relied on to do his work well and on time. He recently joined a reflective practice group at his workplace and recorded this practice story on audiotape to share with his colleagues.

I am new at reflective practice, so I realize I have a lot to learn about how to do it. Let's see – um, my work is as a community nurse, and I really love it. I haven't been registered all that long, but I know I prefer working in the community to working in hospitals. It feels much better going into people's homes where it is friendly, rather than the formality of hospital work. I've been asked to tell a practice story about an event in my work that gave me reason to feel concern. Here goes.

I have been caring for a man, Adam, who is dying from an AIDS-related illness. He lives with his partner, Roger. They have a large circle of flamboyant friends, some of whom I meet when I visit to care for Adam. Adam and Roger live out of town in a trendy rural village and their home looks like something out of vogue living – very tastefully furnished, yet quirky. Anyway, I have worked hard at overcoming my Christian values about homosexuality, and I think I've done a pretty good job of caring for Adam.

The other morning – Sunday, I arrived as usual around 10 a.m. and no one answered the door. I went around the back of the house and used the spare key under the garden gnome to open the door. As I walked in I called out to Adam. I could hear a muffled cry from the bedroom. Adam was in there, on the floor, and he couldn't get back into bed. He'd been on the floor since 10 p.m. the previous night when Roger went out to a dance party. Roger didn't come home and he left Adam all that time to fend for himself!

> ### Critical friend response
>
> Critical friend: *What gave you reason for concern in this story?*
> Stewart: *Isn't it obvious?*
> Critical friend: *Not necessarily. You tell me.*
> Stewart: *Well, Adam was very ill and Roger just left him and went out dancing. That's pretty poor form in my book. How could you leave your partner alone for 12 hours and not care about how he is?*
> Critical friend: *What judgements are you making in this story?*
> Stewart: *What do you mean?*
> Critical friend: *Play back your story and look at the any judgements you are making about Adam and Roger, and your role in caring for Adam. It may help you to use the lead-in phrase: It seems as if I feel that . . .*

Allen *et al.* (1986: 23) described three paradigms for generating knowledge within nursing and midwifery: the empirico-analytical paradigm, Heideggerian phenomenology and critical social theory. These paradigms align with Habermas's technical, practical and emancipatory categorizations of 'knowledge-constitutive interests' respectively, which will be discussed later in this chapter.

Parse (1985) categorized her own work into the simultaneity paradigm and claimed that it was a human science approach to nursing, which views a person as a unitary being in continuous mutual interrelationship with the environment. This paradigm aligns knowledge with the concept of holism and the interconnectedness of people and their environment.

Although each of these approaches has merit, the approach taken in this book is to use the categories suggested by Habermas (1972) of empirical, interpretive and critical paradigms of knowledge. As you read further in this chapter, you will notice that these three forms are able to explain human knowledge as cognitive interests, aspects of social existence, reflection and foci of learning. At this stage, however, I will describe empirical, interpretive and critical knowledge so that you can see how they relate to the kinds of reflection highlighted in this book.

Reflector

Of the examples given in this section, which forms of knowledge resonate with you and your practice? Why do they 'ring true' for you?

Empirical knowledge

Empirical knowledge is generated and tested through 'the scientific method': a set of rules for gaining knowledge through a systematic and rigorous procedure. Scientific enquiry ensures that knowledge can be tested over and over again and found to be accurate and consistent (reliability). It also ensures that it tests what it actually intends (validity), rather than other factors that are there as extra or unnoticed (extraneous variables). To achieve this, scientific knowledge is rendered as free as possible from the distorting influences of people, such as their prejudices, intentions and emotions (subjectivity). In other words, empirical knowledge needs to show that due consideration has been given to achieving objectivity.

Another requirement of empirical knowledge is that the only research questions that can be asked legitimately are those which can be structured in ways that can be observed and analysed (by empirico-analytical means) and measured by numbers, percentages and statistics (quantified). This is why research using the scientific method is also referred to as empirico-analytical and/or quantitative research. The scientific method reduces areas of enquiry to their smallest parts (reductionism) in order to study them. This idea assumes that all empirical knowledge is waiting to be discovered and assembled, as absolute knowledge. The reason empirical knowledge is reductionist is that it reduces areas of interest to their smallest parts. It also attempts to find cause and effect links between certain objects and subjects (variables), which are controlled and manipulated carefully. Empirical knowledge confirms or disputes the degree of certainty in cause and effect relationships, by demonstrating significance statistically. This allows empirical knowledge to claim to be predictive and generalizable with some confidence that the conclusions are truthful, real and trustworthy, and not happening by chance. The outcomes are achieved mainly through rational deductive thinking processes, which move systematically from broad to focused inferences.

Practice story

A group of midwives working in a neonatal intensive care unit were concerned about whether frequent handling of the neonates for procedures was resulting in the babies developing hypothermia. They knew that compromised neonates have difficulty maintaining their body temperature, because of factors associated with prematurity and low birth weight, but they also believed that touch is important for bonding and comfort for neonates experiencing intensive care procedures. The midwives decided to undertake an investigation as part of their routine care of the neonates, to focus on the effects of handling, by noting

> *temperature changes in the neonates. Their observations of the neonates' temperature change patterns over a 48-hour period showed that temperature changes occurred in relation to procedural handling. To demonstrate this hypothermic effect to their colleagues the midwives used the technical reflection process (see Chapter 5) to present a sound argument at the multidisciplinary meeting that handling of neonates results in decreased temperature recordings, and that procedural handling needs to be restricted, to allow opportunities for parents' touch.*

In summary, the scientific method generates and validates empirical knowledge through rigorous means such as reliability, validity, and control and manipulation of variables, to produce objective data that can be quantified to demonstrate the degree of statistical significance in cause and effect relationships. The outcomes of this method for the generation of empirical knowledge include description of what is, prediction for what might be, and change through new knowledge discoveries. The success of empirical knowledge is evident in nursing and midwifery through the constant evolution of newer and safer technical nursing and midwifery procedures.

Reflector

Think of two examples of work procedures that represent empirical knowledge. How can you be sure that you can 'trust' these procedures to be safe and effective? It might help you to judge each procedure against the criteria for empirical knowledge described in this section.

Interpretive knowledge

People are the focus of interpretive knowledge, because this form of knowledge features their perceptions of their life experiences and their ability to communicate them. The underlying concepts of interpretive knowledge include interpersonal understanding through attention to lived experience, context and subjectivity.

Lived experience means knowing, through living a life in a particular time, place and set of circumstances. Humans have the potential for reflecting on lived experiences. Other living beings such as animals may also have lived experiences, but they are unable to communicate them through spoken language and reflection. Therefore, lived experience in this sense is described in terms of human existence only. A philosopher named Dilthey (1985) suggests that lived experience is awareness of life without thinking about it, a pre-reflexive consciousness of life. He explains (p. 223) that 'lived experience does not confront me as something perceived or represented; it is not given to me, but the reality of the lived experience is there-for-me because I have reflexive awareness of it, because I possess it immediately as belonging to me in some sense. Only in thought does it become objective'. From this description, you can see that Dilthey thinks that lived experience happens before reflection, like a grasp of events not requiring objective thought. It is only through reflection, however, that sense is made of lived experience.

In agreement with Dilthey's understanding of lived experience, Dreyfus (1979 in Benner and Wrubel 1989: 83) claims that 'we are able to move around in the everyday world because our understanding is always situated and our actions are typically only as orderly as the situation demands'. Novel situations may be managed with reference to like situations of which people have had previous experience. This seems true of nursing and midwifery practice. Practitioners are very familiar with the work setting and circumstances, and thus they feel ready for what may transpire as part of the work day. Nurses and midwives have a knack of knowing what to do and how to do it in certain unforeseen circumstances. One explanation for this is the interpretive knowledge they have developed through their lived experience of being a practitioner.

Reflector

What is your lived experience of nursing and midwifery in relation to the ways in which you practice your work? It might help to think about the values that guide your practice and determine the way you relate to people in your workplace. Do you 'walk your talk' about how to be an effective nurse or midwife? For example, if your think that honesty is a necessary value for practice, are you always honest in every situation? If your lived experience of your practice does not fit with your espoused values, how does that make you feel?

Context means all of the features of the time and place in which people find themselves, in which their lives are located and their realities are embodied. People live their daily lives in the moment, yet they also remain connected to their past and future (Heidegger 1962). People cannot help but be placed, and involved in, a particular time and place, which gives a sense of familiarity. Context provides relative stability for daily activity, because so many things can happen in an ever-changing world. Nurses and midwives work out what to do and how to do it in any situation by making personal applications to their own life issues, worries and stories, and to their sense of time, habits and favoured rituals and patterns of behaviour in various groups. They also pay attention to how they feel and what sense they make of it based on experience.

Subjectivity refers to the individual's sensing of inner and external events, which is appropriate for themselves. Subjectivity includes personal experiences and 'truths' that may or may not be like other people's subjective experiences and 'truths'. 'Intersubjectivity' refers to how individuals take account of one another in the social world to make sense of their experiences. Nursing and midwifery occur in social contexts in which intersubjective meanings are generated, because clinicians interpret their work experiences from their respective person-to-person viewpoints.

Practice story

Returning to Stewart's practice story, recounted earlier in this chapter, he reflected on the judgements he made about Adam and Roger and his role in Adam's care. He said to the reflective group: 'My critical friend really got me thinking when she asked me to reflect on the judgements I made about Adam and Roger. At first I thought: "Judgements? What judgements?" and then I realized I made plenty of judgements, that's for sure, but it took me a while to work out just what they were. She suggested I use the phrase "It seems as if I think/believe . . ." I replayed the story I recorded and then I wrote my responses in my journal. Here's what I wrote.'

It seems as if I think I work according to my Christian values. It seems as though I have judged homosexuality as against my faith. Even though I am actively working on adjusting my Christian values in caring for Adam, it seems as if I see homosexuality as a 'special case', or a kind of perversion, that needs adjustment, and for me it takes a lot of effort to accept. Seeing Adam and Roger together helps me to see that theirs is a loving relationship, like any other relationship, so it has been good for me to see them both up close, and to realize that many of my fears about homosexuals are unrealistic. I have been thinking a lot about my reaction to finding Adam on the floor and it seems as if I think that Roger was thoughtless in leaving him alone for so long. This is where I am starting to see my worst judgement. It seems as if I believe I know what is OK for Adam and Roger. In other words, I don't know what they had decided about the dance party. Maybe Adam knew Roger would not be driving home. It was just bad luck that Adam fell out of bed, poor man. It doesn't make Roger a 'baddie', and I realize I am in no position to make judegments about the way they interpret their relationship – or anyone's relationship for that matter.

In summary, interpretive knowledge emerges from the perspectives of people engaged personally in their lives and it includes and values what people feel and think. Judgements as to the usefulness and 'truthfulness' of people's accounts are based on relative indicators, such as the nature of lived experience, context and subjectivity.

Critical knowledge

Critical knowledge is derived from some key ideas in critical social science, which emerged from the social and epistemological needs that presented after World War I. In a nutshell, a group of philosophers of the Frankfurt School decided that a way of generating knowledge other than through the scientific method was needed to open up new thinking about human knowing and experience, in order to prevent future wars and domination by oppressive regimes. Critical knowledge has the potential to be emancipatory – that is, it can free people from the oppression of their entrenched social and personal conditions.

The need for emancipation comes from the assumption that certain people, in the circumstances in which they find themselves, may suffer oppression and constraints of some kind, by other people and regimes. Freedom from oppression comes from being aware that it is happening in terms of historical, social, political, cultural and economic determinants and from finding the means to do something about it. Critical knowledge and theorizing seek to look into what is promoted as the status quo of various repressive social contexts, to discover and expose the forces that maintain them for their particular advantages. This means that critical theorists look at the way life is and ask how it might be different and better for the majority of people, not just for the privileged few.

Critical knowledge includes consideration of lived experience, context and intersubjectivity; other related key ideas are false consciousness, hegemony, reification, emancipation and empowerment. You will see that the first three words describe the oppressive potential of social life, and the last two provide some optimism about how repressive circumstances can be overcome.

False consciousness is the 'systematic ignorance that the members of . . . society have about themselves and their society' (Fay 1987: 27). Critical knowledge attempts to critique firmly held individual and collective ignorance to change this self-defeating consciousness and transform society itself. For example, the women's movement of the twentieth century finally identified and challenged women's oppression by men after centuries of assimilating male dominance. One of the reasons western women remained oppressed for so long was the firmly held ignorance of the oppression itself, perpetuated by the unquestioned acceptance of male-dominated cultural practices. Nurses and midwives might relate to the concept of false consciousness as clinicians working in bureaucratic settings where oppressive daily rituals remain unquestioned, because they are unnoticed. For example, nurses and midwives may continue to accept power structures in their workplace, such as interpersonal relationships that keep them subservient to doctors and administrators, because in trying to maintain their employment they do not even think to 'rock the boat' and critique and challenge oppressive forces. The difficulty with false consciousness is the systematic ignorance itself, because it is sustained by unawareness, so it takes deep and sustained reflection to even uncover some issues as problematic.

Hegemony means the ascendancy or domination of one power over another. In a critical social science interpretation, it refers to the ways in which some social systems, and the people in them, give the impression that they are unassailable, and that the conditions they have produced are not only good, but also appropriate for the people over whom they have control. In nursing and midwifery, this might mean that nurses come to think that the hospital bureaucracy is not only necessary, but also conducive to their welfare, and that the oppressive elements within it, such as dominating relationships and difficult work conditions, cannot and should not be changed. Thus, hegemony would have nurses and midwives believe that they can do little to change their work lives. Hegemonic influences maintain the status quo and are resistant to change, so clinicians need to critique taken-for-granted assumptions about everyday practices, in order to identify and change them in their workplace.

Reflector

Can you identify hegemonic practices where you work? What are they? Why are they so powerful? What, if anything, can be done about them? If your responses to this reflector are pessimistic of change at this point, take heart, as emancipatory reflection, as described in this book, may provide some optimistic options for action.

Fay (1987: 92) explains that reification means 'making into a thing'. He defines it as 'taking what are essential activities and treating them as if they operated according to a given set of laws independently of the wishes of the social actors who engage in them'. These laws of social life are assigned a power of their own. For example, a female nurse or midwife may assume that, as a woman, it is a given that she will be subordinate to doctors who are often males, so she acts in accordance with that assumption and fetches, carries, cleans up and generally accedes to the doctors' orders. Reified practices are rich sources of reflection and they can be identified and changed through systematic questioning and action.

Emancipation means freedom, and it infers that one is free *from* something and free *towards* something. Critical knowledge claims to be helpful in emancipating people to be liberated from their present oppressive conditions to be freed towards empowering conditions. Emancipation for nurses and midwives, therefore, can mean that they experience freedom from the limitations of their own and other people's expectations and roles, to be free to adopt expansive self-aware and socially aware practices.

Empowerment is the process of giving and accepting power. Critical knowledge is geared towards helping people to find their own power, to liberate them from their oppressive circumstances and self-understandings in those circumstances. Empowerment for nurses and midwives may come about when they have used reflection to work through a radical critique of their personal and professional roles and conditions and they have liberated themselves to other possibilities. In a practical sense this may be something seemingly simple, such as being the patients' advocate, or demonstrating and asserting their worth as nurses or midwives in the health team. While these examples may not seem extraordinary, they can amount to major changes in daily practices that in turn open up other opportunities for being empowered and empowering others.

Practice story

Five nurses – Ken, Bobby, Dianne, Bev and Alan – formed a reflective practice group. Through discussion of their practice stories, they realized that even though they worked in different specialty areas, they had a common issue they all faced: of lacking the courage to speak up in some clinical situations in which people in authority exercised power over them. Even though the stories differed according to the settings in which the nurses worked, they acknowledged the same sense of helplessness and frustration, especially when attempting to act as patients' advocates with other members of the multidisciplinary team. The nurses decided to use the emancipatory reflective process (see Chapter 7) to work through their issue of lacking assertive skills. Through continued reflection they identified specific instances in which they acted according to the belief that it is disrespectful to speak up against seniority, even if there is reasonable cause to do so. They traced this value to childhood influences of families, school and church, all of which influenced conformity to the ideal of respecting elders. They discussed why they felt hesitant to speak up in the patients' favour at work even when it was reasonable to do so, the power relations that were involved and other constraints operating in the practice stories they shared. This process resulted in small yet significant personal insights that were applicable directly to changing practice from silence to assertion when clinical situations required someone to speak up for the patients' rights.

Reflector

Think about your recent practice. In what small or grand ways have you helped other nurses or midwives to gain some sense of emancipation in their work? In what ways has anyone offered you the means to feel liberation of some sort in your work? If the outlook is bleak and few emancipatory events happen where you work, you may find that reflective practice heightens your awareness for liberating change for you and your colleagues.

In summary, critical knowledge is potentially liberating for individuals and groups of people, when they realize that they may be living under systematically entrenched misunderstandings about themselves and their social situations. As people and clinicians, nurses and midwives are subject to oppressive social structures, which can be transformed through critical reflection and action, the results of which constitute critical knowledge.

Knowledge and human interests

Jurgen Habermas, a prominent philosopher and sociologist, expounded a compelling critical theory of knowledge and human interests. These ideas are central to how I formulated the three kinds of reflection. My description of Habermas's ideas is derived from some of his work (Habermas 1972) and from other writers who have supported his work (Mezirow 1981; Fay 1987).

As a critical theorist, Habermas argued that human knowledge could be categorized as technical, practical and emancipatory, based on primary cognitive interests. He suggested that these areas are 'knowledge-constitutive interests', because they determine what humans count as important knowledge. He based this on his reasoning that humans have constructed experience socially, and that knowledge and social existence represent identifiable human interests. In other words, he claimed that knowledge and how we judge it to be 'truth' (epistemology) is constructed according to the sense we make of our existence and how we live socially (ontology). He argued that these interests in knowledge are based on aspects of social existence, such as work, human interactions and power relationships. He connected technical interests to work, practical interests to interaction and emancipatory interests to power. I have adopted the categorizations of these interests to name the types of reflection described in this book.

Technical interest and work

In Habermas's view, technical interest in work creates 'instrumental action' through which people control and manipulate their environments. This means that people act in accordance with technical rules to generate empirical knowledge. I explained empirical knowledge previously in this chapter, but you may recall that it relates to finding information, which can be proven to be correct or incorrect according to the rules of the scientific method. The empirical-analytical sciences have been developed to assist in understanding technical interests relating to work. These sciences are identified readily by their use of quantitative research methods, which allow them to generalize results and predict future tendencies for similar effects and outcomes to occur. For nurses and midwives, this means that technical interest is associated with task-related competence, such as clinical procedures. There is an increasing call in nursing and midwifery for evidence as a basis for better practice and many of the work practices that need to be improved require technical interest using objective and systematic lines of enquiry, so this interest fits well with technical reflection, to be described later.

Practical interest and interaction

Practical interest involves human interaction, or 'communicative action', which involves reciprocal expectations about behaviour, which are defined and understood by the people concerned. Social norms, or sets of expectations for behaviour, are created over time by people who are in consensus as to what is expected in certain situations. The social norms are enforced through sanctions, which ensure that people recognize and honour their responsibilities in reciprocal behaviour. If this sounds complex, think of it as in a nursing or midwifery context, where communicative action translates to something as familiar as the communication patterns that are set up by clinicians with other people. For example, the ways in which you communicate may differ between people – you may communicate in a certain way with patients' relatives in a waiting room and in a different way with doctors at the unit desk.

Practical interest in communicative action requires understanding it according to the people involved. Its main intentions are to describe and explain human interaction, so this kind of interest is situated in the 'historical-hermeneutic sciences', which are concerned with interpretation and explanation. Some examples of these sciences are history, aesethics and literary studies. Practical understanding is mediated through language, which describes and explains the area of interest. Previously I referred to this kind of knowledge as interpretive knowledge, because it intends to understand human interaction through understanding the meaning of experience. Practical interests abound in nursing and midwifery and they can be reflected on systematically through practical reflection, described later in this chapter.

Emancipatory interest and power

Emancipatory interest is rooted in power and creates 'transformative action'. It involves the interpretive elements as described previously in practical interest, because people interpret themselves in terms of their roles and social obligations. However, the main intentions of emancipatory interest are motivated by 'transformative action' which seeks to provide liberation from forces which limit people's rational control of their lives. These forces are so influential and taken for granted that they give people the strong impression that they are beyond their control.

The modes of enquiry for exploring and critiquing emancipatory interests associated with power are the critical social sciences. Some examples include critical forms of sociology, politics and feminism. Critical theorists suggest that people must become conscious 'of how an ideology reflects and distorts moral, social and political reality and what material and psychological factors influence and sustain the false consciousness which it represents – especially reified powers of domination' (Mezirow 1981: 145). The kind of radical critique suggested by Mezirow is necessary for nurses and midwives as they examine the effects of power in their work settings and how situations become entrenched and taken for granted and continue to constrain work relationships and practices. Thus, I have adopted the label of emancipatory reflection to uncover and potentiate emancipatory interests at work.

In summary, in this book I have chosen to refer to three types of reflection, which are derived from Habermas's technical, practical and emancipatory 'knowledge-constitutive interests'. This is not a novel decision, as similar approaches have been taken in education and research. Habermas connected technical interests to work, practical interests to human interaction and emancipatory interests to power. Technical interest in work creates 'instrumental action' through which people control and manipulate their environments. Practical interest creates human interaction or 'communicative action', which involves reciprocal expectations about behaviour, defined and understood by the people involved. Emancipatory interest is rooted in power and creates 'transformative action' through which people can free themselves from forces which limit their rational control of their lives. In the next section, I connect Habermas's 'knowledge-constitutive interests' to technical, practical and emancipatory reflection.

Table 4.1 may help you to distinguish the features of each paradigm according to the cognitive interests related to the kind of reflection, the aspects of social existence, and the action and learning involved.

Three types of reflection

Nurses and midwives engaged in daily practice have the advantage of living their practice, in that they have opportunities to look every day at their practice to learn from it. When nurses and midwives reflect on what they do, they can make sense of their practice, and imagine and/or bring about changes (Freshwater 2002a, 2002b; Johns 2002; Taylor 2004). The kinds of change they desire might direct the kind of reflection they use.

Table 4.1 Three paradigms of knowledge with associated cognitive interests, aspects of social existence, action and learning involved

	Paradigm of knowledge		
Critical	*Empirical*	*Interpretive*	
Cognitive interests related to the kind of reflection	Technical	Practical	Emancipatory
Aspect of social existence	Work	Interaction	Power
Action involved	Instrumental	Communicative	Transformative
Learning involved	Task-related competence	Interpersonal	Transformative

In this section I highlight the advantages and limitations of technical, practical and emancipatory reflection. I also suggest that each type is as important as the others and that a type or combination of types may be used according to the requirements of a clinical situation. Because each of these ways of reflecting is important, I have devoted a chapter to each of them in this book. All I am intending to do in this section is to give you a brief introduction to the individual features of technical, practical and emancipatory reflection.

Technical reflection

The influence of the scientific model on empirical knowledge is apparent in daily practice. Many innovations and evidence-based adaptations in nursing and midwifery have been possible because of empirical knowledge, which is gained through empirical research and technical reflection.

The scientific method and rational, deductive thinking and reflection allow you to generate and validate empirical knowledge through rigorous means, so that you can be assured that work procedures are based on scientific reasoning. If clinical questions and issues are complex, as they tend to be when they are related to competency in practice, technical reflection may accompany empirical research projects, which are based on reliability, validity, and control and manipulation of variables. The technical reflection thus instigated will produce objective data that can be quantified to demonstrate the degree of statistical significance in cause and effect relationships. Technical reflection allows you to adapt and improve work procedures. You may also be able to predict likely outcomes for similar procedures. Technical reflection helps you to improve your instrumental action through technical control and manipulation in devising and improving procedural approaches to your work.

Although technical reflection offers a great deal of important knowledge in relation to providing evidence for the competency of work practices and procedures, by itself it will not be sufficient to interpret the meaning of what it is like to exist and work in settings that rely on making sense of their interpersonal communication patterns and behaviours. Technical reflection by itself will not assist you in understanding the social interactions and consensual norms that govern the communication of the people undertaking and receiving the procedures, because it does not have an interest in human interaction and communicative action. Also, technical reflection by itself will not raise your awareness of power relationships between the givers and receivers of procedures and it will not provide a radical critique of the unexamined assumptions about social, economic, historical and cultural influences that underlie the instrumental action in procedural activities, because it does not have an interest in power and transformative action.

Technical reflection methods and processes are explained in detail in Chapter 5.

Practical reflection

Interpretation for description and explanation are the key outcomes of practical reflection, which focuses on human interaction in social existence. Communicative action in nursing or midwifery relates to shared communication of norms and expectations.

Practical reflection offers a means of making sense of human interaction. Through the medium of language, practical reflection helps you to understand the interpersonal basis of human experiences and offers you the potential for creating knowledge, which interprets the meaning of lived experience, context and subjectivity. It also offers you the potential for change, based on your raised awareness of the nature of a wide range of communicative matters pertaining to nursing and midwifery.

However, practical reflection will not offer you the objective means to observe and analyse work procedures through a scientific method, because it does not have an interest in instrumental action. Also, practical reflection will not offer you a radical critique of the constraining forces and power influences within nurses' and midwives' work settings. The reason for this is that, although practical reflection can raise awareness through insights into communicative action, it does not have transformative action as its primary concern.

Practical reflection methods and processes are explained in detail in Chapter 6.

Emancipatory reflection

Emancipatory reflection involves human interaction, but its focus is on how people interpret themselves politically in terms of their roles and social obligations. Emancipatory reflection leads to 'transformative action', which seeks to free nurses and midwives from assumptions and oppressive forces which limit them and their practice.

Emancipatory reflection provides you with a systematic means of critiquing the power relationships in your workplace and offers you raised awareness and a new sense of informed consciousness to bring about positive social and political change. Emancipatory reflection also offers nurses and midwives the potential to identify their own misguided and firmly held perceptions of themselves and their roles, to bring about positive change. The process of emancipatory reflection for change is praxis. Praxis in nursing and midwifery offers clinicians the means for change through collaborative processes that analyse and challenge existing forces and distortions brought about by dominating effects of power in human interaction.

Even though emancipatory reflection provides a critique of power in your work setting and relationships, it will not offer you a central focus on the technical interest of procedures at work, because it does not have an abiding and primary interest in instrumental action. Also, even though it begins with analyses of social interactions and consensual norms that govern human communication, emancipatory reflection is more concerned with examining the distortions that occur in communicative action than it is with generating a rich description of the meaning of human experience as it is lived by people involved in the practice of nursing and midwifery.

Emancipatory reflection methods and processes are explained in detail in Chapter 7.

Choosing a type of reflection

No type of reflection is better than another; each has its own value for different purposes. This is the same as saying that no one form of knowledge is superior to another. For example, empirical knowledge was once valued over other types. For a long time, nurses and midwives thought they had to imitate the medical model and the scientific method in the way they thought about and researched their work. As a consequence of dominant scientific approaches, a culture developed which included specific traditions, such as the use of objective language in conversations and nurses' and midwives' notes, and reductionist approaches to people requiring specific attention to affected body parts. Added to this was a strong belief that the only kind of research that was useful and valid was quantitative, because it involved prediction, control, numbers and statistics, which were seen to serve medical practice well, and could thus benefit nursing and midwifery. Some nurses and midwives have 'moved on' from the days of medical domination and scientific rationality, but many more may not be aware of the other choices they can make in making sense of their practice.

All kinds of knowledge can be generated through reflection, and nurses and midwives can benefit from a range of reflective processes. The first set of questions you should ask yourself in choosing a specific type or combination of types of reflection consists of: 'What do I want to know through reflection?' 'Why do I want to know it?' 'What questions will stimulate and guide my reflections and lead me to the answers I am seeking?' 'Is my primary focus on work procedures, human interaction or power relationships, or a combination of these interests?'

Practice story

Nancy is a midwife working in a hospital setting. She has 20 years of experience in all areas of midwifery, but she prefers to work in antenatal units. For some time she had noticed prejudicial attitudes from some of her midwife colleagues in relation to teenage pregnancies. Nancy also acknowledged a sense of growing frustration herself, especially when multiple pregnancies occur for some individuals, due to lack of contraception. Nancy formed a midwives' reflective practice group and suggested that they reflect collectively on the issue of teenage pregnancies and their attitudes towards them. The midwives required statistics on the incidence of teenage pregnancies and parenting, and they also needed to look at their own tendencies to make negative judgements about the situation. The group realized that there may not be simple explanations for the issue and that a combination of reflective processes was needed, such as technical and practical reflection.

In the section above I described the features of technical, practical and emancipatory reflection. I think that finding a balance for using types of knowledge and reflection is important, because knowledge exists for all sorts of purposes and the reflective means nurses and midwives use will depend on what they need to achieve. Returning to a point I made previously, the categories of reflection are artificial and contrived for convenience – they do not exist in isolation from one another and they are not mutually exclusive. Remember this as you read on through this book, so that your choices can be informed by broader considerations than choosing one type of reflection over another. If you can develop a reflective consciousness based on balance and context, it will serve you well in deciding how to reflect on any issue which presents itself in your practice.

Critical thinking and reflection

This section describes a particular form of thinking that has been used for many decades by nurses and midwives: critical thinking. Thinking is essential for reflection. The ability to think in a systematic and rational way separates humans from other species and gives people reflective consciousness. Thinking is integral to reflection, and the kind of thinking required for making sense of personal and work events can differ according to the demands of the situation and the enormity of the task. For example, searching for answers to difficult questions about quantum physics is a different cognitive task and uses complex thinking processes, relative to deciding what to wear to a concert, or when to get out of bed in the morning. When thinking takes on complex proportions, it is of a more critical nature. Authors (e.g. Bandman and Bandman 1995; van Hooft et al. 1995) have described critical thinking and emphasized its use in nursing and midwifery. All of these authors agree that critical thinking is essential for safe practice and that rationality is its first requirement. This section defines critical thinking, and describes its component parts, skills and attitudes, and how they relate to reflection. Technical, practical and emancipatory reflection all require some degree of critical thinking, but the most obvious application is in technical reflection.

Definitions of critical thinking

According to Bandman and Bandman (1995: 7) critical thinking is 'the rational examination of ideas, inferences, assumptions, principles, arguments, conclusions, issues, statements, beliefs, and actions'. They clarify their definition by stating that critical thinking includes scientific reasoning, the use of the nursing process, decision-making and reasoning about issues. Adding further specifications to the definition, they make it clear that critical thinking is reasoning in which we analyse the use of language, formulate problems, clarify and explicate assumptions, weigh evidence, evaluate conclusions, discriminate between good and bad arguments, and seek to justify those facts that result in credible beliefs and actions.

Van Hooft et al. (1995: 6–7) identify the first important element of critical thinking as rationality. In supporting their prioritization, they use the Bandman and Bandman (1995) definition, but they follow this up with some important qualifying statements which describe the nature of critical thinking and thinkers. They summarize critical thinking as being rational, practical as well as theoretical, and conducive to dialogue, and describe critical thinkers as committed, self-aware and sympathetic to the commitments of others. This adds some human aspects to the definition of critical thinking which are missing from Bandman and Bandman's definition. These authors tend to feature rationality as an objective process, and to understate the subjective qualities of the people possessing the capacity for rational thought.

Wilkinson (1996: 26) defines critical thinking as 'both an attitude and a reasoning process involving a number of intellectual skills' and places rationality at the head of the list of characteristics. Interestingly, Wilkinson's account of critical thinking has the strongest human emotion content in that, while she acknowledges the central role of rationality, she also emphasizes the subjective side of critical thinking by describing the skills and attitudes of critical thinkers.

Component parts

Whereas the definitions of critical thinking may be useful in their comprehensiveness, they introduce many words which require definition, such as reasoning, scientific reasoning, assumptions and argumentation.

Reasoning refers to the act of drawing conclusions from *premises*, which are statements leading up to end findings or summary statements. Premises show a discernible pattern of thought, which follows logically from a former idea. For example, reasoning often includes 'if-then' statements, such as: 'If nurses work on improving their own patterns of communication, then they will be better able to develop therapeutic relationships with patients'. Reasoning may have many steps in the pathway between the original and end statements. The more complex the reasoning, the greater the need for more premises or propositions to make and support a stronger argument.

In this context, an *argument* is not a quarrel; rather, it means a well thought out and delivered defence of a point of view supported by sound reasoning. Not all premises in an argument may be stated openly – they may be hidden as *assumptions*, which may be discerned as 'gaps' in the logic of arguments. It is not difficult to recognize assumptions in an argument because people tend to make them frequently, in the often-mistaken belief that others will be able to 'fill in the gaps' through their own knowledge and experience of the topic being discussed.

Words such as *because, hence, since, so, therefore* and *thus* may be used to maintain the flow of the argument and indicate the connections between the ideas expressed in the statements used to support the conclusions. For example, reasoning may be presented thus: communication is an important interpersonal skill, which all people need, because it is integral to everyday life. Since midwives care for women who may not be able to express their concerns about motherhood, it is especially important for midwives to refine their communication skills; therefore, professional development sessions should include opportunities to improve knowledge and practice communication skills.

Scientific reasoning refers to a certain kind of argument which reflects the assumptions underlying 'the scientific model'. The main features of scientific knowledge are that it claims to be objective (free from emotionality), systematic, rigorous in terms of the way in which it is organized and validated, and able to predict and explain relationships between variables. Typically, the scientific approach to reasoning is to state a problem, give a preliminary hypothesis setting out the expected relationships between variables, collect more facts in order to formulate a hypothesis, deduce further consequences, test those consequences, and finally apply the findings to confirm or disconfirm the hypothesis (Bandman and Bandman 1995).

This kind of reasoning is advantageous in thinking through the consequences of adaptations to nursing and midwifery procedures, so that they can be made more effective and based on sound scientific reasoning, rather than folklore or some other untested assumptions. Scientific reasoning of this kind is structured into quantitative research designs to ensure that methods produce credible and dependable results. As this book cannot deal with all that is inferred by the mention of research, I suggest that you consult some research texts if you would like to pursue these ideas (e.g. Crookes and Davies 1998; Roberts and Taylor 2001; Young *et al.* 2001).

Skills and attitudes

According to Wilkinson (1996), the cognitive skills required for critical thinking include decision-making and problem-solving methods. Nurses and midwives make decisions constantly about the best ways of achieving clinical goals. Problem-solving involves assessing, planning, implementing and evaluating the best courses of action in given situations so that the most effective care can be negotiated. Wilkinson suggests that methods of problem-solving might include intuition, as described by Benner (1984) and Benner and Tanner (1987), the scientific method and the nursing process. Intuition is part of expert clinical practice and is acquired through years of knowledge and experience when patterns and cues from prior like instances present rapidly and completely to an expert's consciousness. The scientific method was described earlier in this chapter, and the nursing process is a well documented problem-solving one, which has been used by nurses and midwives for many decades. If you need to explore this method further, read Wilkinson (1996), because she explores the nursing process through a critical thinking approach.

The attitudes suggested for critical thinking include thinking independently, intellectual humility, courage, empathy, integrity and perseverance. Wilkinson (1996: 29–32) also suggests that other attitudes required are faith in reason, fair-mindedness and the need to explore thoughts and feelings. Unsurprisingly, independent thinking requires critical thinkers to be able to think and to 'stand up' for themselves. Nurses and midwives must be able to be autonomous, because so many work decisions must be made quickly for the best results. Intellectual humility means being prepared to own up to what you do not know, so that you do not act deceptively. Intellectual courage is needed when critical thinkers are prepared to reassess their own ideas in the face of new information, which is based on sound reason and evidence. Intellectual empathy is the ability to imagine yourself 'in the place of others in order to understand them and their actions and beliefs' (p. 30). Intellectual integrity is about being honest and consistent in your thinking. Intellectual perseverance is about being determined to sort through issues and options to overcome confusion and complexities. Faith in reason refers to a belief in the soundness of rationality and allows critical thinkers 'to distinguish intuition from prejudice' (p. 31). Fair-mindedness occurs when critical thinkers 'consider opposing points of view and listen with an open mind to new ideas' (p. 31). Finally, Wilkinson (pp. 31–2) suggests that 'all feelings are based on some kind of thinking, and all thought creates some kind of feeling'. Knowing this, critical thinkers consider their own and the other person's feelings, in order to understand the presenting behaviour.

Reflector

Think of an example of a work situation when you used critical thinking. In what ways did you portray the attitudes suggested for critical thinking of thinking independently, intellectual humility, courage, empathy, integrity and perseverance?

Although van Hooft *et al.* (1995: 5) deal extensively with the intellectual skills needed for critical thinking, they also make it clear that 'critical thinking does not consist only of rational cleverness. It includes empathy and sensitive perception'. Maintaining dogged attention to the need for rationality, Bandman and Bandman (1995: 7–8) do not describe the skills and attitudes of the critical thinker as such; rather, they provide a checklist of the functions critical thinkers should perform. They suggest that critical thinkers:

- use the process of critical thinking in all of daily living;
- discriminate among the uses and misuses of language in nursing;
- identify and formulate nursing problems;
- analyse meanings of terms in relation to their indication, their cause or purpose and their significance;
- analyse arguments and issues into premises and conclusions;
- examine nursing assumptions;
- report data and clues accurately;

- make and check inferences based on data, making sure that the inferences are at least plausible;
- formulate and clarify beliefs;
- verify, corroborate and justify claims, beliefs, conclusions, decisions and actions;
- give relevant reasons for beliefs and conclusions;
- formulate and clarify value judgements; and
- evaluate the soundness of conclusions.

The relation of critical thinking to reflection

Reflection requires thinking of some kind. I have already defined reflection as the throwing back of thoughts and memories in cognitive acts such as thinking, contemplation, meditation and any other form of attentive consideration, in order to make sense of them, and to make contextually appropriate changes if they are required. In the latter part of this chapter, I focused on critical thinking as useful for certain issues in nursing and midwifery. Critical thinking has been described and endorsed at length by authors convinced of its necessity in making informed clinical decisions based on rationality. There is much more to reasoning than I have overviewed in this chapter – in fact, it is the subject of several books (e.g. Bandman and Bandman 1995; Rubenfeld and Scheffer 1995; van Hooft *et al.* 1995). Reasoning of this kind is quite complex and requires your considered attention to do it well.

Critical thinking gives you more choices about the ways in which you choose to reflect. If you require careful, fully analytical reasoning to assure you of the conclusions you have drawn in relation to some objective issues in your practice, critical thinking processes are worthy of your attention. Whatever you do in reflection, some kind of reasoning will almost invariably be involved, even if it is only to make direct connections between events to find patterns and themes in your work.

Other ways of 'thinking' in reflection

Reasoning will almost invariably be involved in considering choices, but there are other ways of 'thinking' that are less acknowledged. For example, we also 'think' through intuitive grasps, creative expression and inner knowing that is not easily rationalized, such as contemplation and meditation.

Sometimes connections are made between events with what appears to be no conscious thinking. It is as though the answers are already there just as the questions are posed or even a split second before they are asked. It is possible to have an intuitive grasp such as: 'I've got it! I know!' Some people explain this phenomenon by appealing to the effects of experience, while others claim that it is independent of experience – they would say that *it just is*. Whatever the source of knowing, either through experience or direct awareness, however gained, intuitive grasps can occur and, having happened, are worthy aspects of reflection. The reason for needing to explore intuitive grasps further is that the conclusion thus gained may not turn out to be reliable over time, with more circumstances and information. If intuitive grasps are to be acknowledged – and I consider that they are worthy of acknowledgement – they can be balanced with further reflection that tries to find some other evidence for the conclusions which have come so rapidly. Time may show that the grasps were groundless, or conversely they may reveal deep knowing of unquestionable value. My suggestion is that they be noticed and explored to see if they can add to the outcomes of reflection. It is too easy to dismiss things that cannot be explained objectively, but if they are entertained in a tentative way until further information is gained, they might prove to be complementary to methods of thinking based on some form of rationality.

Reflector

Think of a practice situation in which you *just knew* something was wrong with a patient without even checking that person's vital signs. How did you know without objective evidence?

Reflection can be facilitated through creative expression. Whether the expression precedes or follows reflection is a moot point, but that it *can* occur is sufficient cause to admit it into the ways in which 'thinking' can be done. For example, I may not know where to start in reflecting on how I feel about the death of a patient I have nursed for some time, so I could paint a picture and see what manifests from the spontaneous depiction of my subconscious-ness. Alternatively, I could write a poem and let it wander until it tells me how I feel about the death. Maybe I could even allow my body to tell me in a private dance as I think of the person. I could sing a song I create in the moment, noticing the words I sing and the sound of the music I let flow out of me. The ways in which I can reflect creatively on anything in my clinical practice and my life are limited only by my imagination and my motivation to try something novel.

Other forms of reflective thinking or inner knowing which cannot easily be rationalized are contemplation and meditation. Much has been written about these forms of reflecting (Brennan 1987, 1993; Houston 1987; Capra 1988, 1992; Judith 1992) and it is not my intention to go into issues such as their worthiness, methods or how or why they are done. The contradiction here is that they facilitate reflection by clearing the mind of excess thoughts, making the way clear for focused and uncomplicated reflection. The value of these forms of reflection is in clearing away the debris of too much rationality, so that a different starting point in thinking is reached, allowing different perspectives to be gained. This is in contradiction to other forms of reflection, such as those described in this book, which engage you actively in posing and exploring questions about yourself and your practice. I raise other forms of thinking beyond rationality here for you to consider, so you can find out more about them, and if they strike you as interesting, you may decide to admit them to your range of possibilities.

Summary

In this chapter I cautioned you about the use of categories and introduced three types of reflection you can use in your work and adapt to your life if you wish. As the basis for understanding how knowledge is related to reflection, I introduced some nursing and midwifery authors who have categorized ways of knowing. Empirical, interpretive and critical knowledge and Habermas's 'knowledge-constitutive interests' were connected, so that you could see how they relate to the kinds of reflection highlighted in this book. Technical, practical and emancipatory reflection were introduced to highlight their relative merits, so that you can decide on which type or combination of types of reflection to use for your practice issues. The chapter concluded by describing critical thinking and other ways of thinking that are integral to all types of reflection.

Key points

- It is a tricky business to put ideas into neat, fixed categories, because concepts do not necessarily fit in 'boxes' – however, when potentially complex phenomena are in focus, structures for thinking, such as theories, models and categories can be used gainfully.
- Empirical knowledge comes from technical reflection, interpretive knowledge comes from practical reflection, and critical knowledge comes from emancipatory reflection.
- It is important to consider these categories as ways of creating a temporary framework on which to hang certain broad principles, because it would be shortsighted to have an absolute conviction that there are only three forms of knowledge and reflection.
- The categories are ways of structuring your thinking until you have the confidence you need to disregard the conceptual boxes, so that you can roam freely in open fields of uncategorized knowledge and reflection.
- Knowledge specializations have developed into finer and finer distinctions within humanities and sciences, responding to two implicit

concerns of human knowledge and existence, explored through epistemology and ontology.

- Epistemology concerns itself with knowledge generation and validation, meaning that it tries to ascertain how to make new knowledge and how to judge whether it is trustworthy and 'true'.
- Ontology is the study of meaning of the human existence.
- There are many ways of thinking about knowledge and existence and, historically, in nursing and midwifery, several approaches have been suggested (e.g. Carper 1978; Parse 1985; Allen *et al.* 1986; Chinn and Kramer 1991).
- Empirical knowledge is generated and tested through 'the scientific method'.
- Empirical knowledge outcomes are achieved mainly through rational deductive thinking processes, which move systematically from broad to focused inferences.
- People are the focus of interpretive knowledge, because this form of knowledge features people's perceptions of their life experiences and their ability to communicate them, based on their interpersonal understanding through attention to lived experience, context and subjectivity.
- Lived experience means knowing, through living a life in a particular time, place and set of circumstances.
- Context means all of the features of the time and place in which people find themselves, in which their lives are located and their realities are embodied.
- Subjectivity refers to the individual's sensing of inner and external events, which is appropriate for themselves.
- Critical knowledge is derived from some key ideas in critical social science, such as false consciousness, hegemony, reification, emancipation and empowerment.
- False consciousness is the 'systematic ignorance that the members of . . . society have about themselves and their society' (Fay 1987: 27), so critical knowledge attempts to critique firmly held individual and collective ignorance to change this self-defeating consciousness and transform society itself.
- Hegemony means the ascendancy or domination of one power over another, and given that hegemonic influences maintain the status quo and are resistant to change, clinicians need to critique taken-for-granted assumptions about everyday practices in order to identify and change hegemonic practices in their workplace.
- Fay (1987: 92) explains that reification means 'making into a thing', by 'taking what are essential activities and treating them as if they operated according to a given set of laws independently of the wishes

of the social actors who engage in them'. Therefore reified practices are rich sources of reflection, so they can be identified and changed through systematic questioning and action.

- Emancipation means freedom, and it infers that one is free from something and free towards something; therefore, critical knowledge claims to be helpful in emancipating people to be liberated from their present oppressive conditions and moved towards empowering conditions.

- Empowerment is the process of giving and accepting power, therefore critical knowledge is geared towards helping people to find their own power, to liberate them from their oppressive circumstances and self-understandings in those circumstances.

- Jurgen Habermas claimed that knowledge and how we judge it to be 'truth' (epistemology) is constructed according to the sense we make of our existence and how we live socially (ontology), and that these interests in knowledge are based on aspects of social existence, such as work, human interactions and power relationships.

- Habermas connected technical interests to work, practical interests to interaction and emancipatory interests to power, and these categorizations are adopted in this book to name technical, practical and emancipatory reflection.

- There is an increasing call in nursing and midwifery for evidence as a basis for better practice and many of the work practices that need to be improved require technical interest using objective and systematic lines of enquiry, so this interest fits well with technical reflection.

- Practical interest involves human interaction, or 'communicative action', involving reciprocal expectations about behaviour, defined and understood by the people involved, so practical interests in nursing and midwifery can be reflected on systematically through practical reflection.

- Emancipatory interest is rooted in power and creates 'transformative action', so emancipatory reflection can uncover and potentiate emancipatory interests at work.

- Technical reflection helps you to improve your instrumental action through technical control and manipulation in devising and improving procedural approaches to your work.

- Practical reflection helps you to understand the interpersonal basis of human experiences and offers you the potential for creating knowledge by interpreting the meaning of lived experience, context and subjectivity, and the potential for change, based on raised awareness of the nature of a wide range of communicative matters pertaining to nursing and midwifery.

- Emancipatory reflection leads to 'transformative action', which seeks to free you from taken-for-granted assumptions and oppressive forces, which limit you and your practice, by critiquing the power relationships in your workplace and offering you raised awareness and a new sense of informed consciousness to bring about positive social and political change.
- No type of reflection is better than another; each has its own value for different purposes.
- All kinds of knowledge can be generated through reflection, and nurses and midwives can benefit from a range of reflective processes.
- Technical, practical and emancipatory reflection all require some degree of critical thinking, but the most obvious application of critical thinking is in technical reflection.
- Bandman and Bandman (1995: 7) define critical thinking as 'the rational examination of ideas, inferences, assumptions, principles, arguments, conclusions, issues, statements, beliefs, and actions'.
- Reasoning refers to the act of drawing conclusions from premises, which are statements leading up to end findings or summary statements.
- An argument is not a quarrel; rather, it means a well thought out and delivered defence of a point of view supported by sound reasoning.
- Not all premises in an argument may be stated openly – they may be hidden as assumptions, which may be discerned as 'gaps' in the logic of arguments.
- Scientific reasoning refers to a certain kind of argument, which reflects the assumptions underlying 'the scientific model'.
- The cognitive skills required for critical thinking include decision-making and problem-solving methods and attitudes include thinking independently, intellectual humility, courage, empathy, integrity, perseverance, faith in reason, fair-mindedness and the need to explore thoughts and feelings.
- Critical thinkers use the process of critical thinking in all of daily living to: discriminate among the uses and misuses of language in nursing/midwifery; identify and formulate nursing/midwifery problems; analyse meanings of terms in relation to their indication, their cause or purpose and their significance; analyse arguments and issues into premises and conclusions; examine nursing/midwifery assumptions; report data and clues accurately; make and check inferences based on data, making sure that the inferences are at least plausible; formulate and clarify beliefs; verify, corroborate and justify claims, beliefs, conclusions, decisions and actions; give relevant reasons for beliefs and conclusions; formulate and clarify value judgements; and evaluate the soundness of conclusions.

- Reasoning will almost invariably be involved in considering choices, but there are other ways of 'thinking' that are less acknowledged, such as 'thinking' through intuitive grasps, creative expression and inner knowing that is not easily rationalized, such as contemplation and meditation.

5   Technical reflection

Introduction

This chapter reviews information connected directly to technical reflection, including the reasons why this process is used for specific purposes and why it creates different outcomes in terms of knowledge of, and practical answers to, clinical problems. The relationships are explained between empirical knowledge and the scientific method, and how technical reflection fits with these ideas. The connections between technical reflection and evidence-based practice are described and you will find that the two processes are highly complementary. The chapter also describes the technical reflection process, practice stories, critical friend responses, and other examples of how technical reflection can be used by reflective nurses and midwives.

Technical reflection is important, because it admits into the realms of reflection systematic thinking processes that are capable of bringing about sophisticated levels of argumentation, much needed to secure improvements in clinical policies and procedures. Therefore, this chapter justifies the value of technical reflection, based on its validity as a form of knowledge and its usefulness for clinical practice. The process of technical reflection has been developed through an eclectic approach, borrowing ideas from Bandman and Bandman's (1995) view of scientific reasoning and the functions of critical thinkers, the features of critical thinking and thinkers described by van Hooft *et al.* (1995) and the problem-solving steps of the nursing process (Wilkinson 1996).

There are some important points to note before continuing. Although scientific reasoning and critical thinking have clear and distinctive purposes in generating and validating empirical knowledge, critical thinking also has wide applications and it may be helpful in any of the forms of reflection described in this book. However, critical thinking is most likely to be useful when you are raising questions in your practice about technicalities related to the form and usefulness of your work procedures and policies.

Also, remember that technical reflection may be used as a process in itself when you are working alone or with colleagues through observation and critical thinking, or it may be used in conjunction with research projects based on scientific reasoning that demand reliability, validity, and control and manipulation of variables. Alternatively, if a question posed as a reflective task is less complex and does not require a research project *per se*, technical reflection alone can lead to answers based on observation and sound arguments that incorporate rational aspects of critical thinking. It is also possible that technical reflection could become part of mixed methodology research, such as an action research project, using empirical methods to examine procedure 'X' as part of a larger collaborative group process. You need to exercise caution in determining whether a clinical problem is focused, and whether it can be resolved sufficiently by technical reflection alone. If there is any doubt as to whether the information generated is sufficient and effective, you may need to consider extending your reflections into a formal research project.

Practice story

Michael, an RN aged 35 years, had been working in acute care settings for all of his 14 years of postgraduate experience. He used technical reflection to help him work through a clinical issue involving a hospital's policy relating to on-call physicians.

In Michael's story about Lorna, the clinical problem was how to manage a critically ill patient throughout the night and early morning hours, to balance her need for rest and lung secretion drainage. The 'procedure' or clinical task at hand was to manage Lorna's shortness of breath when she awoke at 0430 hours, so Michael performed a blood gas saturation and listened to her chest. He then phoned the physician with the results of the assessment; the physician directed Michael to turn off the intravenous infusion, obtain blood cultures, give intravenous Lasix, and insert an indwelling catheter. In testing the blood gas saturation and listening to Lorna's chest, Michael assessed the degree of lung congestion. In informing the physician, Michael requested medical assistance to relieve Lorna's dyspnoea.

In following the physician's directions, Michael instituted measures to relieve pulmonary congestion. The outcomes of the interventions were not successful immediately, as evidenced by the lack of diuresis, poor air entry and low blood oxygen saturation. In view of these indicators, Michael rang the physician again. This time, he was directed to administer more Lasix and oxygen, and to repeat the blood gases at 0700 hours. He could not understand the physician's rationale for withholding the blood gas measurement for 1.25 hours, although he suspected that it was to allow the physician more time to sleep.

Michael's immediate problem was to prevent Lorna from having a cardiac arrest until he could check her blood gas levels at 0700 hours. When the results were available at the designated time, they indicated Lorna's critical condition and she was transferred to a major intensive care unit within the hour.

The clinical problem was the management of critically ill patients during the night shift when physicians need to be woken from their sleep to give directions for medical care. Working through the technical reflection process, Michael was able to reach sound conclusions for an argument to a clinical administrative committee that an extra nurse was needed on evening shifts, and that nurses need to develop open dialogues with physicians. After a process of individual and group technical reflection, the hypothesis was confirmed that meeting the needs of ill patients on the night shift is related directly to the provision by the hospital of better resources and to improvements in nurse-doctor communication.

Critical friend response

Acting as a critical friend, I discussed with Michael the assumptions he was making in his practice story. Our conversation was along these lines:

Critical friend: *Michael, you said that you could not understand the physician's rationale for withholding the blood gas measurement for 1.25 hours, although you suspected that it was to allow the physician more time to sleep.*

Michael: *Yes, well it sure crossed my mind that the physician was 'sitting on her' a bit too long, possibly so he could get more sleep.*

Critical friend: *So, you felt that wasn't reasonable – for the physician to withhold the blood gas measurement for 1.25 hours?*

Michael: *Absolutely not! I could see she was not OK, and all her physical signs backed that up. It was not as though I had not communicated my concerns to the physician. I made it as clear as it could be, without actually demanding that he come in and see her for himself.*

Critical friend: *Why couldn't you demand he come in?*

Michael: *Because that's how we play the game. You give the physician all of the data, and she or he makes the decisions about treatment. In the meantime, I'm the one checking constantly*

> *on Lorna, hoping against all hope that she can survive until I can get her transferred out.*
>
> Critical friend: *So what are your assumptions in this case – that is, what are the things you have not said explicitly, but they underlie what you have said?*
>
> Michael: *Well, I suppose – that's a hard one – I suppose one assumption is that I am very capable of knowing when a patient's condition is deteriorating. Also, another assumption is that the physician's non-attendance was related to his own need for sleep – maybe he thought I was overstating the case. It's hard to say.*
>
> Critical friend: *And you said before that you could not demand he come in and see her for himself. What assumptions are you making there about your professional relationship with the physician?*
>
> *The conversation continues . . .*

Review of previous ideas

Understanding the basis of technical reflection relies on information given earlier in this book, so you may choose to revisit Chapters 1 and 4. However, as background to this chapter, here are some essential points to tie the ideas firmly together.

Before you practise technical reflection it may help you to understand why this process is useful for specific purposes and why it creates specific outcomes in terms of knowledge of, and practical answers to, clinical problems. Integral to this understanding is the relationship between empirical knowledge and the scientific method, and how the process for technical reflection fits with these ideas. This section provides an epistemology explanation, which describes how empirical knowledge is generated and validated.

Empirical knowledge rests on evidence from direct observation and it is generated and tested through 'the scientific method'. Some scientists claim the scientific method is *the* method of knowledge generation and validation, because it has enjoyed great success in the last 200 years or so in relation to technological innovations in areas such as medicine, psychology, physics, chemistry, biology, genetics, environmental sciences, engineering, architecture and so on. In fact, the proponents of the scientific method have such confidence in it that they claim empirical knowledge is the yardstick against which all other epistemological methods should be measured. The scientific method has been and continues to be very successful, because it uses strict criteria for setting up its enquiry and judging its truthfulness through rigorous and systematic measures including reliability, validity, and control and manipulation of variables.

Through the scientific method, data are quantified to demonstrate the degree of statistical significance in cause and effect relationships. In other words, information is converted into a numerical form, which can be measured and counted, so that it is possible to predict mathematically that the occurrence of a behaviour or experimental response is significant, and not just happening by chance. To achieve this kind of predictive ability, scientific knowledge is rendered as free as possible from the distorting influences of people, who may skew the results with their prejudices, intentions and emotions. To avoid subjectivity of this kind, empirical researchers demand objectivity, meaning they strive to ensure that there is no involvement of prejudices, intentions and emotions in the conduct of the project. In summary, the scientific method creates empirical knowledge, which can claim to be predictive and generalizable with some confidence that the conclusions are truthful, real, trustworthy and not just happening by chance.

The new or amended knowledge outcomes achieved by using the scientific method are mainly through rational deductive thinking processes, which move systematically from broad to focused inferences. Scientific reasoning refers to a certain kind of rational argument which underlies the scientific method. The scientific approach to reasoning is to state a problem, give a preliminary hypothesis setting out the expected relationships between variables, collect more facts in order to formulate a hypothesis, deduce further consequences, test those consequences, and finally apply the findings to confirm or disconfirm the hypothesis (Bandman and Bandman 1995). Scientific reasoning provides a systematic approach to working through complex problems in an objective manner designed to keep the enquirer on track and provide a means whereby other people can use a similar process to test whether the results can be repeated with the same results (replicated).

Reflector

Think of situations in which scientific reasoning is essential in your work. Why is it the best approach to problem-solving in these situations?

In Chapter 4, critical thinking was defined as the ability to think in a systematic and rational way. Scientific reasoning is aligned closely with critical thinking, in that the two processes share many characteristics and often lead to similar outcomes. Critical thinking is essential for safe clinical practice and, according to many authors, rationality is its first requirement (Bandman and Bandman 1995; van Hooft *et al.* 1995; Wilkinson 1996). However, some authors stress that critical thinking is not just about rationality and emotional detachment for intellectual 'purity'. Even though van Hooft *et al.* (1995: 6–7) are keen to define the first important element of critical thinking as rational thinking, they emphasize that it is practical as well as theoretical – that it is conducive to dialogue and that it includes empathy and sensitive perception. They also describe critical thinkers as committed, self-aware and sympathetic to the commitments of others. The addition of practicality, dialogue, empathy and sensitivity in critical thinking, and self-aware and altruistic features in critical thinkers, gives critical thinking a 'human touch' that elevates it above a pure exercise of scientific rationality as described previously. Even so, critical thinking borders on scientific reasoning, because of its emphasis on rationality and scientific reasoning.

Chapter 4 also introduced the philosophy of Jurgen Habermas, whose ideas have been applied to practical areas such as curriculum (Mezirow 1981). Habermas is of interest to nurses and midwives because he had important things to say about the interests people have in their work, communication and power relations. When we consider technical reflection, we are focusing on what he had to say about work and procedures. In Habermas's view (1972), technical interest in work creates 'instrumental action' through which people control and manipulate their environments. This means that people work with intention, so that by keeping a 'hold' on situations they can achieve what they want. Therefore, people act in accordance with technical rules to generate empirical knowledge. In other words, they figure out the best ways of creating and following procedural steps in technical situations and claim that their results have been achieved through systematic and direct observation.

In nursing and midwifery, technical interest is associated with task-related competence, such as clinical procedures and policies. As you can see, this is another way of talking about empirical knowledge, rationality, the scientific method, critical thinking and problem-solving. The scientific method's influence on empirical knowledge is apparent in daily practice, because nurses and midwives have technical interest in their work. Many innovations and evidence-based adaptations in nursing and midwifery have been possible because of empirical knowledge, gained through empirical research, using processes described previously. Technical reflection fits into this discussion because it is a way for you to integrate ways of thinking, to allow you to adapt and improve procedures and policies. You may also be able to predict likely outcomes for similar procedures and improve many work practices through objective and systematic lines of enquiry.

Technical reflection fits well with evidence-based nursing (Pearson *et al.* 1997; Shorten and Wallace 1997), which claims that practice needs to be based on research findings, rather than on rituals, traditions, whims and unfounded beliefs about what should or could be done in certain clinical situations. If you have been practising for some time now, you can probably remember how nursing or midwifery procedures have changed over time. For example, in nursing you may have witnessed the transition from 'double nursing' of patients post myocardial infarction, to getting them out of bed and ambulating as soon as possible. In midwifery, you may have changed from undertaking 'peri' washes of bedfast women to encouraging them to ambulate to the bathroom to attend to their own perineal showers. At times, you may have wondered whether what you were doing was working at all and whether you had any technical justification for doing it. The evidence-based movement in nursing and midwifery is testing the validity of long-standing procedures, and it is replacing old untested and unproven approaches with newer research-based alternatives. Technical reflection is a systematic process for raising questions relating to procedures and policies providing strong argumentation based on scientific reasoning; therefore, it is highly complementary to evidence-based practice.

Reflector

Think of a clinical procedure you have undertaken for some time now that you suspect is outmoded in some way. Why do you continue to perform that procedure in the same way, even though you suspect it is outmoded? What is needed for the performance of that procedure to change in your workplace?

The process of technical reflection

This section presents a process to assist you in using technical reflection in thinking about issues relating to a clinical procedure. Chapter 2 suggests many different methods for reflecting, and I emphasized that these methods may be used alone or in combination to assist you in letting your thoughts flow during reflective processes. Reflection does not have to be a solo effort. If you work better in groups, you can enlist a team or committee and go through reflective processes collaboratively. Technical reflection works well in groups and committees, when the process is used systematically and carefully. You may find that one 'run through' by yourself is a good idea, even if it just helps you get your thoughts together before a clinical meeting. Also, once you know how the process works, you can guide your colleagues through it, using this book as a reference.

Practice story

Marcia, aged 26 years, had been practising midwifery in hospital settings for five years. Through her educational and practice experiences she was keen to learn as much as she could about how to facilitate effective breastfeeding. In her workplace she noticed that many midwives were quick to intervene in actively guiding and sometimes forcing babies to attach to a mother's breast, often resulting in babies struggling and crying. She suspected that some techniques of breast attachment, although well meant, were ineffective and that the midwives working in the unit needed to review their approaches to effective breastfeeding techniques.

Marcia raised the issue at a midwives' clinical meeting and offered to facilitate a technical reflection exercise to assist them to work collaboratively through the issue. In the discussion preceding the reflective process, the midwives agreed that they had learned their practice ideas about breastfeeding from many sources, they did not always check on research-based evidence for changing their approaches, and that they mainly worked on a one-to-one with mothers, so they were not aware of other midwives' practices in facilitating breastfeeding. By guiding them through the technical reflection process, Marcia was able to stimulate discussion and create a forum in which midwives were willing to use scientific reasoning to provide a sound argument for standardizing their approaches to facilitating breastfeeding based on the most recent research.

Critical friend response

Acting as a critical friend, I discussed with Marcia the application of the technical reflection process in her workplace. Our conversation was along these lines:

Critical friend: *Marcia, did it take some courage to raise the issue of breast attachment with your colleagues?*

Marcia: *It sure did, especially when I first noticed the problem and I was wondering how to approach it with the other midwives.*

Critical friend: *Why's that?*

Marcia: *Well, I have been working there for five years, but some of the midwives have been practising for 23 plus! I respect their knowledge and skills and the last thing I wanted to do was to tell them their own business!*

Critical friend: *So, how did you go about it?*

Marcia: *Well, I knew I needed to put a convincing case forward to them, as objectively as I could, and to provide as much evidence as I could that the latest trends in midwives assisting in breastfeeding are 'hands off the breast'. Some of the midwives have been guiding babies to the breast for most of their working lives, so I knew they would need to be convinced that the baby is just as capable of finding the nipple with the mother managing the alignment and coaxing the baby's*

> *mouth around the areola. Anyway, I worked it all through as a test case using the technical reflection process, and that gave me a systematic approach to arguing my position.*
>
> *The conversation continues . . .*

The technical reflection process presented in this section encourages you to reflect on issues which require rational thinking for specific, manageable problems. As mentioned previously, if your clinical issues are especially complex and require protracted work to solve them, you may need to use technical reflection in conjunction with an empirical research design.

The outcomes of technical reflection can be immediate, if the process has been shared with, and the findings endorsed by, the key people who are in a position to influence and ratify nursing and midwifery practice. You may find that this process has many applications. For example, you could use technical reflection to think critically through your own practice issues, or it could be used in groups as a guide for a clinical policy and practice meeting agenda, as an outline for analysing technical issues in ward/unit clinical discussions, and/or as part of the methods of formal research. In whatever situations you use it, technical reflection has the potential for allowing you to think critically and reason scientifically, so that you can critique, adapt and improve procedures and policies. You may also be able to predict likely outcomes for similar procedures and improve many work practices through objective and systematic lines of enquiry.

I now present a process to assist you in using technical reflection in thinking about issues relating to a clinical procedure or policy. There are many different methods for reflecting, including writing, audiotaping, creative music, dancing and so on. These methods may be used alone or in combination to assist you in letting your thoughts flow during reflective processes.

Using the method(s) of your choice, consider the following questions. Respond as carefully as you can, making sure that you attend to every step along the way. Use as many words as necessary to explain your position thoroughly, but keep to the point, so that you do not cloud the issue with extraneous information.

Think of a practice or procedure, referred to here as 'Procedure X', that has been established for some time, the value of which you have cause to question.

Assessing and planning

In this part of the process, set up the premises for rational thinking by making an initial assessment of the problem and by planning for the development of an argument.

- What is Procedure X?
- Why is Procedure X done?
- How is Procedure X done?
- When is Procedure X done?
- What are the outcomes of Procedure X?
- Why do you believe that Procedure X is of questionable value?
- How do you propose to amend Procedure X?

From your responses to the previous questions, state the problem, giving a preliminary hypothesis about the expected relationships between the variables you have identified. If you are unable to state a hypothesis at this point you may need to spend more time assessing the problem, and you may need to collect more facts related to Procedure X.

- What words and language are associated commonly with Procedure X?
- Why are certain words and language associated commonly with Procedure X?
- Is there any evidence of misuse of words and language in Procedure X?
- Could the words and language associated commonly with Procedure X be stated differently?
- What health care problems are associated with Procedure X?

Implementing

In this part of the process, develop an argument by analysing the issues and assumptions operating in the situation.

- What arguments are made to support the continuation of Procedure X in its present form?
- What health care assumptions underlie the support of Procedure X in its present form?
- What premises support the argument for Procedure X in its present form?
- Do these premises follow logically to provide sound conclusions?
- If not, why not?
- What inferences have been made and in what ways are they plausible in supporting Procedure X in its present form?

Now is the time to formulate and clarify your own beliefs about Procedure X as stated in your hypothesis.

- What arguments are made to support the discontinuation of Procedure X in its present form?
- What health care assumptions underlie the opposition to Procedure X in its present form?

- On what premises are these arguments for opposing Procedure X in its present form based?
- Do these premises follow logically to provide sound conclusions?
- If not, why not?
- What inferences have been made and in what ways are they plausible in opposing Procedure X in its present form?

To test the consequences of the position that Procedure X is of questionable value in its present form, you need to implement some changes, or 'apply the findings' of rational deliberation in the practices associated with Procedure X. The changes would need to be based on the results of rational discussion and decision-making, but they might include factors such as the time of day, the frequency of the procedure, preparations for Procedure X, the sequence of the method and activities following Procedure X.

Evaluating

In this part of the process, you review the problem in the light of all the information gained through the process of technical reflection.

- What information has been gained to date through implementing the technical reflection process?
- In what ways can you verify, corroborate and justify claims, beliefs, conclusions, decisions and actions taken in this process?
- What are the reasons for your beliefs and conclusions regarding this issue?
- What are your value judgements about this issue?
- To what extent can you claim that the conclusions you have reached are sound?
- What other possible consequences may transpire due to the conclusions reached by this process?

Make a succinct statement to either confirm or disconfirm the hypothesis as stated at the outset of this process.

You have just been through the technical reflection process to generate empirical knowledge, to amend and improve a clinical procedure. Congratulations!

An example of technical reflection

If you lost your way in the previous section, or found parts of the process difficult to follow, this section provides an example of technical reflection to assist you. The example responds to questions listed in the technical reflection process above.

A very common problem we see in many nursing settings is the tendency nurses have to want to get everyone showered/washed/bathed by 10 a.m. For ease of reference, we will simply refer to the problem as the need to attend to patients' hygiene needs by 10 a.m. This example shows how the technical reflection process works when it is applied to question the soundness of, and necessity for, the procedure of nurses wanting to attend to patients' hygiene needs by this set time.

Assessing and planning

In this part of the process, set up the premises for rational thinking by making an initial assessment of the problem and planning for the development of an argument.

- What is Procedure X? The procedure is attending to patients' hygiene needs by 10 a.m.
- Why is Procedure X done? To have all the patients clean and tidy by 10 a.m.
- How is Procedure X done? Patients may be showered, washed in bed or bathed, depending on their condition and willingness.
- When is Procedure X done? Between coming on duty of a morning around 7 a.m. until 10 a.m.
- What are the outcomes of Procedure X? The patients are clean and tidy by 10 a.m., ready for doctors' rounds, visitors, and other procedures and appointments.
- Why do you believe that Procedure X is of questionable value? The procedure is of questionable value because it serves the purposes of the nurses and the ward routines, rather than the expressed wishes of individual patients.
- How do you propose to amend Procedure X? The proposed amendment is to undertake hygiene care at any time of the day the patient prefers, and to cease the procedure of having all the hygiene needs completed by 10 a.m.

From your responses to the previous questions, state the problem, giving a preliminary hypothesis about the expected relationships between the variables you have identified. If you are unable to state a hypothesis at this point you may need to spend more time assessing the problem, and you may need to collect more facts related to Procedure X.

The problem of nurses needing to attend to patients hygiene needs by 10 a.m. is counterproductive and needs to be ceased, because hygiene needs will be better met if patients indicate their preferred method of hygiene at any time of the day that suits them.

- What words and language are associated commonly with Procedure X? The procedure of meeting hygiene needs by 10 a.m. is associated with nurses' statements such as: 'We need to have everyone done by morning tea', 'There are five washes and two showers this morning', 'How many sponges have we got?'
- Why are certain words and language associated commonly with Procedure X? The words and language associated with meeting patients' hygiene needs by 10 a.m. relate directly to getting the work done, on time.
- Is there any evidence of misuse of words and language in Procedure X? The 'misuse' of words and language is in the tendency to reduce patients to tasks to be done and to approach hygiene needs as being specific to the needs of the ward, not the person, who is the patient.
- Could the words and language associated commonly with Procedure X be stated differently? Yes, if the statements used commonly are looked at carefully, nurses may identify their tendency to speak of patients' hygiene needs in terms of work to be done, on time. For example, differently stated the sentences could be: 'We need to attend to patients' hygiene needs, how and when they prefer', 'Five patients have indicated they want to have a wash and two patients have indicated they would like a shower, sometime today', 'How many people have indicated they would like a wash in bed?'
- What health care problems are associated with Procedure X? Lack of patient hygiene may result in patients feeling uncomfortable at least, and developing bedsores at worst, but this range of problems are not necessarily related to the time of day when hygiene needs are met.

Implementing

In this part of the process, develop an argument by analysing the issues and assumptions operating in the situation.

- What arguments are made to support the continuation of Procedure X in its present form? Nurses who support the continuation of meeting all of the patients' hygiene needs by 10 a.m. argue that it helps patients to feel clean and comfortable and if patients are clean and comfortable then it will assist them in all aspects of their healing process.
- What health care assumptions underlie the support of Procedure X in its present form? That all patients will be willing, cooperative and pleased to comply. Assumptions may also be that nurses want to continue the procedure, as it suits their purposes to have the bulk of the work done early in the day, and it also fits with the established ward routines of meal times, doctors' rounds, visitors and so on.

- What premises support the argument for Procedure X in its present form? The premises are as stated previously: patients will feel clean and comfortable, and that will assist them in all aspects of their healing process.
- Do these premises follow logically to provide sound conclusions? If not, why not? No, because the nurses' assumptions have not been made explicit. In addition, patients' healing processes can be facilitated by various means, and given that hygiene is only one of those important aspects, then it follows that it does not matter if the wash, shower or bath is taken after 10 a.m., indeed, it may be what the patient prefers.
- What inferences have been made and in what ways are they plausible in supporting Procedure X in its present form? The inference is that *if* patients' hygiene needs are met by 10 a.m. *then* patients' healing processes will be helped. This inference is plausible in the sense that patients require hygiene care, but it is not plausible in specifying the time of day, as it does not necessarily follow that hygiene needs must be met by that time for the patients' benefit.

Now is the time to formulate and clarify your own beliefs about Procedure X as stated in your hypothesis.

- What arguments are made to support the discontinuation of Procedure X in its present form? That although patients require hygiene care, this does not have to be attended to before 10 a.m., or at any particular time, because patients are usually in the best position to decide when they would prefer to have a wash, shower or bath.
- What health care assumptions underlie the opposition to Procedure X in its present form? Assumptions opposing the procedure are that patients have a right to choose and nurses will be willing to comply with their wishes in relation to hygiene needs. The previously unexpressed assumptions are also challenged that nurses who continue the procedure are actually using it to serve their own purposes and to maintain the routines that meet the needs of a busy ward on a morning shift.
- On what premises are these arguments for opposing Procedure X in its present form based? That patients require hygiene care, the time is unimportant, and patients who are able to do so are in the best position to decide when they would prefer to have a wash, shower or bath.
- Do these premises follow logically to provide sound conclusions? If not, why not? Yes.
- What inferences have been made and in what ways are they plausible in opposing Procedure X in its present form? One inference is that *if* patients who are able are encouraged to decide when they want to have their hygiene needs met, *then* the nurses' work is in response to patients' needs, rather than the reverse. Another series of connected inferences is

that *if* the procedure is changed, *then* the ward work will not be compressed into three very busy hours in the morning, and *if* that is so, *then* nurses may find that the ward is less chaotic and that there is more time to spend with patients. *If* there is more time to spend with patients, *then* nurses and patients have the potential to create therapeutic relationships in which healing and well-being are promoted.

To test the consequences of the position that Procedure X is of questionable value in its present form, you need to implement some changes, or 'apply the findings' of rational deliberation in the practices associated with Procedure X. The changes would need to be based on the results of rational discussion and decision-making, but they might include factors such as the time of day, the frequency of the procedure, preparations for Procedure X, the sequence of the method and activities following Procedure X.

Evaluating

In this part of the process, you review the problem in the light of all the information gained through the process of technical reflection. We will assume that the procedure has been changed and the nurses have had two weeks to get accustomed to responding, for those patients able to decide, to patients' preferences for the time and mode of their hygiene needs.

- What information has been gained to date through implementing the technical reflection process? Although the first week of the changed procedure resulted in some nurses expressing frustration, anger, impatience and anxiety, the majority of the nurses have noticed that the patients are happy with the amended procedure, and for those patients newly admitted who did not witness the transition there is an acceptance that they are well suited to decide when and how they will have their hygiene needs met.
- In what ways can you verify, corroborate and justify claims, beliefs, conclusions, decisions and actions taken in this process? The amended procedure has resulted in less movement and noise in the ward between 7 a.m. and 10 a.m., allowing some patients to continue to sleep and rest if they prefer. Even though nurses have other patient care responsibilities, such as assisting with meals, monitoring observations and so on, more time is available for being with patients to converse and provide company that would not have otherwise been possible.
- What are the reasons for your beliefs and conclusions regarding this issue? The issue of the timing of hygiene needs has been related to the often unexpressed need of nurses to have their work done on time, and also to maintaining a balance of who does the work and when. For example, it

has been a cultural expectation that nurses on the morning shift 'will do the washes and showers', leaving the afternoons and evenings free for other procedures that are done then, such as receiving new patient admissions, monitoring patients' progress, administering medications and so on.

- What are your value judgements about this issue? That patients have the autonomous right to choose when hygiene needs are met. Nurses should value responding to patient needs rather than dictating them, and they are influenced by the moral principle of beneficence to do only good to the patient.
- To what extent can you claim that conclusions you have reached are sound? The conclusions are sound, in that the amended procedure has resulted in greater benefits to patients, because it fulfils the patients' rights for autonomy and respect and the nurses' moral obligation to provide them. Also the ward is quieter and more conducive to rest and therapeutic outcomes.
- What other possible consequences may transpire due to the conclusions reached by this process? That other unexamined ward procedures and routines may be questioned and changed through a technical reflection process that enlists the nursing process, scientific reasoning and critical thinking.
- Make a succinct statement to either confirm or disconfirm the hypothesis as stated at the outset of this process. The hypothesis is confirmed that the problem of nurses needing to attend to patients' hygiene needs by 10 a.m. is counterproductive and needs to be ceased, because hygiene needs will be better met if patients indicate their preferred method of hygiene at any time of the day that suits them.

Summary

Questions about clinical procedures can be answered quickly and effectively through technical reflection. This chapter reviewed some previous information given in this book, connected directly to technical reflection, explaining some of the reasons why technical reflection is used for specific purposes and why it creates practical answers to clinical problems. The relationships were reviewed between empirical knowledge and the scientific method, and how the process for technical reflection fits with these ideas. The connections were described between technical reflection and evidence-based practice and it was suggested that the two processes are highly complementary.

Technical reflection is based on a form of empirical knowledge generation, which is useful for clinical practice. Technical reflection as an amalgam of Bandman and Bandman's (1995) view of scientific reasoning and the functions of critical thinkers, the features of critical thinking and thinkers described by van Hooft *et al.* (1995) and the problem-solving steps of the nursing process (Wilkinson 1996). The chapter provided an example of technical reflection so you can see how the process can be applied to clinical procedures and policies in your work.

Key points

- Questions about clinical procedures can be answered through technical reflection.
- For nurses and midwives, technical interest is associated with task-related competence, such as clinical procedures, therefore technical reflection involves empirical knowledge, rationality, the scientific method, critical thinking and problem-solving.
- The evidence-based movement in nursing and midwifery is testing the validity of long-standing procedures and is seeking to replace old untested and unproven approaches with newer research-based ones.
- 'Assessing and planning' is the part of the technical reflection process in which you set up the premises for rational thinking by making an initial assessment of the problem and begin planning for the development of an argument.
- 'Implementing' is the part of the process in which you develop an argument by analysing the issues and assumptions operating in the situation.
- 'Evaluating' is the part of the process in which you review the problem in the light of all the information gained through the process of technical reflection.
- The outcomes of technical reflection can be immediate, if the process has been shared with, and the findings endorsed by, the key people who are in a position to influence and ratify health care practice.
- In whatever situations you use it, technical reflection has the potential for allowing you to think critically and to reason scientifically, so that you can critique and adapt present procedures to better ones as necessary. You may also be able to predict likely outcomes for similar procedures and improve many work practices through objective and systematic lines of enquiry.

6   Practical reflection

Introduction

This chapter reviews some information connected directly to practical reflection, before guiding you through the practical reflection process, practice stories, critical friend responses and other examples of how practical reflection can be used by nurses and midwives.

When I turned my attention towards practical reflection, I realized that this would involve an adjustment of what has been used previously in the work of Smyth (1986a, 1986b) and Street (1991), with an adaptation to emphasize the communicative nature of this type of reflection. Therefore, practical reflection retains some of the questions used previously within the process of experiencing, interpreting and learning. Experiencing involves retelling a practice story so that you experience it again in as much detail as possible. Interpreting involves clarifying and explaining the meaning of a communicative action situation. Learning involves creating new insights and integrating them into your existing awareness and knowledge.

Practical reflection is important in itself. The reason for this is that there is immense value in reflecting for the purposes of interpreting and learning from work life. Although change may not be an explicit aim of practical reflection, it is still possible, through new insights that follow from raised awareness. However, while practical reflection is helpful, it has limitations in what it can offer you. Through the medium of language, practical reflection will help you to understand the interpersonal basis of human experiences and will also offer you the potential for creating new knowledge which interprets the meaning of your lived experience, context and subjectivity. You can experience changes through practical reflection, although that is not its primary aim. The changes will be based on your raised awareness of the nature and effects of a wide range of communicative matters pertaining to your practice.

However, practical reflection will not offer you the objective means to observe and analyse work procedures through a scientific method, because it does not have an interest in instrumental action. Also, practical reflection will not give you a process for making a radical critique of the constraining forces and power influences within your work settings. The reason for this is that, although practical reflection can raise awareness through insights into communicative action, unlike emancipatory reflection it does not have transformative action as its primary concern.

Practice story

Cathy, aged 40 years, has had 15 years of midwifery practice in a variety of clinical settings ranging from the remote Australian outback to large city hospitals in New York and Paris. This practice story is about a busy day on the postnatal ward, when Cathy received a handover from a student midwife, who had not started discharge arrangements for a mother with her twins. This resulted in a great deal of work for Cathy, involving 'double the paperwork', the problem of the complex and lengthy process for discharging a baby with clicky hips, and a referral of the mother to the community nurses for care of a gaping wound.

Critical friend response

Although Cathy did not state her response to this situation explicitly, I inferred that she was not very pleased with the communication on a number of counts. I based this impression on my experience as a midwife and on the way Cathy had identified certain people and listed the activities she had to undertake to manage a 'successful discharge'. Cathy referred to 'a student midwife', who knew about the impending discharge, 'but hadn't even started discharge'. I explored my sense of the situation with Cathy. The conversation was along these lines:

Critical friend: *Cathy, how did you feel about the student midwife not completing some of the discharge preparations?*

Cathy: *I would have thought that was pretty obvious!*

Critical friend: *You tell me.*

Cathy: *Well, it's hard to put a name to it, but I guess I was very frustrated and angry.*

Critical friend: *I thought that might be so, because you wrote in your journal: 'Junior staff possibly overwhelmed with procedures of discharge and paperwork'. Anything else?*

Cathy: *A bit put upon, I suppose.*

Critical friend: *Meaning?*

> Cathy: *Well, I had enough of my own work to do, let alone having to finish off the morning shift's work! Why are you interested in how I was feeling?*
>
> Critical friend: *Sometimes it is useful to let out your feelings about how a situation affects you, because you can acknowledge it to yourself and other people, and begin to see how things could be different.*
>
> Cathy: *But how do I get from being angry and frustrated to making changes in my practice?*
>
> *The conversation continues . . .*

Review of previous ideas

In Chapter 4 I described practical reflection in relation to interpretive knowledge and practical interests. Practical reflection is related to interpretive knowledge, because it centres on people and values their perceptions of their life experiences and their ability to communicate them. People communicate through language, symbols, ceremonies, rituals, art forms and other behavioural practices. Of all the means of communication, the main way of making and sharing meaning is through speaking words that convey ideas, concepts, theories, propositions and so on. One of the most important reasons for language and interpersonal discussion is the communication of human experience, because people assign significance to what is happening within their own bodies and lives, and to similar concerns of other people. Practical reflection focuses on human experience and communication to make sense out of these phenomena through experiencing, interpreting and learning from them.

Interpretive knowledge centres on people, because of their perceptions of their life experiences and their ability to communicate them. The underlying concepts of interpretive knowledge include interpersonal understanding through attention to people's lived experience, context and subjectivity.

Lived experience means knowing what it is like to live a life in a particular time, place and set of circumstances. It involves the interpretation of experiences, which make up the fabric of human existence, once they have been opened up to reflection. It is only through reflection that people can make sense of their lived experiences, because time must elapse – whether it is moments or years – to sort through the meaning of experiences. Daily life is always moving forward towards the next experience and it is so easy to get caught up in it and to just let it happen. If you think of what it is like to be a human, the movement forward of life is within a body in a social world, and in respect to everything which occurs as part of living. In a sense, we are propelled forward by the prospect of tomorrow, and we cannot help but accumulate experiences along the way. This being so, there is a need to make sense of lived experience, in order to prepare for further forward movement by reflecting on what has happened, why and how, so that we can learn in the present and project these new insights into the future. Therefore, lived experience is an important concept in understanding interpretive knowledge and how it fits into practical reflection.

Context means all of the features of the time and place in which people find themselves, in which they locate their lives. If you think now of your context, how would you describe it? My context presently is that I am living on the far north coast of New South Wales, Australia. This is where I work as an academic and where I reside with my partner and son. My context is also described by my age, gender and social and political affiliations, such as my friends, colleagues and other relationships and my work and home interests. I could go on to describe more and more of my context and the more I describe, the broader and deeper my context would become. I cannot help but be connected to my context in all of its features, because I relate to it as part of myself and, in turn, it tells me who I am. Interpretive knowledge is explained in part by context, because it situates people in their experiences and gives them some markers for making sense of their lives. This is also how it relates to practical reflection.

Subjectivity refers to the individual's sensing of inner and external events, which includes personal experiences and truths, that may or may not be like other people's subjective experiences and truths. In this book I am using the word 'subjectivity' in an uncomplicated way, which tries to avoid the tangle philosophical thought has put it into in trying to differentiate it from objectivity. In relation to interpretive knowledge, subjectivity is the means through which individuals sense phenomena inside and outside themselves. Therefore, it is a form of knowledge within the person as subject – that is, the person who relates towards objects of attention. Subjectivity is a part of interpretive knowledge, because the person as the knower, who makes sense of his or her experiences, creates it.

Intersubjectivity refers to how individuals take account of one another in the social world to make sense of their experiences. We tend to live in social circumstances and therefore we need to take account of other people and their experiences. Interpretive knowledge is formed in part by people in dialogue with one another, negotiating the sense they make out of experiences by sharing and contesting meaning in human communication.

In summary, interpretive knowledge emerges from the perspectives of people engaged actively in their lives and it includes and values what people feel and think. Judgements as to the usefulness and 'truthfulness' of the accounts are based on the relative indicators, such as the nature of lived experience, context and subjectivity.

In Chapter 4 I also introduced the idea of practical interest, derived from the work of Jurgen Habermas. To some extent, I have already linked practical interest and interpretive knowledge, but you may find further explanation useful at this point. Practical interest involves human interaction or 'communicative action', which involves reciprocal expectations about behaviour, which are defined and understood by the people involved. In other words, and put into the negative if it did not exist, we would have no means of making sense of communication if we did not agree on what certain words and symbols mean. Through this lack of consensus, it follows that we would not have a common basis for agreeing on the relevant action needed in certain circumstances.

In a work setting, communicative action translates to something as familiar as the communication patterns that are set up by clinicians and the people with whom they come into contact. Communicative action in nursing or midwifery relates to agreeing on and acting upon shared communication norms and expectations. Social norms, or sets of expectations for behaviour, are created over time by people who are in consensus about what is expected in certain situations. The social norms are enforced through sanctions, which ensure that people recognize and honour their responsibilities in the reciprocal behaviour. Thus communicative action is a rich source of interest for practical reflection. As the main intentions of practical interests are to describe and explain human interaction, they are concerned with interpretation and explanation through practical reflection, which in turn creates interpretive knowledge.

Reflector

When you are next at work, watch what happens when people are speaking with one another. Do certain combinations of people relate in a 'typical' fashion (e.g. nurse with nurse, nurse with doctor, nurse with relative, nurse with patient and so on)? Are there any noticeable patterns in the ways nurses relate to people in authority, as opposed to people at their occupational level or below in the work setting hierarchy?

The process of practical reflection

At this point, you may find it helpful to refer to Chapter 2, in which I suggested some prerequisites for reflecting. There are many strategies for reflecting, which you can use alone or in combination. If you have been reading through this book sequentially, by now you will be equipped with some of the literature which affirms the usefulness of reflective practice and some stories from other nurses and midwives who have begun reflecting on their practice.

You may also have undertaken a 'warm up' exercise, in which I encouraged you to think about the person and professional you are now in the light of childhood memories and rules for living. In the previous chapter, you may have also applied technical reflective processes to procedural work requiring improvement through rational processes. We are now at the point at which it is time to reflect on some practice incidents, which could benefit from practical reflection.

The focus of your stories is you, so that you can gain new insights from your experiences. In the exercise that follows, you will reflect on your own work setting and practice, because these stories require you to be active and central to what is happening. You can use the process as a means of exploring any questions and concerns related to the interpersonal basis of your work experiences. When you have recorded one scenario, you can go on to reflect on as many as you choose. Although a daily reflective habit is excellent, if you can manage only one focused attempt each week that will be useful. You might find that your reflection is more a matter of quality than quantity. As I explained previously, it is important to keep a compilation of all your reflections, because you will need them to compare your insights over time. They will show you your main issues and how you are working through them using reflective processes.

In considering these questions, you are making an interpretation of human interactions in your practice. You will begin to see that, even though you are often at the centre of the action, you are certainly not the only person contributing to the situation. Human communication is complex and by looking at the relationships and shared norms you will raise your awareness about your own values and actions, and how they relate to those held and done by other people. This means that you will have a greater understanding of your own communication patterns and those of the people with whom you work.

Think of an incident at work in which you were undertaking your usual work activities involving interpersonal communication, that you felt did not go well. In other words, the situation did not develop the positive outcomes you had envisioned. Write your responses in your journal or record them through audiotape or videotape, ensuring that you can review your answers for later analysis.

Experiencing

Experiencing involves retelling a practice story so that you experience it again in as much detail as possible.

In this part of the process, it is important to recall the sights, sounds, smells, people and any other features which had a bearing on the incident. It might help if you shut your eyes and take yourself back in your imagination to that time.

Alternatively, you might like to begin the process by getting ready emotionally through creative means, such as by playing music, painting or any of the other strategies mentioned in Chapter 2.

When you have a clear image of the situation, write down or represent creatively a full description of the experience. Refer to yourself in the first person, so that you remain engaged centrally and actively in the story. Let your thinking flow so that you portray your head image as faithfully as possible. Respond to the following questions to build up a thick description of the experience:

- What was happening?
- When was it happening?
- Where was it happening?
- Why was it happening?
- Who was involved?
- How were you involved?
- What was the setting like, in terms of its smells, sounds and sights?
- What were the outcomes of the situation?
- How did you feel honestly about the situation?

Let the reflection end when it exhausts itself, then review what you have written or represented in some other creative form. Compare the image in your head with your representation of the event. How do the image and the representation of the reflection compare? If the words or other means of creative expression do not do justice to your head image, go back and elaborate further to ensure that you have encapsulated the experience as well as you possibly can.

Interpreting

Interpreting involves clarifying and explaining the meaning of a communicative action situation.

You should have before you a fully descriptive scenario of situational and communicative aspects of your experience. To make sense of the story, you will need to revisit the account to locate yourself and the communication patterns that were set up with the other people. To find the communicative action features in the story, read the account or review the creative representation and ask yourself:

- What were my hopes for the practice outcomes in this story?
- How were my hopes related to my ideals of what constitutes 'good' practice?
- What are the sources in my life and work for my ideas and values for communicative aspects of my practice?
- In what ways do I embody them now in the way I communicate at work?

- What was my communicative role in this situation?
- To what extent did I achieve my communicative role?
- How did my interpretation of my role affect my relations with the people in the situation?
- What are the shared communication norms and expectations in this situation? In other words, how did everyone else in the story interpret their roles and what did they seem to expect in the situation?
- To what extent were social norms, or sets of expectations for behaviour, operating in this situation?
- What sanctions were in place to ensure that people in this situation recognized and honoured their responsibilities for maintaining socially approved reciprocal behaviour? In other words, what system of rewards and penalties was in place to maintain accepted behaviours? Remember, the sanctions or coercive measures may have been obvious (explicit) or hidden (implicit), but they nevertheless operated as ways of authorizing and controlling the situation.
- Were the usual communicative norms and sanctions altered in this situation?

Learning

Learning involves creating new insights and integrating them into your existing awareness and knowledge.

- What does this scenario tell me about my expectations of myself?
- What does this scenario tell me about my expectations of other people?
- What have I learned from this situation?
- What kinds of adaptations are possible in my work relationships?
- How do I fit these new insights into my present ways of regarding communicative action in my work?

Record your responses to these questions and discuss them with a critical friend. When you are ready, apply your new learning to your work situation.

An example of practical reflection

Kierrynn, aged 42 years, is experienced in acute and intensive care nursing. Her practice story relates to a shift in ICU, when a child with acute leukaemia was admitted. The story is retold here from Kierrynn's discussion in a reflective practice group and her journal entries.

Experiencing

Experiencing involves retelling a practice story so that you experience it again in as much detail as possible.

- What? When? Where? Why? Who? How were you involved? What was the setting like? I was working in ICU and a child I'll call Karl was admitted. I felt a sense of terror, as I always do when a child is admitted, because when a sick child comes in, it creates such an awesome sense of responsibility in me. I was relieved when the child's care was allocated to a senior nurse, Betsy, who I felt could handle Karl's care, especially when he needed a platelet transfusion. Even so, I felt the need to check on the infusion procedure for platelets, sensing that Betsy may not have been aware of how to do the procedure properly. I don't know why I sensed that – I just did. The information was not in the ward, so I went to locate it elsewhere, and I was away about five minutes before I arrived back with the brochure. The platelets had come from a larger hospital five hours by road south, so they were very precious and would have been difficult to replace if anything had gone wrong. Karl's parents were present sitting beside his bed, the ICU was fairly silent, and I suddenly realized that the platelets were not going through and I truly feared they would soon be coagulating.
- What were the outcomes of the situation? As the nurse in charge of that shift, I took control of the situation, by quietly suggesting to Betsy that she get another filter, while I gently moved the platelets in the transfusion bag, to minimize coagulation. I could feel myself getting increasingly stressed, and when the parents asked if anything was wrong I covered up by replying that it was a faulty filter. The after hours Nurse Unit Manager was contacted by phone and she was not impressed about having to find another filter, and asked me why it was necessary. I could not speak out loud on the phone, as the ward was quiet and the parents were listening.
- How did you feel honestly about the situation? I thought: 'Why couldn't Betsy admit she didn't know how to prepare the filter?' I also wondered what the parents thought. After it was all over, I asked myself: 'Why do I take so much responsibility for others?' I felt so annoyed at Betsy for not speaking up and admitting that she did not know how to prepare the filter, as it would have saved so much time, energy and worry.

Interpreting

Interpreting involves clarifying and explaining the meaning of a communicative action situation.

- What were my hopes for the practice outcomes in this story? I hoped we could care for Karl effectively, that he would soon feel better, and that his parents would rest assured he was in good hands.
- How were my hopes related to my ideals of what constitutes 'good' practice? Good practice for me is when things go as planned, with good patient outcomes, through high-quality nursing care.
- What are the sources in my life and work for my ideas and values for communicative aspects of my practice? I always try to communicate openly and honestly and to do the best I can. I learned these values from my parents and the Catholic Church, and I suppose, from friends and family I respect as being open and truthful.
- In what ways do I embody them now in the way I communicate at work? I always try to be open and honest at work, even if I have to confess to a mistake, or try that little bit harder to assert myself if I hold a position I believe is in the patient's best interests.
- What was my communicative role in this situation? My role was in two main different directions: I had to communicate with Betsy; and I had to respond to Karl's parents. Even though the NUM was annoyed about having to find another filter it was a passing annoyance and I didn't really worry too much about that. She took my apology well.
- To what extent did I achieve my communicative role? Well, not at well. No, I'd say I bombed out all round.
- How did my interpretation of my role affect my relations with the people in the situation? With Betsy: I was in charge that shift, but Betsy actually has more years of experience than me. Betsy does not like to work in charge, so I took it on that shift. So, even though I was in charge, I was pussy-footing around Betsy, because I assumed she'd know enough to do the procedure well. With Karl's parents: My role with Karl's parents was as nurse to relatives. They have a right to assume that nurses caring for their son know what they are doing, and I was keen to show that we did, so I was maintaining a professional air of confidence with them.
- What are the shared communication norms and expectations in this situation? In other words, how did everyone else in the story interpret their roles and what did they seem to expect in the situation? With Betsy: I imagined that Betsy would have admitted that she did not know how to transfuse the platelets, and I guess she could not see the need to do so. Maybe she thought she knew what she was doing, or maybe she was bluffing her way through, hoping all would turn out well. I really can't speak for Betsy. I know that I expected her to know the procedure, yet somehow I had a sinking feeling that she did not. With Karl's parents: The parents were understandably anxious for Karl's welfare and they were watching us all like hawks. They have a right to ask questions, which they did, especially when they picked up that something was going wrong

with the transfusion. I wanted to cover up for Betsy and for myself, so when they asked me what was wrong, I told them it was a faulty filter – obviously, that was a lie – or can I call it a white lie?

- To what extent were social norms, or sets of expectations for behaviour, operating in this situation? With Betsy: I was not going to risk making a scene by making a fuss about the mistake. It was easier for me to just work hard to fix the mistake as quickly as I could. Nurses try to cover up for one another I think. At least, I tend to cover up for my colleagues. I don't know why that is. Maybe it is about keeping up appearances of being professional, even when things are going wrong. The strange thing with Betsy and me, is that even now, I have not broached the subject with her – even though we now are well out of the hearing range of the parents and we have both had time to think about it. With Karl's parents: As I said before, they have certain rights as relatives: to ask questions, to be assured of good care and so on. The interesting thing for me though, is that I was so convinced of the need to cover up and maintain a professional front, that I was willing to lie to them about the filter. Wow! That bears some thinking about! For whom was I covering up? For Betsy? For me? For us both?

- What sanctions were in place to ensure that people in this situation recognized and honoured their responsibilities for maintaining socially approved reciprocal behaviour? In other words, what system of rewards and penalties was in place to maintain accepted behaviours? Remember, the sanctions or coercive measures may have been obvious (explicit) or hidden (implicit), but they nevertheless operated as ways of authorizing and controlling the situation. With Betsy: If I'd risked tackling Betsy about the way she was managing the transfusion, I would have had to do it ever so carefully, within the hearing of the parents. Like it or not, Betsy had some intimidating power over me, because she has been practising longer than me and she enjoys lots of respect with her peers. I could not risk asserting myself against all that! With Karl's parents: In their case, it was a matter of needing to be seen as effective. It is important to me that nurses are respected for doing a great job and I wanted to protect that reputation in our case. If we had lost their confidence, they would have been very anxious about us caring for Karl, and I could not risk that.

- Were the usual communicative norms and sanctions altered in this situation? With Betsy: No, I guess not, because this is the way it is usually played out – do your best, but cover up for one another if something goes marginally wrong. It is not necessarily OK, but it is the way it tends to be between nurses. Obviously, we own up straight away if serious errors occur, like a medication mistake, but with marginal errors with no serious consequences, we have a tendency to cover for one another. With Karl's parents: Here again, the scene played out pretty much as it might elsewhere, under similar circumstances. Nurses cannot know everything, but somehow we are meant to be invincible and to never make mistakes, so when mistakes happen, we do not broadcast them to the public.

Learning

Learning involves creating new insights and integrating them into your existing awareness and knowledge.

- What does this scenario tell me about my expectations of myself? I expect myself to be able to handle most situations. I try very hard to make everything OK for everyone when I am at work. I expect myself to be able to assert myself and to be honest and open in my communication with everyone, but I do not always achieve that, it seems.
- What does this scenario tell me about my expectations of other people? With nurses: I expect nurses to be open and honest with me also. I was really annoyed with Betsy for putting me through all that – a scene which could have been averted if she'd only admitted to not knowing what she was doing, so we both could have read the information and undertaken the procedure effectively. With parents: I expect parents to be concerned and I uphold their rights to expect good care and to ask questions, but in this case it did not result in me sticking to my values about being open and honest with them.
- What have I learned from this situation? With nurses: I really need to look at how I communicate with my peers, especially those who I feel have some power over me. I need to become more assertive. If I had approached her earlier, in a gentle but earnest way, maybe Betsy might have admitted to not knowing the procedure and maybe we could have had a very different outcome. I was in charge, but I did not assert myself. Even if I am not in charge in future, I need to find ways of communicating more openly with my peers, especially if it is on professional issues that need our attention. With parents: Well, that's a hard choice – do I always tell the whole truth or do I save parents the whole truth, for whatever reasons?
- What kinds of adaptations are possible in my work relationships? With nurses: It's a two-way street – assertion requires me to be assertive, but the other needs to be willing to listen to my position. I can definitely afford to feel more confident about my own clinical expertise and I can work on making the situations in which I communicate more conducive to open and honest talk. With parents: Knowing that I chose to cover up rather than to stand by my values to tell the truth is a real eye-opener for me. It is hard for me even to admit to it, but I realize that it is a complex matter. My adaptations here that I can make are to become more aware

of how I communicate with relatives and to be more reflective-in-action about what is happening and my choices at that time.

- How do I fit these new insights into my present ways of regarding communicative action in my work? With nurses: I know now that I need to work on being more assertive and to find the courage to find my voice when I need to speak up with my peers. I am more aware now of my communication patterns under stress and I am working on adjusting my usual patterns to include options for being more direct, but in a thoughtful and supportive way. With parents: I would like to imagine that I could apply my values of openness and honesty to every situation, but that may not always be possible, or even advisable. There are shades of grey, I realize, but I need to be aware of when I am hiding behind my professional identity rather than trying to uphold my values. I have no answers for this one yet, but I hope to approximate my values with my practice as much as I can. Who knows? One day I may even be able to admit to myself and to parents that I am an excellent nurse, even though I do not know everything, and I am not invincible!

Summary

This chapter reviewed some information connected directly to practical reflection, before guiding you through the practical reflection process. Communication is complex because it involves human beings with mixed motives and agendas. In the complexity of nursing and midwifery practice, communication becomes even more challenging. Practical reflection can assist you to make your way through the maze of human communication work. I hope you find it useful for your practice.

Key points

- Practical reflection is derived from the work of Smyth (1986a, 1986b) and Street (1991), with an adaptation to emphasize the communicative nature of this type of reflection.
- Practical reflection retains some of the questions used previously by Smyth and Street, within the process of experiencing, interpreting and learning.
- Experiencing involves retelling a practice story so that you experience it again in as much detail as possible.
- Interpreting involves clarifying and explaining the meaning of a communicative action situation.

- Learning involves creating new insights and integrating them into your existing awareness and knowledge.
- Although change may not be an explicit aim of practical reflection, it is still possible through new insights that follow from raised awareness.
- Through the medium of language, practical reflection will help you to understand the interpersonal basis of human experiences and it will also offer you the potential for creating new knowledge, which interprets the meaning of your lived experience, context and subjectivity.

7   Emancipatory reflection

Introduction

This chapter reviews some information connected directly to emancipatory reflection, before guiding you through the emancipatory reflection process, practice stories, critical friend responses and other examples of how emancipatory reflection can be used by nurses and midwives.

Beyond objective reasoning provided by technical reflection, and awareness and description offered by practical reflection, is a critical view of your practice and the constraints within it. If you are thwarted by the power relationships within your practice and work setting, you may need to adopt emancipatory reflective processes to bring about transformative action.

Although I am aware of the potential of emancipatory reflection to bring about positive changes, I am also very aware of the enormity of the task which faces any reflective nurse or midwife who 'takes on the system' to change the status quo. In fact, I am so aware of the inherent dangers in the process that I have warned teachers of reflective practice that they should be careful about sending clinicians out prematurely to bring about change through reflective practice, without ongoing support to fight 'big battles for small gains' (Taylor 1997). With this in mind, I suggest that you find a colleague with whom to work collaboratively on your emancipatory issues. A critical friend may also be helpful, as he or she can act as a colleague, keeping you company on this journey of reflective practice.

Emancipatory reflection is only as liberating as the amount of effort you are willing to invest in making a thorough and systematic critique of the constraints within your practice. Emancipatory reflection will help you to analyse critically the contextual features which have a bearing on your practice, whether they are personal, political, sociocultural, historical or economic.

Personal constraints involve some unique features about you as a nurse or midwife, into which you may or may not have insights. Political constraints are about work relationships and power struggles that happen day to day. The features of the workplace and how people define their entire ways of being together in that setting constitute sociocultural constraints. Historical constraints are those factors that have been inherited in a setting, which have the potential to cause difficulties. Economic constraints have to do with a lack of money in settings in which the health dollar is being made to stretch further and further. Nursing and midwifery practice can include some or all of these constraints, depending on particular work settings and the people interacting in them.

Emancipatory reflection is based on the work of Smyth (1986a) and Street (1991), even though they did not name the process 'emancipatory reflection' as such. Of all the types of reflection, it is the richest, but riskiest, in terms of what it tries to achieve and the courage it requires to use it effectively. It requires clinicians to make a deep, systematic and direct analysis of their work to locate the reasons effective practice is constrained. Given the hegemonic and reified conditions in work settings and relationships, this is no small task. Even so, the process has effects and rewards that can be so impressive as to change the habitual ways you define yourself and go about your daily work.

Practice story

Esther, aged 35 years, is an experienced midwife working in a country hospital with accredited birthing facilities. This is Esther's story about caring for a critically ill newly-birthed young woman before she was transferred to a larger hospital. The following excerpt is from Esther's reflective journal:

A woman was admitted for an elective induction of labour at 38 weeks gestation. She was exceptionally obese and hypertensive. She had obvious ankle oedema. On examination, her Bishop's score was unfavourable for artificially rupturing her membranes. I had looked after this woman when a similar situation had arisen in her previous pregnancy, and she was transferred to a larger hospital for intrapartum care . . . Now the same nightmare scenario was repeating itself! I was really pissed off, as whomever (and I knew who) had completed her antenatal booking had either not recognized her at-risk condition, or done anything about it, i.e., phoned the GP/obstetrician or discussed the situation with the hospital manager. Therefore, this woman had presented inappropriately again!

When the GP arrived, he was to phone the hospital manager. The GP arrived, ignored the request to phone the hospital manager and went to see the woman. He disagreed with our findings of hypertension. He examined her vaginally and lo, her membranes ruptured! Quite a coincidence – I don't think! However, the liquor was heavily meconium stained, and the foetal heart rate, extremely difficult to locate because of her obesity, became erratic, bradycardia, tachycardia and some Type 11 dips.

Critical friend response

I offered my support as a critical friend to Esther. When Esther revisited the story to see what she could locate in terms of political motives and outcomes, she had plenty of justification for feeling that the woman was mismanaged by the midwife, who booked her in as low risk, and the doctor who Esther felt acted inappropriately in giving medical care. In doing this, however, she jumped quickly to conclusions without engaging in a more tentative process. For example, Esther wrote: 'Collusive behaviour between some midwives, inept GPs and gutless management ensures that the status quo remains, inept, dangerous practice continues and obstetric/midwifery care is sometimes poor, depending on the mid-wife and GP involved'. Whereas this judgement may or may not have some 'truth' and merit, it is important at this point for Esther to identify her involvement in the scenario by looking at her part with the eyes of an interested observer standing back from the action.

Esther could make explorations tentatively, using the detector statement of: 'It seems as if I tend to act according to my belief that . . .' *By completing this sentence as often as she needs to, she could find the basis for the events in practice that 'push her buttons' and make her react each time they come up in some form or another. For example, it seems as if Esther has standards of care which may or may not be met by midwives and doctors, which she applies to management situations. Only Esther can apply this tentative exploration of herself in other respects. For instance, she may see that it seems as if she has certain unexamined ideas about how she views 'good' practice, or that her frustration at incompetence may be connected to a deeply personal part of her life. I raised these ideas with Esther, purely as conjecture, acting as a critical friend.*

Esther's practice story and a critical friend response continues later in this chapter.

Review of previous ideas

Chapter 4 explained that critical knowledge is derived from some key ideas in critical social science which have the potential to be emancipatory – that is, to have freeing possibilities. In particular, critical social science has the potential to free people from the oppression of their social and personal conditions by questioning the status quo of various potentially repressive social contexts, to discover and expose the forces that maintain them for the advantages of particular people or regimes. This means that it looks at the nature of powerful relationships in life and asks how they might be different and better for the majority of people, not just for the privileged few. There are many key ideas in critical social science, but the ones included in emancipatory reflection are false consciousness, hegemony, reification, emancipation and empowerment. Many of these ideas are related, and they describe the depth and scope of forces which can keep people controlled and subordinated.

False consciousness is the 'systematic ignorance that the members of . . . society have about themselves and their society' (Fay 1987: 27). Ignorance of oppressive forces means that they remain unchallenged. Hegemony means the ascendancy or domination of one power over another, and it refers to the ways in which some social systems, and the people in them, give the impression that they are unassailable, and that the conditions they have produced are not only good, but also appropriate for the people over whom they have control. Nursing and midwifery settings have hegemonic influences operating within them that maintain false consciousness, but emancipatory reflection helps you to see where they are and how they create and maintain their power to work against you.

Fay (1987: 92) explains that reification means 'making into a thing' and he defines it as 'taking what are essential activities and treating them as if they operated according to a given set of laws independently of the wishes of the social actors who engage in them'. These laws of social life are assigned a power of their own, thus becoming accepted and unquestioned as givens. When practices become reified, they are immensely resistant to change because they are so deeply entrenched and accepted that they are embedded in the matrix of practice and thereby become relatively impervious to identification and critique.

Emancipation means freedom, from your own and from other people's expectations and roles, and to adopt other self-aware and socially aware practices. Empowerment is the process of giving and accepting power, to liberate people from their oppressive circumstances. Emancipatory reflection alerts you to the possibilities of emancipation and gives you the means to empower yourself and others.

In summary, critical knowledge is potentially liberating for individuals and groups of people, when they realize that they may be living under mis-understandings about themselves and their social situations – misunder-standings which have been developed and held systematically. As people and practitioners, nurses and midwives are subject to oppressive social structures which can be transformed through critical analysis and action. Emancipatory interest is rooted in power and creates 'transformative action' which seeks to provide emancipation from forces which limit people's rational control of their lives. These forces are so influential and taken for granted that people have the strong impression that they are beyond their control.

Emancipatory reflection involves human interaction, but it emphasizes how people interpret themselves within their roles and social obligations. Emancipatory reflection leads to 'transformative action', which seeks to free you from your taken-for-granted assumptions and oppressive forces which limit you and your practice. Emancipatory reflection provides you with a systematic means of critiquing the status quo in the power relationships in your workplace and offers you raised awareness and a new sense of informed consciousness to bring about positive social and political change. It also offers you freedom from your own misguided and firmly-held perceptions of your-self and your roles, to bring about change for the better. The process for change is *praxis*, which offers clinicians the means for change through collaborative processes that analyse and challenge existing forces and distortions brought about by the dominating effects of power in human interaction.

Reflector

How do you define a 'good day' at work? Think about whether you identify a day at work as 'good' because it is unremarkable in the sense that not much goes wrong? If this is so, look closely at your 'good day' and see whether it contains unexamined issues of power. If you are alerted to the practices involved in a 'good day', you may uncover aspects of your work that have become hidden and silenced through hegemonic influences.

The process of emancipatory reflection

Daily work incidents are imbued with power. If you look closely, you will begin to see subtle and not so subtle examples of power-plays within health care settings that are taken for granted as 'just the way things are'. Emancipatory reflection provides a process to construct, confront, deconstruct and reconstruct your practice. *Construction* of practice incidents allows you to describe, in words and other creative images and representations, a work scene played out previously, bringing to mind all the aspects and constraints of the situation. *Deconstruction* involves asking analytical questions regarding the situation, which are aimed at locating and critiquing all the aspects. *Confrontation* occurs when you focus on your part in the scenario with the intention of seeing and describing it as clearly as possible. *Reconstruction* puts the scenario together again with transformative strategies for managing changes in the light of the new insights.

There are many constraints operating in work settings, including cultural, economic, historical, political, social and personal, which may affect the ways in which you are able to interpret and act at any given moment.

Reflector

Review the description of practice constraints in Chapter 1. What are they? How do they weigh against effective practice? What kinds of constraint operate at subtle levels in your workplace? How can you recognize them? What effects do they have on your practice?

You are a central character in your practice stories, reflecting on your own practice as it relates to other people and determinants of the situation. When you have reflected on one scenario, you can go on to reflect on as many as you choose. Keep a record of all your reflections; they will be interesting to compare, because they track your reflective journey, and they will show you your main issues and how you are working through them using reflective processes.

Choose an incident in which you were not entirely happy about the outcomes of your involvement, that is, you felt that you did not make a difference of a positive nature to someone in your care. The incident should also exemplify an imbalance of power and cooperation between people. The situation can involve as many people as you like, but you should be central in the activity. The following steps guide you through the reflective writing processes of construction, to describe the situation as fully as possible.

Constructing

In order to construct an incident in which you felt that you did not make a difference of a positive nature and there was an imbalance of power and cooperation, it might help to shut your eyes and take yourself back in your imagination to that time. You could also use other strategies to enhance your memory, such as those described in Chapter 2. When you have a clear image of the situation write down, or represent creatively, a full description of the experience. If you respond to the following questions you will be able to build up a thick description of the event:

- What was happening?
- When was it happening?
- Where was it happening?

- What was the setting like, in terms of its smells, sounds and sights?
- Why was it happening?
- Who was involved?
- How were you involved?
- What were the outcomes of the situation?
- How did you feel honestly about the situation?

Now you need to review your construction of the situation:

- Is your description or creative representation as rich and full as possible?
- Does it capture the scene as faithfully as possible?

You might like to go back and elaborate further to ensure that you have described the experience as well as you possibly can. As you may have noticed already, a rich and full description at the outset provides more information on which to reflect.

Deconstructing

If you have been able to capture the context, you should have before you a fully descriptive scenario of the interactions and inherent power relations in an aspect of your practice. The reason I have described power relations as 'inherent' is that they will be there, but they may not be explicit at this point, especially as this story may not be able to capture all of the people's intentions and behaviours. Even if you use this process to describe a story in which events appear to go well, there may be implicit power plays operating. A critical view of practice helps you to see the power relations which bubble away, possibly just under the surface of what is apparent immediately. With this in mind, revisit your account or creative representation and see what you can locate in terms of political motives and outcomes.

Identify your involvement in the scenario by looking at your part with the eyes of an interested observer standing back from the action. When you locate aspects of your contributions to the interaction, investigate your motives and actions by musing tentatively: '*It seems as if I act according to my belief that . . .*' By completing this sentence as often as you need to, you will find the stimuli in practice that 'push your buttons' and make you react each time they come up in some form or another. The chances are that you will find these themes in your reflection, even though initially your practice stories appear to have little relation to one another.

Express yourself as clearly as you can, so that your observing self-identifies, frankly and honestly, the person you have represented as yourself in the scenario. Write down or audiotape any observations you make, so that you can revisit them. Alternatively, you might like to write poetry or use some other creative means to respond to this part of the process. At this point, however, you need to be as clear in your mind as possible about what your musing means, so you need to make a note of your responses and interpret your creative reflections as they 'speak' to you.

Confronting

To become aware critically you need to remain vigilant and take a critical view of practice. Even when situations appear relatively positive, power interests may mediate them. To confront these power issues you need to ask questions such as:

- Where did the ideas I embody in my practice come from historically?
- How did I come to appropriate them? In other words, how did I take them on?
- Why do I continue now to endorse them in my work?
- Whose interests do they serve?
- What power relations are involved?
- How do these ideas influence my relationships with the people in my care?
- What cultural, economic, historical, political, social and/or personal constraints are operating in this practice story (adapted from Smyth 1986a)?

In being prepared to ask these questions, you are making a critical analysis of your practice world. You will begin to see that even though you are often at the centre of your world, you are certainly not the only determinant of the situation. The world in which you exist and act is influenced by historical, sociocultural, economic and political determinants, which to greater and lesser extents constrain the ways in which you are free to interpret and act in any given moment. The realization that you are 'not alone' in your practice can free you from bitter self-recriminations and raise the possibilities of new awareness. At some stage it may also be possible to transform the repressive conditions which cause you to act in certain ways.

Reconstructing

Reconstructing puts the scenario together again with transformative strategies for managing changes in the light of new insights. Given that you have been able to follow the process of systematic enquiry outlined so far, by now you may have realized that there may be contradictions in what you *say* you think, say and do, and what you *actually* think, say and do.

The only remaining step in the process is to free yourself to the possibilities of using your raised awareness in reconstructing your world. There may be a lot of time, space and effort between raised awareness and change, but if you do not allow yourself to imagine the possibilities of transformation, then nothing will be possible. If you dare to imagine and to plan to act in ways that are capable of transforming your world, then you will have attempted to break free from the taken-for-granted assumptions which maintain the status quo.

The final question to be posed is:

- In the light of what I have discovered, how might I work differently?

As you imagine some different ways of acting, don't forget that you are not alone in your work setting. Consider how historical, sociocultural, economic and political determinants might play a part in the way you are able to work. Begin to imagine or make some adjustments to some of the situational constraints as part of your plan of action for change.

Practice story

Continuing on with Esther's practice story of caring for a woman at risk, Esther then confronted her practice. To become more aware critically, she confronted the power issues by asking herself where the ideas she embodies in her practice came from historically, how she came to appropriate them and why she continues to endorse them now in her work. Although Esther came close to answering these questions, she veered off and did not quite address them.

For example, she concluded: 'The interests served are definitely those of maintaining the status quo, i.e. medically dominated birthing. The power relations are that of oppression – of birthing women and midwives on the one hand – and domination by GPs. Women are given very little choice or information, therefore informed decision-making re-birthing is limited. My relationship with the women in my care while practising midwifery is definitely influenced by the power relations. There continues to be a dilemma where my strong belief in advocacy is challenged by both the GPs and in a more insidious way, by some midwives . . .'

Critical friend response

In response to what I thought might be a tendency for Esther to reach conclusions rapidly, during a phone call one day in which she was describing her experience of becoming a reflective practitioner, I asked her to put herself into the picture. It seemed to me that in her quest to name the problem and put things right, Esther did not involve herself, but seemed to draw conclusions about other people's motives and behaviour. Our conversation was along these lines:

Esther: *You asked before about where I am in the story – my emotions, how I felt, that kind of thing.*

Critical friend: *Yes Esther, have you come up with anything yet?*

Esther: *When you asked me that, my voice became chokey and I almost started crying. I know that I keep a lot of my emotional stuff damped down regarding my midwifery practice, or I'd be constantly angry, a blubbering mess, or both, most of the time.*

Critical friend: *Yes, I hear what you are saying, but tell me what in particular makes you angry.*

Esther: *I get angry at the injustice. I whittle away at injustices for clients and staff little by little. I could not live with integrity if I didn't.*

Critical friend: *Give me an example of the injustice.*

Esther: *One injustice is that doctors don't listen to the requests and observations of experienced midwives.*

Critical friend: *What makes that an injustice?*

Esther: *Their unwillingness to listen, or to even consider the possibility that we have weighed up the clinical situation very carefully, and, for example, when we say a woman has hypertension, she* has *hypertension, not only evidenced by her vital signs, but also through her past pregnancy history.*

Critical friend: *Given that people such as doctors will determine what they will do as doctors, and given that midwives are in the best position to influence midwifery care, what are the* mid-wifery issues *in this story that you can work on, that might somehow assist in levelling out the midwife-doctor power imbalance?*

The conversation continues . . .

An example of emancipatory reflection

Jenny, aged 38 years, is an experienced nurse with 15 years in total of experience in acute nursing care, and in the last five years she been in a senior nursing management position that has allowed her to keep her clinical proficiency while influencing practice management. As such, Jenny is a respected member of the health care team, especially the nurses, who often ask her to assist them in solving complex clinical problems. Her clinical nursing and management role also requires her to communicate often with doctors in forming clinical guidelines for procedures.

Jenny is also a member of a reflective practice group, who are using action research to work through the clinical issue of the need for assertion, especially in situations in which there are power imbalances. Jenny told her practice story about meeting with two doctors to look at possible changes to some clinical guidelines.

Constructing

- What? When? Where? Why? What was the setting like? Who was involved? How were you involved? As part of my role as the clinical nurse manager, I had to meet with two doctors during the week. The intention of the meeting was to review the present guidelines for emergency resuscitation and to make any changes that might be necessary in the light of new research-based evidence for best practice. We met in one of the rooms in the education centre around 1 p.m., and the meeting was to last for around an hour or so. It was quiet and private in the room and with only three of us in the subcommittee I felt outnumbered as the only nurse.
- What were the outcomes of the situation? All seemed to be going well until the doctors bamboozled me with generic names of recently marketed drugs. I know the names of most drugs, of course, but I don't always use their generic names for simplicity's sake. Some new drugs have come onto the market recently, but they are not necessarily in common use in hospital settings as yet. They began talking among themselves as though I was not there. Their tactic effectively silenced me and I was unable to contribute much after that, because they kept the subject on medications, rather than sticking to the task of reviewing the entire procedure, not just the drug therapies.
- How did you feel honestly about the situation? I honestly felt as though it was a case of 'We'll show this hot-shot nurse! Thinks she's smart, does she?' I felt like it was two against one and I felt overwhelmed and out-numbered. I also felt patronized and I felt that they were trying to get rid of me, as inconsequential to any decisions they might make.

Deconstructing

A member of the reflective practice group asked Jenny to identify her involvement in the scenario by looking at her part with the eyes of an interested observer standing back from the action. Jenny located aspects of her contributions to the interaction by investigating her motives and actions and musing tentatively: *'It seems as if I act according to my belief that . . .'* By completing this sentence often she found some of the stimuli in her practice that 'push her buttons' and make her react each time they come up in some form or another.

Jenny said: 'It seems as if I act according to my belief that doctors should respect nurses' knowledge and skills. I was indignant that these doctors used the generic names to keep me out of the conversation and to silence me. Therefore, following on from that, it seems as if I value being part of a multidisciplinary team, but I don't really feel like an equal in it. Also, by remaining silent because of their exclusion tactics, it seems as if I am willing to comply with their dominance over me. Possibly, somewhere deep inside me I must hold the thought that doctors know more than me and that they have the power when it comes to multi-disciplinary teams, despite all the rhetoric we perpetuate that we all contribute as equals in multidisciplinary teams, such as in this committee.'

Confronting

Jenny knew that to become aware critically she needed to remain vigilant and take a critical view of her practice. To confront the power issues she responded to the following questions:

- Where did the ideas I embody in my practice come from historically? From my practice story I can see that I value the ideas of respect, col-laboration and equality. Historically these values come from growing up in a large family, having to share and cooperate with one another. As I became an adult I realized that valuing respect, collaboration and equality were good markers for life, so I have continued to uphold them. Even so, this story shows me that I also embody passivity to power, that is, in the face of lack of respect, collaboration and equality, I do not necessarily always assert my right for these values to be honoured or reciprocated.
- How did I come to appropriate them? I took on the ideas of respect, collaboration and equality as I developed expertise and confidence in my work relations. Most of the time I actively embody them in my relation-ships with people at work, but sometimes they are not that obvious in my practice.
- Why do I continue now to endorse them in my work? I continue to endorse respect, collaboration and equality now in my practice, because they work for me most of the time, and they help me to work as an effective multidisciplinary team member. I suppose I feel that if I embody these values I might become a role model for other people. This means that if I show other people how to be respectful, and to work collabora-tively and with equality, they might catch on and treat me and other people in the same way. Widely spread across the entire organization, respect, collaboration and equality can only have good effects that are advantageous for everyone.
- Whose interests do they serve? They are positive values that should ideally serve everyone's interests, in that they form a good foundation for relating to one another in the multidisciplinary team. I must admit also, that they serve my purposes, because if I can model them, they might

flow back to me and make my work life a lot happier. Just imagine, if people in power in the hierarchy embodied these values, there would be less 'grandstanding', egos would be in check, and it would take a lot of anxiety away from me, if I could come to work each day and know everyone was enacting their roles with respect, collaboration and equality.

- What power relations are involved? Respect, collaboration and equality do not work when everyone in the multidisciplinary team does not value or embody them, and this is demonstrated very well in my story, when doctors used language to hammer home their clinical superiority. They used their medical power over me to obliterate any possibility of respect, collaboration and equality. In fact, I could go so far as to say that they sensed my willingness to embody these values and took advantage of me, *because* of them. In other words, sensing my willingness to be respectful and to collaborate in equal terms with them, they seized that as their opportunity to turn the situation around to their advantage, and to make me look weak and passive for trying to embody these values.

- How do these ideas influence my relationships with the people in my care? They influence my work relationships by giving me some values on which to make my decisions and act ethically, in relation to the people with whom I come into contact. For example, I care for my patients with these values in mind – they deserve my respect and we collaborate in the planning of their care, as equals in terms of our shared humanity. Patients may look to me to have extra knowledge and skills that they do not possess, but that does not mean that I use that expertise to talk down to them, or treat them like lesser beings.

- What cultural, economic, historical, political, social and/or personal constraints are operating in this practice story? Let's see – in my practice story about the doctors using their knowledge as power over me, I consider that the cultural constraints operating between us had to do with how we see ourselves in terms of the symbols and rituals that denote our different practices. For example, doctors use medical language as a device to maintain distance and to exert authority and superiority. While I may have considerable skills in speaking in medical terminology, and I am able to decode the vast majority of it, in my story these doctors used their knowledge of recently marketed generic drug names to intentionally leave me behind in the conversation. That left me with the alternative to speak up and ask for a decoding or translation of their medical language, or to remain silent. I was feeling patronized and I did not want to give them the satisfaction of knowing that their cultural strategy to distance and exclude me from the conversation had in fact worked. There were no economic constraints operating in this situation that I can see. Economic constraints happen often in clinical settings, but not in this case. Rare, isn't it! The historical constraints are those that we have perpetuated from long ago, when doctors were indisputable 'lords of the manor' and no one dared to question that. Historically, doctors have enjoyed a great deal of professional power in the hospital hierarchy and some still hanker for those days when their word was not questioned and we nurses ran around willingly as handmaidens to them. Times have changed and we now acknowledge other professionals' knowledge and expertise by forming multidisciplinary teams. However, history holds a strong influence over the present day and some doctors may not have moved on much from being the dominant member of the health team. Nurses have historically come from a tradition of subservience to doctors and I realize that my response to these doctors shows me that the constraints of history still have an influence on me. The political constraints were the power and prestige differences, acted out by two doctors shutting out one nurse, in a political manoeuvre managed through language. Professional politics are not always explicit I know, but in this case it was a blatant attempt to put me in my place. I'm sure they felt they were totally capable of revising the resuscitation guidelines without any help from a lowly nurse, even if she is the best nurse this hospital can offer! The social constraints are how we relate to one another as people and professionals, within the hierarchy. I am sure that these doctors did not see me as their social equal. They enjoy far higher salaries than me, drive around in luxury cars, live in the best suburbs, are members of the best clubs, stay within their own social circles, and maintain their social distance by not associating with nurses outside working hours. These factors all act as constraints in a work setting in which there is rhetoric about the equal contributions of members of the multidisciplinary health team. Of course they do not see me as their equal – not in any way – culturally, historically, politically or socially. The personal constraints relate to my inability to rise above the patronizing exclusion tactics of these doctors, to assert myself in that situation. I am a shy person by nature, even though my clinical expertise gives me confidence at work. Sometimes the shy and passive person comes out at work, because it is easier and less confronting to remain silent when the stakes are high and political forces are blatantly active in clinical situations.

In being prepared to ask these questions, Jenny began to see that even though she was at the centre of this story, she was not the only determinant of the outcome. She realized that the unsatisfactory outcome was more than from her personal inability to make the situation better, rather it related to the constraints operating in this situation, such as the historical, sociocultural and political factors.

Reconstructing

Jenny realized that there were contradictions in what she *said* she thought and embodied, and what she *actually* thought, said and did. She realized that she espoused the values of respect, collaboration and equality, but it was not always possible to live by these values at work, nor was there much hope of seeing them enacted and reciprocated routinely in her work setting. She was then ready to take the final step in the process of emancipatory reflection, to free herself to the possibilities of using her raised awareness in reconstructing her practice world.

The final question Jenny posed to herself was: In the light of what I have discovered, how might I work differently? Jenny reflected that in future cases of this nature, when she becomes aware of power tactics to silence her, it might be possible to speak up and ask for more information, for example: 'Could you please tell me the medications to which you are referring?' This will require her to be honest and to risk feeling vulnerable, but the sincere attempt to open up dialogue and clarify meaning could also be interpreted as mature communication embodying her values of respect, collaboration and equality among professionals.

Jenny decided that if she has a good sense of what may come up as points of discussion in similar meetings with doctors or other members of the multidisciplinary team, she could spend more time preparing herself by reviewing clinical knowledge to make her ready for most contingencies. This might mean spending time reading recent research and literature, or discussing complex ideas or new treatment regimes with peers, to make her conversant with the latest thinking in specific areas.

Jenny imagined that in situations in which the main focus of the meeting is being circumvented by other people's power agendas, she could try getting the discussion back on focus by identifying the diversion and reminding the other people of the primary intention of the conversation. This kind of assertive communication takes courage, but it is nevertheless a communication skill that can be used intentionally and with success when discussions are digressing from the main focus.

Jenny also decided that it might be appropriate sometimes to respond to a politically overwhelming situation with an assertion of her own expertise and the professional credibility she brings to the discussion. For example: 'As a nurse with X years of experience in Y, I have the responsibility for Z. Therefore, I am well placed to offer advice on A, B and C'.

Summary

This chapter reviewed some information connected directly to emancipatory reflection, before guiding you through the emancipatory reflection process. When you are thwarted by the power relationships within your practice and work setting, you may need to adopt emancipatory reflective processes to bring about transformative action. By working through the process systematically, you may find yourself liberated from self-recriminations, as you realize that personal constraints are not the only determinants of situational outcomes. Nurses and midwives work in settings that are replete with cultural, economic, historical, political and social constraints, all of which may contrive to make your practice less than you might ideally envision.

Key points

- If you are thwarted by the power relationships within your practice and work setting, you may need to adopt emancipatory reflective processes to bring about transformative action.
- Emancipatory reflection is only as liberating as the amount of effort you are willing to invest in making a thorough and systematic critique of the constraints within your practice.
- Emancipatory reflection will help you to analyse critically the contextual features which have a bearing on your practice, whether they are personal, political, sociocultural, historical or economic.
- Of all the types of reflection, emancipatory reflection is the richest, but riskiest, in terms of what it tries to achieve and the courage it requires to use it effectively.
- Emancipatory reflection leads to 'transformative action', which seeks to free you from your taken-for-granted assumptions and oppressive forces, which limit you and your practice.
- Emancipatory reflection provides you with a systematic means of critiquing the status quo in the power relationships in your workplace and offers you raised awareness and a new sense of informed consciousness to bring about positive social and political change.
- Emancipatory reflection also offers you freedom from your own misguided and firmly held perceptions of yourself and your roles, to bring about change for the better.
- The process of emancipatory reflection for change is praxis, which offers clinicians the means for change through collaborative processes that analyse and challenge existing forces and distortions.
- Emancipatory reflection provides a process to construct, confront, deconstruct and reconstruct your practice.
- Construction of practice incidents allows you to describe, in words and other creative images and representations, a work scene played out previously, bringing to mind all the aspects and constraints of the situation.

- Deconstruction involves asking analytical questions regarding the situation, which are aimed at locating and critiquing all the aspects of that situation.
- Confrontation occurs when you focus on your part in the scenario with the intention of seeing and describing it as clearly as possible.
- Reconstruction puts the scenario together again with transformative strategies for managing changes in the light of the new insights.

8 Reflective practice in research and scholarship

Introduction

This chapter provides practical information on how to incorporate reflective practice into research methodologies and nursing or midwifery scholarship. Reflective methods and processes fit well with all qualitative research methodologies, and this chapter identifies possible applications before focusing on specific projects involving action research. The chapter also describes how to foster scholarship by preparing your research findings for conference presentations and journal articles, because research worth doing is worth sharing to improve practice and to extend disciplinary knowledge.

Research is important in any human service providing health care, because humans require and deserve high-quality management of their health needs. Ideally, nurses and midwives are mindful of the complexity of their practice and they attempt daily to provide safe and effective care based on the latest research evidence. Reflective methods and processes not only guide practice, they can also provide evidence for supporting practice changes.

Scholarship in nursing and midwifery is generated and validated through scientific means. 'Science' in this sense is '*scientia*', meaning knowledge in general, not the specific knowledge of an empirical type originating from the scientific method, described in Chapters 4 and 5. This means that *scientia* allows for many types of knowledge that contribute equally to the disciplinary content of nursing and midwifery. Thus, reflective methods and processes in practice provide empirical, interpretive and critical knowledge for scholarship in nursing and midwifery.

Incorporating reflective practice into research methodologies

This section reviews foundational research knowledge before connecting research methodologies to reflection. Research attempts to find new and amended knowledge using systematic data collection and analysis approaches. You may need to consult recent research texts (Crookes and Davies 1998; Roberts and Taylor 2001; Young *et al.* 2001), because this section cannot cover the detailed complexity inherent in nursing and midwifery research methods and processes. As a basis for understanding the connections between reflection and research, it is important to review the main types of research, because they make certain assumptions about how knowledge is generated and verified.

Types of research

It is advisable for a beginning researcher to reduce the complexity of research by thinking of it as fitting into three main types: empirico-analytical (quantitative), interpretive (qualitative) and critical (qualitative) (Roberts and Taylor 2001).

Empirico-analytical (quantitative) research uses numbers and statistics as its main investigative tools, to observe and analyse through the scientific method. The scientific method uses rigorous rules for research, to test something over and over again and be consistently accurate (reliability), and to test what it actually intends to test (validity) rather than other things that are there unnoticed (extraneous variables). To achieve this, the scientific method demands objectivity, to eradicate the distorting influences of people, such as their ideas, intentions and emotions (subjectivity), to produce scientific knowledge. The scientific method only asks research questions that can be structured in ways that can be observed and analysed (by empirico-analytical means), and measured by numbers, percentages and statistics (quantified), hence the categorization of empirico-analytical and/or quantitative research. Research areas examined through quantitative research include cause and effect relationships, incidences and percentages of occurrences and trends. Examples of empirico-analytical research methods are randomized controlled trials, experimental designs, surveys and questionnaires. All of these methods require strict attention to details, which can be found in most quantitative research texts (e.g. Polit *et al.* 2001).

Reflector

Which type of reflection – technical, practical or emancipatory – combines best with quantitative research methods? Why?

Qualitative research can be interpretive or critical (Roberts and Taylor 2001), and uses words and language as its main exploratory tools. Qualitative researchers are interested in questions that involve human consciousness and subjectivity, and they value humans and their experiences in the research process. Qualitative research involves finding out about the changing (relative) nature of knowledge, which is seen to be special and centred in the people, place, time and conditions in which it finds itself (unique and context-dependent). Qualitative research uses thinking that starts from the specific instance and moves to the general pattern of combined instances (inductive), so it 'grows from the ground up' to make larger statements about the nature of the phenomenon being investigated. Rather than starting with a statement of anticipated relationships (hypothesis), qualitative research begins a project with a broad statement of the area of interest, such as: 'This research explores the nature of the nurse/midwife-patient/mother relationship'. The measures for ensuring validity in qualitative research involve asking participants and other people if the experience resonates with them. Reliability is often not an issue in qualitative research, as it is based on the idea that knowledge is relative and dependent on all of the features of the people, place, time and other circumstances (context) of the setting. People are valued as sources of information and their expressions of their personal awareness (subjectivity) are valued as being integral to the meaning that comes out of the research. Qualitative research makes no claims to generate knowledge that can be confirmed as certain (absolute) or even predictive.

Reflector

Which type of reflection – technical, practical or emancipatory – combines best with interpretive qualitative research methods? Why?

Interpretive qualitative research aims mainly to generate meaning, that is, to explain and describe, in order to make sense of phenomena of interest. Examples of interpretive qualitative research include historical methods, grounded theory, phenomenology and ethnography. Qualitative critical research also generates meaning and aims openly to bring about change in the status quo. Examples of qualitative critical research include action research, critical ethnography, feminist research and discourse analysis. Qualitative interpretive and critical research have many similarities, but they differ in terms of their intention to bring about social and political change. By working collaboratively with participants as co-researchers to systematically address research problems, qualitative researchers try to find answers and use them to bring about change. Further details on these and other qualititive interpretive and critical research can be found in Streubert Speziale and Rinaldi Carpenter (2003) and Roberts and Taylor (2001).

Reflector

Which type of reflection – technical, practical or emancipatory – combines best with critical qualitative research methods? Why?

It becomes immediately obvious from the preceding overview of foundational ideas that qualitative research fits best with reflection, as both are concerned with the description of human experience for the possibilities of increased understanding, raised awareness and change. Reflective processes may be the main framework for the project, or they may be integrated into other research approaches.

Possible applications of reflection in research

Reflective processes may be used solely as the research approach, or they may be integrated into other research approaches. This section describes both options, to open up the potential for creative reflective processes in research.

The reflective research approach

A research project may use reflective methods and processes solely as its organizing and procedural framework. This is because reflective approaches assume certain principles of knowledge generation and validation that fit well with the qualitative research paradigm. The validation for this position has been provided already in this chapter. Briefly, reflective practice generates objective (through technical reflection) or subjective (through practical and emancipatory reflection), context-dependent, relative knowledge that resonates as 'truth' for the individual and for other people who recognize similar experiences. The value of reflective knowledge of an interpretive or critical form is raised awareness, insight and potential for change and improvement.

The forms of reflection described in this book can be used as data collection methods in research projects. For example, a project examining the effectiveness of a clinical procedure could use technical reflective processes to facilitate critical thinking and problem-solving. The information gained through individual or collective discussions using objective argumentation is data. These processes could be used alone or in combination with other quantitative methods, such as experiments and structured observation. Research participants could keep reflective journals or use the questions posed by technical reflection as a stimulus for group discussion. The aim of research using technical reflection would be to satisfy the need for rational adaptations to work procedures and to maintain evidence-based practice.

Practical reflection may be used in any project which intends to explore the meaning of phenomena in nursing and midwifery. For example, a project may explore the meaning of illness as it is experienced. In this case, practical reflection could be encouraged in research participants by asking them to tell a story about the experience of their illness. The questions posed in the reflective process could facilitate the telling of the story to ensure that a rich description is achieved. Alternatively, the researcher or research team could keep reflective logs about their experiences of providing care for people.

Emancipatory reflection fits well with critical research, which aims to expose power relations and change the dominant forces constraining nurses' and midwives' practice. For example, a group of nurses or midwives could form an action research group and work collaboratively to bring about changes in their practice according to what matters most to them. This might mean that each person keeps a reflective log, parts of which are shared in the group to assist in deciding on the direction of the project. The group would work together to assess clinical problems and to suggest and trial strategies for change.

A reflective research approach can be used for projects based solely on the assumptions, methods and processes of reflection. As stated previously, the epistemological assumptions of reflection are that knowledge is partially objective or subjective, context-dependent and relative, making no claim as absolute or certain 'truth', but rather as socially constructed representations of 'truth' that provide tentative answers to issues and problems and to 'useful for now' descriptions of meaning and experience.

There is no 'correct' or 'best' reflective research method. Even so, taking the types of reflection in this book as examples, it is possible to construct a creative method to undertake research. The basic eight steps in the method are to: identify the issue/problem/phenomenon for reflection; decide on the reflective method; clarify its intent; plan the stages in a research proposal; follow the method and use the process; generate insights, institute changes and improvements and continue to reflect on outcomes; report on outcomes; and use the outcomes in practice as evidence.

Step 1: identify the issue/problem/phenomenon for reflection

Practice is a rich ground in which to find puzzles to be solved. Issues and problems can be in relation to the wider health environment, for example, research questions can be raised about governmental structures and processes for health, legal and ethical guidelines for health care and the organizational structures and systems in which you work. Research questions can also be raised about your local professional context, such as the department, ward or unit in which you work. The specific nature of the research questions will depend on the issues you locate there, for example, research questions could be about policies and procedures, interpersonal relationships, and/or power-plays. Other local issues for reflective research could be those found often in nursing and midwifery, which are described in Chapter 1.

Reflector

Turn to Chapter 1 and review the issues often faced by nurses and midwives. Are any of these issues familiar to you? Choose one and write two research questions in relation to it. This will be the issue you will work on, in order to follow a reflective research process. Write it down as Step 1.

Step 2: decide on the reflective method

In this step you choose the type of reflection that best suits the exploration of your clinical issue. Given that this book sets out three types of reflection, use one of them as the basis for demonstrating this approach to reflective research. Is your issue about policies and procedures, interpersonal relationships or politics at work? Is it a combination of all or some of these? When you make this decision, remember that this book describes technical reflection for policy and procedural issues; practical reflection for interpersonal communication issues; and emancipatory reflection for issues involving unequal power balances.

Reflector

Decide on a reflective method to suit the issue you chose in Step 1. Write it down under the issue as Step 2.

Step 3: clarify the intent of the reflective method

To ensure that the method fits your clinical issue, clarify the intent of the specific type of reflection you are thinking of using in your research. For example, you'll remember that technical reflection offers you the objective means to observe and analyse work procedures through scientific reasoning, because it has an interest in instrumental action. Practical reflection will help you to understand the interpersonal basis of human experiences and offer you the potential for creating new knowledge, because it has an interpretive intent. Emancipatory reflection will give you a method for making a radical critique of the constraining forces and power influences within your work setting, because it has transformative action as its primary concern.

Reflector

What is the intent of the reflective method you have chosen? Is one method enough, or do you need to combine it with one or two other types of reflection to research this issue effectively? Write a sentence or sentences that clarify the intent of the reflective methods you have chosen as Step 3.

Step 4: plan the stages in a research proposal
This step follows the usual stages in any research proposal, that is, the research title, significance, aims, objectives, research questions, background, literature and methodology, and plans for the data collection, analysis, interpretation and dissemination. A timeline and budget may also be necessary. This following description is brief and intended only as an indicator of your need to do further reading (Polit *et al.* 2001; Roberts and Taylor 2001; Streubert Speziale and Rinaldi Carpenter 2003), or seek expert advice, if you have not undertaken research previously.

Significance
The significance of the research is the usefulness of the project and it answers the implicit question: why is this research necessary?

Aims and objectives
Aims are overall intentions and objectives are specific subsets of the intentions.

Research questions
Specific questions related to the research objectives are posed at this point. These indicate the problem focus you are taking in the research.

Background
Sometimes a background statement precedes the literature review, to set the context for how the ideas for the research came into being. It serves the purpose of showing the researcher's interest in the project.

Literature review
The aim of a literature review is to locate the information that is available in peer-reviewed journals and books relating as closely as possible to the aims and objectives of your proposed project. This is done in order to shed light on what is already known about your topic of interest, and/or even to decide whether a new project on the topic is necessary. For example, relative lack of information shows that the project is needed, but finding literature relating to many projects of a high standard, all discovering the same ideas, means that the area is well researched and that it most probably does not need further work presently. Research that is similar to, yet different from, the aims and objectives of your research can also be used, to show how other researchers have tackled parallel research questions. Undertaking a critically focused literature review takes practice, and texts are available to help you (Polit *et al.* 2001; Roberts and Taylor 2001; Streubert Speziale and Rinaldi Carpenter 2003). The main objectives are to locate, analyse and critique relevant literature in terms of its methods, processes and findings, in order to locate strengths and weaknesses in previous projects and thus bring a clearer focus to your pro-

posed project. The length of a literature review varies according to its purposes. Whereas a literature review in a thesis may stretch to thousands of words, a literature review in a research proposal may only be one page or within the limit of the funding body or ethics committee. The references may be included immediately after the literature review, or appear in an appendix attached to the proposal.

Methodology

Methodology refers to the theoretical assumptions underlying the choice of methods. This means that in the proposal under the word 'methodology' there will be a short description of the theoretical tradition informing the project, in this case, reflective practice and the particular theories informing this research.

Data collection

Full ethical clearance processes precede the commencement of any project involving human participants. The proposal includes the number of participants and access arrangements. It may be necessary to provide a rationale for the number of participants, especially if the proposal is likely to be judged against quantitative criteria of large sample sizes. Ethics committee members may not be aware of the assumptions of the nature of knowledge generated and validated through qualitative research. The extent to which you produce a strongly referenced rationale will depend on the likelihood of it being needed. You might also need to justify your 'sampling' methods, that is, how you will go about accessing the participants.

Be sure to include information on what data you will collect and how you will collect them. Provide examples of the reflective strategies you will use (see Chapter 2). If you are conducting interviews or facilitating discussion, list the questions you intend to ask, even if they are broad guidelines for stimulating conversations.

Data analysis and interpretation

The proposal must set out clearly the methods for sorting (analysing) and making sense of (interpreting) of the data. This is the main way the project will be judged as trustworthy when completed. Therefore, the proposal should be very clear about what you intend to do in order to analyse and interpret the data, so that the people judging the merits of the proposal can consider whether your plans for this phase are reasonable in relation to the rest of the project.

Dissemination of findings

The proposal should contain a plan for the dissemination of findings. This will show that you are aware that the research will be rendered meaningless if the results are not shared with the people who may benefit from them.

The project time frame
The proposal needs to show that you are organized time-wise and that you have allowed enough time to complete the project within the prescribed period. The funding body and/or your organization will want to know what you are going to do, and when, so that they can be assured that the project will be completed on time.

Budget
If you are applying for a research grant to assist you in completing your research, you will need to give careful consideration to the costs involved. Most grant bodies require a detailed budget, outlining costs for the research personnel (research assistants, desktop publishers, clerical assistance and so on); equipment (computer data analysis system, audiotapes and so on); travel at X pence per mile and other costs, such as photocopying, mailing and so on. The grant application will make it clear what they will or will not fund, so be sure to read their information carefully. Funding bodies want to know about each item of research expenditure in your budget, to satisfy themselves that the money is justified and you will use it prudently.

Reflector

Use the stages in writing a reflective research proposal in Step 4 to outline briefly your proposed research, as projected already in Steps 1 to 3 of this section.

Step 5: follow the method and use the process
Bearing in mind the statements you have made already in the research pro-posal you projected in Step 4, review the specific type(s) of reflection you have chosen to research your clinical issue. You may need to merge some or all of the three processes (see Chapters 5, 6 and 7), depending on the complexity of the research issue and the nature of your research questions. This is the time to undertake the research, assuming you have gained ethical clearance and you are ready to proceed with confidence, as an individual or team member researcher, or with research supervision as a student in a research programme.

Reflector

Compile the complete proposal, to include the actual reflective process questions you will be using. Before proceeding, ensure that you have ethical clearance, and that you are competent to conduct research, or you have research supervision from an experienced researcher.

Step 6: generate insights, institute changes and improvements and continue to reflect on outcomes
In this part of the research, you start to generate insights and make changes and improvements, depending on your research aims and objectives and the

processes you have chosen to fulfil them. Document these events carefully, in accordance with participants' accounts of their experiences for practical and emancipatory reflection, and/or in accordance with the scientific reasoning that develops in the case of technical reflection. Reflect on the outcomes, especially on the extent to which the research aims and objectives have been achieved and what further research may be necessary, to extend or more adequately explore other clinical issues.

Reflector

In relation to the research issue you have been exploring in this section, what insights have you gained, and what practice changes and improvements have you made? Have you achieved the research aims and objectives? Is further research necessary?

Step 7: report on outcomes

In this step you prepare to disseminate your research findings. You will find information in this chapter about giving a professional conference presentation and preparing an article for a refereed journal. If you need further help, seek the advice of an expert researcher or academic, who may be willing to assist you in the process.

Reflector

How will you disseminate your research findings? Use the information in this chapter to assist you to begin the first draft of a conference paper and/or a refereed journal article. If you are new to either process, take your first draft to a researcher or academic, who may be willing to assist you further.

Step 8: use in practice as evidence

In this step you explore the possibility of using your research findings in practice. This may happen through the adaptation of existing policies and procedures in your workplace, or you may decide to submit your work to an organization responsible for validating guidelines for evidence-based practice, for example, the Johanna Briggs Institute in Australia.

Reflector

What are your plans for changing practice by using your research as evidence? Consider how your research may be used as a practical guide to practice, based on its validity as evidence for clinical improvement.

> ## Practice story
>
> *Rosie, an experienced midwife working in a hospital, used a reflective research approach to explore 'Constraints midwives experience in facilitating natural childbirth'. The significance of the project was in using a research process that could improve midwifery practice by identifying and reducing or overcoming constraints. The aim was to explore midwives' experiences of the constraints operating against natural childbirth, with the specific objectives of identifying and reducing or overcoming specific social, cultural, historical, political and economic constraints that prevent natural childbirth, in order to improve women-centred care. The research questions were: What is natural childbirth? How do midwives facilitate natural childbirth? What constraints operate against natural childbirth? How can constraints be reduced or overcome that prevent natural childbirth?*
>
> *The background of the project was Rosie's clinical observation of higher intervention rates in the hospital in a two-year period, and her growing sense of ill-ease that many of the interventions were due attendants' anxieties. She collected and reviewed literature on natural childbirth and intervention rates in childbirth. Because she had an explicit change intention, she chose emancipatory reflection as the research method. After ethics approval Rosie interviewed ten midwives using the research questions and the emancipatory reflective process (see Chapter 7). She analysed the interview transcripts with a thematic analysis approach and ensured that each midwife read his or her transcript and the themes and interpretations that came from them.*

Summary

This section described the basic eight steps in the reflective research method. Research knowledge and skills take time to amass, so if you are new to research you may need guidance beyond this section to prepare you to research competently. If you are ready to undertake research, consider using a reflective research approach based entirely on reflective processes, as described in this section.

Reflective processes in other research approaches

Reflective processes can be used in conjunction with other research approaches, for example quantitative (technical reflection), qualitative (practical and emancipatory reflection) or mixed methods of quantitative and qualitative research (technical reflection, plus one or two other types of reflection used in this book). There is no prescription as to how these approaches might be used, as it is up to the researcher to make those choices, based on the fit of the approach to the research aims and objectives. Of course, any approach to reflective practice can be used within a research project if it adds richness to the data, not just the types described in this book. Other reflective processes in research approaches have been admirably demonstrated (e.g. Freshwater 1999a, 1999b; Handcock 1999; C. Johns 2000, 2003; Glaze 2001). Even so, for ease of reference and to demonstrate their value, the types of reflection described in this book will be used as examples for how reflective practice can be used in other research approaches.

For example, a quantitative project using a survey or questionnaire might also use the technical reflection process in a focus group to develop scientific reasoning to support or oppose the continuation of a clinical policy or procedure. A qualitative interpretive research approach using ethnography might also include participants' journals, in which descriptions of the research context are written for later analysis and interpretation, thus adding richness to the description of the culture being studied. The practical reflection process may also be used to explore communicative aspects of the culture of interest. A qualitative critical research approach using action research based on critical theory may use the action research cycles, with a special emphasis on reflection (as demonstrated in the next section). The emancipatory research process could be used in any form of critical research that intends to question the status quo and bring about change in people and organizations.

Researchers may use reflective journaling in any project they are undertaking, as a means of demonstrating rigour or trustworthiness, through documenting the detailed life of the project, and the researcher's and target audience's responses to the process and the findings.

Research students enrolled in research programmes may use reflective processes in the design of their projects. They may also keep a reflective account of their experience as a research student, of the project itself, of the learning that comes about through supervisory meetings, their reactions to literature, and any insights along the way that add richness to the research.

Table 8.1 gives some ideas about how reflective processes may be used in research approaches. The list is to demonstrate possibilities; it is not a prescription, nor is it exhaustive. The possibilities are many, so be creative in deciding how you will use reflective processes in your research.

Table 8.1   Possibilities for using reflective processes in research projects

Paradigm	Methodology	Type of reflection	Processes	Strategies
Quantitative	Empirico-analytical	Technical	Scientific reasoning	Focus groups Committees Consumer groups
Qualitative interpretive	Historical research (oral history, autobiographies)	Practical	Experiencing, interpreting, learning	Journal Audiotape Videotape Photography
	Ethnography	Practical	Experiencing, interpreting, learning	Journal Audiotape Videotape Painting Drawing Photography
	Phenomenology	Practical	Experiencing, interpreting, learning	Journal Audiotape Videotape Painting Drawing Photography
Qualitative critical	Critical ethnography	Emancipatory	Constructing, confronting, deconstructing, reconstructing	Journal Group work Audiotape Videotape Painting Drawing Photography
	Feminisms	Emancipatory	Constructing, confronting, deconstructing, reconstructing	Journal Group work Audiotape Videotape Painting Drawing Photography Dancing Poetry Montage
	Action research	Emancipatory	Constructing, confronting, deconstructing, reconstructing	Journal Group work Audiotape Videotape Painting Drawing Photography Dancing Poetry Montage

Research involving reflection and action research

This section describes how reflection and action research combine to create an effective collaborative qualitative research approach for identifying and transforming clinical issues. Action research is described and a research approach is outlined that applies the ideas of reflection and action research into a transformative process. Two nursing research projects exemplify the effectiveness of reflection and action research.

Nursing has used reflective processes for some time to improve practice (Taylor 2000; Thorpe and Barsky 2001; Stickley and Freshwater 2002; C. Johns 2003), clinical supervision (Todd and Freshwater 1999; Heath and Freshwater 2000; Gilbert 2001), education (Freshwater 1999a, 1999b; C. Johns 2000; Platzer *et al.* 2000a) and research (Freshwater 2001; Taylor 2001, 2002a, 2002b). Midwifery is also a rich source of reflection and midwives have been encouraged to use reflective processes to inform and improve their practice (Taylor 2002a, 2002b). Given that nursing and midwifery are complex practices involving knowledge, skills and human connection, there are many opportunities for using reflection and action research as a collaborative research approach. Reflection is described in detail in this book, so I now introduce action research to demonstrate its synergies with reflective practice.

Action research grew out of World War II (Chein *et al.* 1948), and it had a social change agenda. Kurt Lewin (1946) first used the term 'action research' and in the mid-1940s he used a group research process for community projects in postwar America. Lewin's work is the basis of contemporary versions of action research, including those forwarded by Australian educationalists such as Carr and Kemmis (1984). Action research goes to the site of the concern or practice, and works with the people there as co-researchers, to generate solutions to the problems with which they are keen to deal.

Action research involves a four-stage process of collectively planning, acting, observing and reflecting (Dick 1995; Stringer 1996). Each phase leads to another cycle of action, in which the plan is revised, and further acting, observing and reflecting is undertaken systematically, to work towards solutions to problems of a technical, practical or emancipatory nature (Kemmis and McTaggart 1988; Taylor 2000). The planning and acting phases may include any appropriate methods of gathering and analysing data, such as participant observation, reflective journalling, surveys, focus groups and interviews. Cycles of action research lead to further foci and co-researchers can keep an action research approach to their work for as long as they choose, to find solutions to their practice problems.

Nurses have been using action research successfully in a variety of settings with differing thematic concerns (e.g. Chenoweth and Kilstoff 1998; Keatinge *et al.* 2000; Koch *et al.* 2000). Midwives also have been using action research to assist them in improving their practice (Deery and Kirkham 2000; Barrett 2001; Munroe *et al.* 2002) and education systems (Fraser 2000; McMorland and Piggott-Irvine 2000).

In midwifery, Barrett (2001) used participatory action research processes to work with mothers in their early mothering period, to improve midwifery practice by facilitating mothers' satisfaction with their care and experience of early motherhood, while maximizing their informed choices. Barrett met with the new mothers weekly in a mothers' group and by using company, talk and tea in a supportive social milieu, mothers were able to voice their delights, concerns and fears, and were thereby helpful in assisting midwives to create optimal caring conditions for enhancing early mothering experiences. Deery and Kirkham (2000) used an action research approach to assist midwives to move from hierarchical to collaborative midwifery care, and Munroe *et al.* (2002) used action research to identify their concerns about the overuse of electronic foetal monitoring in labour and to explore different midwife-led care methods.

Fraser (2000) explored the use of action research to bring about curriculum improvements in a local pre-registration midwifery programme and to influence national policy and guidelines for similar programmes. The action research group found that the action research process of problem identification and collaborative solution finding was an important component of curriculum design, to prepare midwives to become competent practitioners. McMorland and Piggott-Irvine (2000: 121) facilitated action research/learning groups in various contexts to 'confront the challenge of assisting people to work and learn together in authentically collaborative ways'. They likened the process to midwifery, in that action research has a 'colaboring' function of 'facilitating the birth of a whole and healthy group process in which honest and bilateral interactions of action and reflection occur'.

Combining reflection and action research

Reflective processes and action research combine well to create an effective collaborative qualitative research approach for identifying and transforming clinical issues, because reflection is part of the action research method of planning, assessing, observing and reflecting. Reflection is drawn out especially in this combined approach of collaborative research, because this distinction gives more importance to the role of reflective processes in helping practitioners to make sense of their practice and to bring sustained improvements to it. This section provides a step-by-step approach to facilitating an action research and reflection group.

Facilitating an action research and reflection group

You can set up an action research and reflection group where you work, and it can stay together for as long as you all have practice issues to research collaboratively. Follow these 13 easy steps and you will be able to undertake action research and reflection where you work.

Step 1: find enough nurses or midwives to form a research group
Two or more people comprise a group, so you do not have to seek large numbers of participants when you set up a research group.

Step 2: ensure the nurses or midwives are ready to make a commitment to the research group
Your colleagues will need to commit to working together through their practice issues, so they will need to meet regularly, for as often and as long as they need to work through the research systematically and to the point at which it offers practice insights and improvements. For this to happen, the nurses or midwives will also need to commit to reflecting on their practice and sharing their thoughts with the group.

Step 3: decide on a venue and a regular meeting day and time
It does not matter where you meet, but it must be a venue that allows privacy so that co-researchers can speak openly and confidentially. There may be a quiet room set aside in your organization for employees, or you may decide to meet in a private home. Decide on a regular day and time, for example, every Friday from 2.30 to 3.30 p.m. for one hour. The specifics of this decision will depend on agreement by the nurses or midwives involved.

Step 4: write a brief research proposal
Write a brief proposal of what it is you are going to do, why, when, how and with whom. The essentials of a proposal include the project's title, background, aims, objectives, data collection and analysis methods, timeline, budget and plans for dissemination (as described previously). Specifics of this process can be found in research texts (Polit *et al.* 2001; Roberts and Taylor 2001; Streubert Speziale and Rinaldi Carpenter 2003). Keep the proposal succinct and in easy to read language, because it is a guide for the group as well as for any other interested audiences, such as a funding body or an ethics committee. Enlist the help of another nurse or midwife from your proposed research group in preparing the proposal, or this first writing step could be a collaborative project for the entire group before you start the action research and reflection project.

Step 5: check on ethics approval processes in your organization
Because you are undertaking research with other human participants, you may
need ethics approval. Check with the ethics committee in your organization
what it required for your submission to them. Write in clear, non-jargonistic
language and enlist the help of another nurse or midwife from your proposed
research group in preparing the ethics submission. Alternatively, the ethics
approval and proposal writing process could be a collaborative project for the
entire group. If you need further help, refer to a research text (see examples
above).

Step 6: get the project underway and decide on who facilitates meetings
When you have the necessary ethics approval you can begin the action
research and reflection group meetings, focusing on the methods and processes to get the project underway. Decide if you will have one facilitator
for every meeting, or if you will use a 'rotating chair' system, in which
everyone takes a turn at guiding the agenda of the regular meetings. You may
decide to keep minutes of meetings as a successive account of the research
process and for information that can be included in the research report for
dissemination.

Step 7: share the business of the first two meetings
At its inception, there are some important foundational processes through
which the group must work together. The areas to be discussed openly include
group processes, and shared understandings of action research and reflective
processes. Group processes are decided by listening to what each nurse or
midwife wants from the group in terms of how they will work together. For
example, they may say that they want to be able to speak openly, with trust
and confidentiality, and that nothing discussed in the group will be open to
public discussion and so on. So that everyone understands the fundamental
ideas in action research and reflection, ensure each nurse or midwife reads this
chapter and any other useful resources and shares in group discussion her or
his understanding of these basic tenets and how they relate to researching
nursing or midwifery practice.

Step 8: share the first reflective task
Take as many meetings as you need to work through the first reflective task. It
is important to begin here, because it gives participants in the research group
confidence in writing or recording their reflections and sharing them in the
group. Use the guide in this book (see Chapter 2) as the first reflective practice
writing task. It is an opportunity for participants to reflect on their own personal, social and historical contexts, so that they can consider the values and
'rules for living' that have contributed to how they now live and practise.
When each participant shares his or her responses, it is important that the

other co-researchers listen attentively and non-judgementally. This may be the first trusting contribution co-researchers make to the group, so it is important to respect and honour the responses for the insights they give into the personal-professional life of the participant.

Step 9: share the practice stories

The next part of the research is to begin to reflect on present or past practice stories. The reason for doing this is to identify a common theme ('thematic concern', in action research language) through which to work collaboratively. Take as many meetings as you need to work through the first part of the process, because it is important that participants share at least two practice stories with the group. Use the guides in this book (Chapters 5, 6 and 7) to reflect on practice stories. The guides assist you to make a critical analysis of an incident at work, according to whether it is primarily of a work procedure, communication or power nature, or any combination of these issues. Keep in mind that the aim of the research group is to locate issues of interest to participants in order to raise awareness and change practice through action research and reflective processes. After the group has worked together for a while, decide on issues that are common to everyone (thematic concerns) and use an action research approach to work through them.

When each participant shares her or his practice stories, it is again important that the other co-researchers listen attentively and non-judgementally. It is not usually a part of nursing or midwifery culture to speak openly about practice stories that did not go well, so be careful to honour the stories, allowing the storyteller to find his or her own insights. Co-researching participants may act as critical friends (see Chapter 2) by asking question for a fuller description, or to encourage a wider exploration of the issue, but they should not offer easy solutions, because it is best to avoid an early foreclosure on possibilities.

Step 10: identify the thematic concern(s)

Keep summary notes of each story and devise a method for analysing their contents. For example, construct a grid with four columns, including 1) story summary, 2) the issue(s), 3) the nurse's or midwife's feelings about the issue(s), 4) how the issue(s) came about. The second column will be most useful in locating the issues to find some thematic concerns common to each participant. For example, the analysis may show that participants have issues relating to relationships, such as with doctors, patients, relatives and so on. The third column will identify the emotions and feelings participants experience in day-to-day practice, which are at the foundation of their perceptions of their practice. The fourth column will locate the various sources of participants' work issues, which affect the ways in which they negotiate their practice conditions. Spend some time discussing the analysis of the stories, with particular interest in the practice issues that are identified. See if there are any issues that come up consistently in the stories. Decide on an issue to research together using an action research and reflection process. If there are several thematic concerns and enough participants in the group to work on them effectively, it is possible to work on many issues at the same time.

Step 11: generate the action plan and begin the action research cycles

This step of the research lasts as long as it takes for the group to reach satisfactory outcomes. The group is now at the point where they are ready to 'do' action research. The main phases of action research are: Plan, Act, Observe, Reflect (PAOR). Participants begin with a thematic concern (common to enough of them to matter) and move through a series of cycles of PAOR until they feel that the issue is solved/acknowledged/challenged or whatever they hope to achieve in relation to it. This is how it works:

Planning

- The group projects a plan in relation to the thematic concern.
- The plan must be flexible to allow for unforeseen effects and constraints.
- The action prescribed by the plan must take account of the social risks involved and recognize the material and political constraints in the situation.
- The plan allows participants to go beyond their present constraints to empower them to act more effectively in the situation.
- The group plans by collaborating openly and honestly with one another and by analysing and improving their understanding of the situation.

Here are some practical notes for creating an action plan. Construct a grid with three columns, including 1) the thematic concern, 2) the source(s) of the thematic concern, and 3) what can be done about it? The second column will be most useful in locating the sources of the thematic concerns, because they are the work aspects that need some adjustment. For example, if a source of the thematic concern is due to economic constraints, a strategy for the action plan may involve inviting a person 'holding the purse strings' to meet with the group to discuss the concern. If the source of a concern in cultural, in its broadest sense of the way people relate to one another, the focus will be on interpersonal relationships. For example, relationships become defined over time in certain ways, and if there are power imbalances, such as one person exerting 'power over' another person, a strategy may be to observe interpersonal interactions at work in order to examine, and work towards changing, the cultural foundations of these relationships.

When the group is discussing the strategies for the action plan, keep in mind the basic principles listed previously. It is very important to maximize the potential for the success of the action plan by making the strategies within it reasonable for managing the risks and ensuring the best possible outcomes. The action plan will be instituted in nursing or midwifery practice and the results of the changed approach to the thematic concern will be noted, through continued PAOR. The action plan will undergo revision until it achieves positive changes in successfully managing the identified thematic concern in practice.

Acting

- The group makes a critically informed, careful and thoughtful variation to practice by putting their plan into action.
- As the strategies in the action plan may be potentially risky, participants need to be flexible and open to change in the light of the real-time situation.
- Acting may involve material, social and political struggle towards improvement and negotiation, and compromise may be necessary.
- Participants may need to be content with modest gains that gradually get bigger based on previous gains (in other words, they may not always be able to 'fix things' the first time).

Observing

- This phase is what makes action *research*. It involves documenting the effects of critically-informed action.
- Participants use their powers of observation and stay responsive, open-eyed and open-minded to see how the plan of action is working.
- Participants record their observations in their journal or by whatever additional means they decide.
- Participants observe the action, the effects of the action (intended and unintended), the circumstances and constraints of the action, and any other issues that may arise.

Reflecting

- Reflection recalls action as it has been recorded in the observation, but it is active in making sense of processes, problems, issues and constraints that may manifest in the strategic action.

- Reflection is aided by group discussion in research meetings so participants can reconstruct the meaning of the social situation and revise the plan if necessary.
- Reflection asks participants to evaluate the effects and the issues and to suggest ways of proceeding.
- Reflection allows reconnaissance for further action research cycles as necessary. Participants keep using the action plan in daily practice until they know they have achieved their aims (plans) relating to the specific issues they raised.

Step 12: write a research report
Use the same structure suggested for the research proposal to write the research report. The front page provides the authors' names (in alphabetical order), positions and qualifications, and the research abstract. The main headings and subheadings under which to write are the title, significance, aims, objectives, research questions, background, literature review, data collection, analysis and interpretation methods and processes, and discussion and conclusions.

The report reiterates much of the information of the proposed research, but in the past tense, because the aim of the report is to give a description of the past events within the project. The report will be written according to the requirements of its target audience, for example, if it is for a funding body the report may be quite lengthy and detailed, but if it is for local dissemination only, it may be short and with just enough detail to describe the project effectively. If you need further help, refer to a research text (see suggestions on p. 179).

Step 13: disseminate the findings
The final step of the process is to disseminate the research findings, so that the action research and reflection process not only helps the participants but also other people with whom it resonates. If participants in the group have not had previous professional publication and presentation experience, ask the help of people who have, and invite them to assist the group in the final stage. Alternatively, the group could learn the processes needed by working together through information for contributors supplied by journals and conference committees, ensuring a fair division of labour throughout the learning process. Practical advice is also given in this chapter.

Nursing research projects using reflection and action research

The methods and processes described in the previous section were developed during projects I facilitated with nurses (Taylor 2001; Taylor et al. 2002).

The first project (Taylor 2001) was entitled: 'Identifying and transforming dysfunctional nurse-nurse relationships through reflective practice and action research'. It aimed to facilitate reflective practice processes in experienced RNs, in order to: raise critical awareness of practice problems; work systematically through problem-solving processes to uncover constraints; and improve the quality of care given by nurses in the light of the identified constraints and possibilities. Twelve experienced female RNs working in a large Australian rural hospital shared their experiences of nursing during three action research cycles. A thematic concern of dysfunctional nurse-nurse relationships was identified, as evidenced by bullying and horizontal violence. The negotiated action plan was put into place and co-researchers reported varying degrees of success in attempting to improve nurse-nurse relationships. This project confirmed the necessity for reflective practice and continued collaborative research processes in the workplace to bring about a cultural change within nurses' collectives and in the places in which they work which weigh against mutual respect and cooperation in nurse-nurse relationships.

The second project (Taylor *et al.* 2002) was entitled: 'Exploring idealism in palliative nursing care through reflective practice and action research'. This project also used a combination of action research and reflective practice processes. Six experienced RNs identified their tendency towards idealism in their palliative nursing practice, which they defined as the tendency to expect to be 100 per cent effective all of the time in their work. Participants collaborated in generating and evaluating an action plan to recognize and manage the negative effects of idealism in their work expectations and behaviours. Participants expressed positive changes in their practice, based on adjusting their responses to their idealistic tendencies towards perfectionism.

Both projects gave nurses a regular forum in which to discuss their reflections on practice and to generate an action plan to bring about change. The benefits of action research and reflection are that there are immediate, practical outcomes for participants, because they can share their experiences with peers, work together on thematic concerns and bring about local changes in their practice. Thus, co-researchers experience participatory research, while developing their reflective skills, and in this sense the research offers them personal and professional gains in lifelong appreciation of their participation.

Summary

This section gave step-by-step guidance in facilitating an action research and reflection group and described two projects which used the approach successfully. Once you are underway with a project of your own, you will find that the group's enthusiasm will keep the process alive and that you will go from one thematic concern to another, solving clinical issues through action research and reflection.

Fostering scholarship

Scholarship in nursing and midwifery is generated through sharing disciplinary knowledge and skills, and the main modes of dissemination are professional conference presentations and publications. This section outlines how to go about preparing your research findings for dissemination.

Presenting your reflective research at a professional conference

For the uninitiated, the prospect may be daunting of standing up in front of a group of people and speaking about your experiences and insights. Public speaking requires courage to endure the scrutiny of your ideas. This section advises you on how to prepare to present your research, by choosing the gathering, writing the abstract, preparing the paper, and preparing yourself on the day and at the presentation. In conclusion, some thoughts are shared of managing afterwards, in terms of praise and critique, and other outcomes such as conversion of the paper into an article for publication.

Choosing the gathering
When you are choosing the gathering at which to speak, think about the theme of the conference, how your presentation contributes, the potential audience and practical aspects such as your availability and any costs involved. When conference organizers send out their advertising material, they describe the theme of the conference and the subthemes which fit within it. Some conferences have a very specific focus, such as 'Reflective practice as evidence-based practice' while others leave the areas open for interpretation, for example, 'Making a difference in practice'.

After reading the advertising material, decide how your presentation would contribute to the conference. You can be creative by making indirect links with conference themes, so don't be deterred by what may appear to be a specific and limited theme. Consider the professional and public mix of the potential audience, and choose a conference at which your presentation will have the most appropriate appeal.

Pay attention to practical aspects. Check the dates and times of the conference to ensure that your diary is free, and that you can cover, or encourage your organization or other agents to sponsor, any costs involved. Submitting an abstract gives the organizers the impression that you are willing and available to be chosen as a conference speaker, and an apparent 'change of mind' on your part may not be received favourably.

Writing the abstract

Unless you are invited as a guest speaker, you will normally need to write an abstract of your proposed presentation. Most organizers provide a space for you to complete an abstract on the conference information sheet, which is returned to them for review and selection procedures. You need to ensure that what you intend to present fits the conference theme and is sufficiently interesting to catch the attention of the selection committee. Many organizers undertake a 'blind review', which means they take the applicant's name and contact details off abstracts and the selection committee judges the merit of the abstract against their selection criteria, rather than in terms of the personal characteristics or reputation of the speaker.

Notice in the guidelines for abstract writing the word limit and any other stylistic features, such as double spacing, and whether it is to be typed and to contain references to literature. Typing should not present a problem by word processing, because you can format the dimensions of the page, type the abstract, make a copy of the computer document, and paste it into the space provided. References are seldom expected in a conference abstract, but if your paper has a particular focus in the literature you will need to cite the work of published authors. You will also need to decide on a title for the paper, and to state clearly your objectives for the session and the general direction of the presentation. It is a good idea to use a selection of the main words in the conference theme within your abstract, to show the organizers that you have considered the relevance of your contribution.

The abstract should represent a commitment to what you present on the day. Conference delegates select their sessions carefully on the basis of the published abstract, and they may be annoyed or disappointed to find the presenter say at the start of the presentation, 'My abstract indicates X, however, today I will be presenting Y'.

Preparing the presentation

You may receive a letter, email or phone call informing you that your abstract has been selected for a conference. Having kept a copy of the abstract and the other conference details, you can refer to them to refresh your memory on your proposed presentation and the conference venue, day and time. The organizers may request a copy of the paper prior to the conference, so that it can be included in the published proceedings. They will give you a timeline for submission and directions for the format, style and form in which to present the paper.

As with all writing tasks, you need to take some time to prepare a plan for the beginning, middle and end of the paper. Feel free to adapt the following approach to suit yourself. If you have a disk copy of the abstract, make a duplicate of the document and use that as the structure for the paper. Use the return key on the computer keyboard to segment out the main ideas of the paper, in the order you have written them. These small segments may become headings or subheadings, but at this point they remind you of where you are going with the presentation. Sometimes the abstract will not reflect all the twists and turns of your talk, so add these areas under appropriate headings, or create a heading to accommodate them. This does not necessarily mean that the paper is different from what you proposed, but that more information has come to light in the period between the abstract submission and acceptance.

Using the headings, write the paper. You don't necessarily have to start at the beginning and finish at the end, even though you have made a plan for the overall paper. Word processors are great for jumping around the text where you fancy, as a thought comes, or a link in the discussion emerges. Try to write according to the 'tone' of the conference. For example, use a casual style of writing and relating to the audience at a highly interactive and experiential conference, or a more formal tone at a conference at which there will be a great deal of serious scholarly debate and the expectation is that you will be clever. If you are not able to judge the tone of the conference, re-read the conference material or contact one of the conference organizers to discuss this with them. Failing that, aim for clarity, midpoint on the 'clever index' and less, rather than more, detail.

How much to write is an important point. It is a sad experience (if the person is about to be stopped by the facilitator) or a frustrating experience (if the person rushes on unabated) to see a nervous presenter galloping through a paper with five minutes to go, having just finished the introduction. With this in mind, practise reading your paper aloud at conference speed to see if it fits well into the time slot allotted to you. With experience you will become adept at timing. I often joke that as a speaker I am like a gas, in that I can expand or contract my talking to fill the available space.

When the paper is ready, keep a copy for yourself to use for the presentation, so that you can write little reminders on it to yourself. For example, make notes such as to thank the organizers for inviting you to speak, or add a bit more information about yourself extra to the introduction, or acknowledge any current major event which may have a bearing on the conference, or insert a reminder to show an overhead transparency or slide, and so on. Such personalized notes on papers can give you a sense of confidence that you have 'covered all your bases', and you can respond to any unforeseen events as they arise, such as power and equipment failures and people walking in late.

One last hint is to look carefully over the paper and imagine the kinds of questions you might be asked at the end of the presentation. If you have included theoretical concepts or references to scholarly work, be sufficiently conversant with them to be able to answer any questions with relative confidence.

Preparing yourself on the day

Before you leave home on the day of the conference, make a quiet and thorough check of all your papers to ensure that you have all the information you need to locate the venue, and that you have your paper and any audio-visual aids you are using. Keep them in sight on the way to the venue, making sure you have them in your grasp when you leave your form of transport. Plan to arrive at the conference venue in plenty of time for your presentation. This will avert last-minute rushes and heart-stopping situations, such as being caught in city traffic ten minutes before you are due on the podium.

When you arrive, register at the conference desk and be recognized as a speaker. You may be given a special name badge or a coloured ribbon to signify your speaker status. The person facilitating your session will probably be looking for you, so make yourself known so that they can rest assured that you are present and ready. Unless you have a burning need to interact with other people before your presentation desist from doing this, as it may accelerate your nervousness. Simply ensure that the facilitator has any aids you may be using if you want assistance with them, agree on the signal to activate help, and sit down quietly. If you are well known to many people there and enjoy some 'celebrity status', you may need to find some silent space outside the building, or you could take a slow and gentle walk to a wash room to brush your hair and check on your appearance. A few deep breaths and an internal affirmation or prayer for help may also be useful at this time. Know that you are there to offer your ideas and that they are worthy of being shared.

Giving the presentation

After the introduction, walk to the podium to give your presentation. Watch your footing as you walk and look up and give a smile (if you can) when you reach the podium. Take some time to position your paper on the lectern and look around the room briefly before you begin. This allows you to see the audience as friendly humans, who are there to support you by listening to what you have to say. It is a privilege to have the attention of people. You have prepared for this moment, you feel honoured to be there, so feel confident to allow your presentation to flow, knowing that it is correct in terms of timing and detail.

If you are very new to public speaking, it might help to stand with your feet slightly apart to give you good balance and to lock your knees ever so slightly to keep you upright. All that remains is for you to read the paper as you practised it. Try to look up as much as possible and direct your gaze to people in various parts of the room. As with any communicative episode, this talk will be more interesting if you can use an appropriate tone, pitch and pace, with an occasional smile. If your mouth gets dry, take a drink of water, even if it means stopping to get the facilitator's attention to assist you. If you try to talk with a dry mouth it may aggravate any nervousness already there. Take notice of this sympathetic nervous system reaction, slow down, take a drink, refocus yourself and continue.

As you progress through the paper, be aware of time passing and ensure that you are keeping the pace correct. If you have practised well and there is just enough detail, your only problem on the day may be too much time, because it may be tempting to speak too rapidly. If this is the case, notice how much time you have remaining and slow down 'in flight', so to speak. When the paper is finished, indicate this by saying 'thank you' and wait to see if questions are to be directed to you.

If you are one of many speakers in a session, the facilitator may prefer to wait until the last speaker has finished before offering opportunities for questions. When you are answering a question, consider your response briefly, ensure that you can be heard, and respond as carefully and helpfully as you can. Sometimes people's questions may be longer than your answer, especially if they are preceding their question with background comment. Simply wait, listen and respond directly. If you get a question you cannot answer, respond as honestly as possible, along the lines of 'I have not thought of that. I cannot answer that at the moment', or 'Although you have made an interesting point, it was not my intention to cover that area specifically in this paper/ project'. Remember that you don't have to have all the answers and a gentle deflection of a question may be preferable to bluffing your way recklessly through uncharted theoretical territory.

Managing afterwards

When your talk is over, there will be applause and then you return to your seat in the auditorium, or accompany the other delegates to a refreshments break, or presentations elsewhere. At this point, you will probably encounter further praise or questions from people who remained silent in question time. On other occasions, people will approach you to make connections and some may want to set up networks so that you can keep in touch in relation to some common interests. If you are not accustomed to 'being in the limelight', you may find the attention disconcerting or overwhelming, but you can handle it graciously with a simple 'Thank you'.

If someone is interested in further debate on the content of your paper, you can make a choice about when to attend to his or her request for discussion. Some questions can be answered with a brief reply, while others demand more time to be dealt with adequately. If the discussion has the potential to be protracted, it is a good idea to negotiate a time in which to meet or to exchange contact details. This ensures that you are not deprived of some quiet time after your presentation, or the chance to attend conference sessions in which you are interested.

Another area you might need to consider is the possibility of transforming your presentation into an article for publication. Most conference papers need to be reworked to accommodate the style and tone of individual journals. Check with the conference organizers about copyright if your work has been published in the conference proceedings, otherwise you are at liberty to submit your paper elsewhere. A conference presentation is an important career event, so ensure that you add it to your curriculum vitae.

Reflector

If you have ever presented at a professional conference, what particular aspects were most challenging for you? Why? How will you adjust your next attempt in view of that experience and the hints provided in this section?

Writing a journal article

You may decide that your reflective insights are worth sharing on a broader stage, so you could consider preparing an article for publication. You could write for a local audience, such as in a hospital newsletter, or you could aim for national and international journals, which have non-refereed and refereed sections. You could write alone or in collaboration with a key person, such as your critical friend or colleagues. You could enlist the assistance of a local nursing or midwifery school, or you could read some books on the subject and do it yourself.

This section gives you some practical advice on how to get started. The first point is to be aware that you are capable of writing for a journal. Don't let self-doubt overtake you. It is compelling to look at other people's articles in journals and think that you cannot attain such standards. Take heart in the knowledge that every author had to start somewhere and go through the experience of submitting work and waiting for feedback. As an editor of a journal I can assure you that editors and referees will be willing to guide you to publish your article. Take some time preparing for the article, then write, and you may surprise yourself.

Choose a journal

You need to choose a journal which would welcome your reflective practice article. Browse in the health professions, nursing and midwifery journal section of your library and find journals which have the kind of style and content aligning well with reflective practice. Notice the section about information for contributors that is often printed inside front or back covers. This tells you what the editor expects of you in preparing a manuscript for submission. Make a photocopy so that you can study it carefully and use it to plot your way through the task of writing an article. Notice the word limits for each category of articles and the preferred referencing style.

Have a clear focus
It is important to be specific about the direction your article will take. You may have some general ideas at first, which you tease out by 'playing' with a working title, and under that tentative heading, then section off a beginning, middle and end, and list some ideas under each main section to 'fill out' the content. Try to list the ideas in the order of their presentation, in flow of discussion or debate. If your creative thoughts come randomly you can insert ideas anywhere in the general structure of the plan, and move them around until you have a reasonable flow of ideas. When you are clear about the focus of your paper, decide on the actual title and prepare the manuscript according to the journal's guidelines.

Writing a descriptive article
The way of writing differs according to the type of article. For example, if you are writing a descriptive article on your experience of being a reflective practitioner, you will be relating a personal story. If you are writing for a scholarly journal and the article is to be peer reviewed, you will need to demonstrate theoretical prowess and the appropriate use of literature to substantiate your work. As with all writing, the article will need a beginning, middle and end. An introduction presents the theme or point of contention of the paper. A middle part provides the 'guts' or substantive part of the article and will relate the main aspects of the experience. A conclusion usually pulls all the ideas together by making a concise analysis of the event and offering insights for further contemplation.

Writing a research article
If you are writing about a research project which focused on reflection or used it as a method, the usual conventions of preparing a research article apply. If you want to present a synopsis of the entire project, your challenge will be to 'do justice' to the project while keeping to the word limit. You will have to make hard decisions about what to put in and take out of the article, so that the essential features of the project remain intact. Essentially, research reports deal with the project's title, background, aims, objectives, data collection and analysis methods and processes, results, implications and discussion. If you are unsure about the specific content of the essential features of a research report, consult a reference on critique of research (e.g. Polit *et al.* 2001 or Roberts and Taylor 2001).

Checking the drafts

The writing phase will take several drafts. You need to check the manuscript for spelling and grammatical errors, attention to referencing conventions and the layout of headings and subheadings. Ensure that ideas flow between sections and that the discussion and conclusion sections are well substantiated with literature and sound reasoning. It is a good idea to invite the critique of friends and colleagues with experience in reading and writing journal articles. After you have adjusted the manuscript according to their feedback, prepare the copies as specified by the journal's guidelines and add other requirements, such as a title page, contact details and so on. Send it with a covering letter to the editor and await feedback.

Receiving feedback

Refereed journals use a process of peer review to judge the worthiness of your paper against the criteria the journal values in acceptable writing. This means that the editor will remove references to your name and identity and send your paper to at least two people who have expertise in the area the article covers. The editor considers the reviewers' feedback and decides what, if anything, needs to be done to amend the paper before it is ready for publication.

In time, a letter or email will arrive from the editor, informing you whether your article is to be published. Sometimes you will receive a rejection. It is possible that you have misjudged the appropriateness of the journal for the type of article you had written, or that it was simply not 'up to scratch'. As odd as it might seem, rejections may be good experiences for you, for what they can teach you about yourself and your responses to feedback and critique. Although rejection may hurt, realize that it is directed at your *writing*, not *you* specifically, and that you can always try again.

A happier message in the editor's letter will be that your article will be published, subject to you making the required changes. Feedback from reviewers will be supplied to assist you in adjusting the manuscript. At this stage, you may consider that there has been a complete misreading of your work (and it can happen!) and you do not want to compromise the article by making changes. You can decide to withhold your work and submit it to another journal. You are under no obligation to inform the editor that you have decided against making the changes as specified. The non-return of your manuscript will signal your lack of further cooperation in the process. You could try to defend your article as written, but the peer review process favours the word of reviewers in judging the merit of scholarly work, even if they 'get it wrong' sometimes. Some editors may negotiate a compromise if they can see the value of what you are arguing, but it is a rare situation that puts the blind review process in question.

Alternatively, the letter may indicate that your article is flawless and ready to publish as is, or it may inform you that the manuscript is not suitable for publication in that particular journal. If you receive notification that it is not suitable for publication, you could resubmit the manuscript elsewhere, after adapting it to another journal's requirements and style. If you want to publish, don't take rejections too much to heart, and don't give up, because 'success begets success'!

Reflector

If you have ever written an article for a professional journal, what particular aspects were most challenging for you? Why? How will you adjust your next attempt in view of that experience and the hints provided in this section?

Summary

This chapter provided practical information on how to incorporate reflective practice into research methodologies and nursing or midwifery scholarship. Reflective methods and processes fit well with all qualitative research methodologies, and this chapter identified possible applications before focusing on specific projects involving action research. The chapter also described how to foster scholarship by preparing your research findings for conference presentations and journal articles. Although it may take some time and work before you feel confident in disseminating research and scholarship contributions to your discipline, don't forget that it can be fun and that confident writing and speaking are within your grasp with practice. They will be even more rewarding if you apply reflective processes to your learning experiences, as you develop your interests in research and scholarship.

Key points

- Reflective methods and processes not only guide practice, they can also provide evidence for supporting practice changes.
- It is advisable for a beginning researcher to reduce the complexity of research by thinking of three main types: empirico-analytical (quantitative), interpretive (qualitative) and critical (qualitative).
- Empirico-analytical (quantitative) research uses numbers and statistics as its main investigative tools, to observe and analyse through the scientific method.
- Qualitative research can be interpretive or critical and it uses words and language as its main exploratory tools.
- Interpretive qualitative research aims mainly to generate meaning, that is, to explain and describe, in order to make sense of phenomena

of interest. Examples include historical methods, grounded theory, phenomenology and ethnography.

- Qualitative critical research also generates meaning and aims openly to bring about change. Examples of qualitative critical research include action research, critical ethnography, feminist research and discourse analysis.

- By working collaboratively with participants as co-researchers to systematically address research problems, qualitative researchers try to find answers and use them to bring about change.

- Reflective processes may be used solely as the research approach, or they may be integrated into other research approaches.

- The basic eight steps in the reflective research method are: identify the issue/problem/phenomenon for reflection; decide on the reflective method; clarify its intent; plan the stages in a research proposal; follow the method and use the process; generate insights, institute changes and improvements and continue to reflect on outcomes; report on outcomes; and use the outcomes in practice as evidence.

- Reflective processes can be used in conjunction with other research approaches, and there is no prescription as to how these approaches might be used, as it is up to the researcher to make those choices, based on the fit of the approach to the research aims and objectives.

- Reflective processes and action research combine well to create an effective collaborative qualitative research approach for identifying and transforming clinical issues, because reflection is part of the action research method of Planning, Assessing, Observing and Reflecting (PAOR).

- The 13 steps to undertake action research and reflection are: find enough nurses or midwives to form a research group; ensure the nurses or midwives are ready to make a commitment; decide on a venue and a regular meeting day and time; write a brief research proposal; check on ethics approval processes in your organization; get the project underway and decide who facilitates meetings; share the business of the first two meetings; share the first reflective task; share the practice stories; identify the thematic concern(s); generate the action plan and begin the action research cycles; write a research report; and disseminate the findings.

- Scholarship in nursing and midwifery is generated through sharing disciplinary knowledge and skills, and the main modes of dissemination are professional conference presentations and publications.

9 Reflection as a lifelong process

Introduction

The maintenance of your reflective practices will require personal and group supports, so that your good intentions materialize into lifelong reflective approaches to your life and work. In this chapter I suggest some ways of maintaining reflective practice by affirming yourself as a reflective practitioner, responding to the critiques, creating a daily habit, seeing things freshly, staying alert to practice, finding support systems, sharing reflection, getting involved in research, and embodying reflective practice.

Maintaining reflective practice

Maintaining reflection will not be easy. People with the best intentions – including myself – throw reflective habits away when life overtakes them. Resolutions are actually about hoping for ideal circumstances. Life seldom runs to plan and many unforeseen obstructions and challenges can get in the way. When you resolve to maintain reflective processes, the trials of life may get in your way and your resolutions may not come to fruition. If this occurs, don't give in and 'throw the baby away with the bathwater'. Keep your resolution alive by holding on to the principle of the idea, even when the fine detail of your intentions go into recess.

Affirming yourself as a reflective practitioner

To maintain reflection you may need to consider ways of affirming your intentions. Your resolution to maintain reflection may falter from time to time, but if you are assured of the value of reflection for your life and work, the central core of your intention will hold. Affirm your worth as a reflective practitioner by acknowledging your insights and how far you have come from whom and how you were when you began, to whom and how you are now. If reflective processes are working, you will be noticing some positive differences in the ways you think about your life and work. If this is so, revel in this recognition and affirm the value of your reflections.

Reflector

On what issues have you reflected since becoming a reflective practitioner? How has reflection helped you as a person and a clinician?

Responding to the critiques

In Chapter 1 I acknowledged the critiques of reflective practice in nursing and midwifery. Even though it has proved successful, critics have perceived limitations in reflective practice. To be assured of the worth of reflection, you may need to respond to the critics, so that your investment in maintaining reflection does not suffer.

For example, there has been criticism of how the nursing profession seized on the idea of reflection (Jarvis 1992), but many years have passed and it is still useful for clinicians. Greenwood (1993) took issue with Schön's idea of reflection that proposed that theories underpinning reflective activity are difficult to articulate, as they are embedded in activity itself. However, even though they are difficult to articulate, they are not impossible, as we have seen from many accounts of people who have been successful (e.g. Freshwater 2002a, 2002b; Johns 2002; Taylor *et al.* 2002).

Even though there may be a high degree of personal investment required by nurses and midwives for successful practice outcomes (Taylor 1997), if they are well prepared for reflection the positive outcomes will outweigh the risks. Barriers to learning must be overcome before midwives and nurses can reflect effectively (Platzer *et al.* 2000b), but these can be negotiated through guided experiences. There may be cultural barriers to empowerment through reflection (Johns 1999), but these can be identified through sensitive exploration.

Negative consequences may ensue when practitioners are pressured to reflect (Hulatt 1995), but this can be averted when personal reflection is not tied to assessment grades. Reflection may be seen to be a fundamentally flawed strategy (Mackintosh 1998), but only in some people's perceptions, so this does not invalidate it for the people with whom it has resonance. There are potential dangers in promoting 'private thoughts in public spheres' (Cotton 2001), so safeguards must be taken to ensure that reflection does not become a mechanism of social control or personal debasement. Reflective processes may have failed to 'address the postmodern, cultural contexts of reflection' (Pryce 2002), but we need to revisit notions of postmodernism and reconnect to reflection as a personal narrative that reveals local truths in a postmodern era.

The criticism no longer holds that there is lack of research evidence to support the mandate to reflect (Burton 2000), as the projects are multiplying rapidly (e.g. see the references at the end of this book). Lack of research will always be cited by people who will never be satisfied with mountains of research – how much is enough?

Ghaye and Lillyman (2000) critically reviewed the foundations and criticisms of reflective practice to question whether reflective practitioners were really 'fashion victims', and having explored the limitations of it, concluded that reflective practice has a place in the postmodern world, because of its ability to explore micro-levels of human interaction and personal knowledge. Useful processes such as reflection survive fashions and endure, long after the passage of time and trends.

C. Taylor (2003: 244) argued that 'reflective practice tends to adopt a naïve or romantic realist position and fails to acknowledge the ways in which reflective accounts construct the world of practice'. It is true that reflective accounts construct the world of practice, but this phenomenon is inevitable if we accept the idea that we co-create our realties. If we accept this conundrum of inevitable influence, we are left with the choice to engage or not engage with socially constructed realities. I vote for reflective practice, as it begins to work its way forward to increased insights and change. To stand still and remain unreflective is not an option if quality of patient care is to be more than rhetoric.

Be prepared to respond to critiques. There are so many ways of seeing that the slightest change of position can reveal new vistas, each with its own shortcomings. There is no end point – no nirvana – no one way of doing things. In this postmodern era we can celebrate difference and partialities. If reflective practice is seen as helpful, but not *the* panacea, we will benefit from what it has to offer us.

Reflector

Which of the above critiques of reflective practice hold some truth for you? How do you respond to these critiques, in order to maintain your reflective practice?

Creating a daily habit

To affirm your experience of reflection it will be important to maintain the everydayness of your reflective practice. It is easy to do something when it is novel. It is another thing to maintain a practice which has lost some of its initial appeal and requires a certain amount of discipline and attention for its continuation.

Just as you wash and feed your body as part of your essential daily activities, it is also possible to find enough space in your day-to-day life for reflection. This does not necessarily mean that you will write in a journal or speak into an audiotape every workday, but it may mean that you will be engaged sufficiently in work to reflect on it in some shape or form. In a practical sense, this may mean that you will use opportunities to take time out from the busyness of life to spend time in quietness.

Silence is the generative home of possibilities. Take time each day to find it, because it will not come to you unless you think it is important enough to seek it actively by doing nothing. It may seem like a contradiction to be active doing nothing, but unless you realize that silence is to be claimed, it will continue to elude you. Being busy can overtake life, so that your body rarely experiences immobility, silence and time for reflective thought. Consider the key activities of your day – simple things like washing, eating and socializing – and be alert to opportunities to be quiet, to go within and to 'just be' in the moment. From this place of quietness comes the potential for deep and effortless thought that springs up from a source of creativity and gives you clues and answers to puzzles that reside within you.

Reflector

When is your best time of day for reflection? In what ways do you seek silence in your life?

Seeing things freshly

Adopting a new way of seeing the events of everyday life can assist in maintaining reflective practice. This may mean that you try actively to keep a fresh perspective on ordinary aspects of life that you would otherwise have taken for granted. For example, what do you see when you open your eyes each morning? Have you ever really looked around the room, noticing its details? Have you ever looked carefully out the window and noticed the colours and moods of morning? As you step into active involvement in the day, start to be aware of all the little details of your life and the people with whom you interact. If these moments and people become a source of interest instead of familiarity, you may see them freshly, with new significance and potential for what and who they are and how they fit into the schemes and patterns of daily life.

Seeing the details of your life freshly will create a sense of constant connection and interest in your relationships to people and your environment. This will be excellent practice for the attentiveness you need as a reflective practitioner. For me, seeing things freshly is possible because I look out at the world from a fairly settled state inside myself, which allows me to focus on details and to be present. This way of seeing is gentle and quiet with wide, childlike eyes of interest. It is not busy and bustling, with the peering eyes of inquisitiveness for personal opportunity. Nurture a way of seeing from a quiet and steady state, which allows you to look around like a tourist visiting a foreign country for the first time. You may learn to see things freshly each day, discriminating between accepting and contesting, and making sense in general of more and more aspects of your life.

Reflector

Stop reading after this sentence and take one minute to look around to notice tiny details in your immediate environment. What benefits can you imagine in seeing things freshly in your practice environment?

Staying alert to practice

The need for seeing freshly in your personal life applies equally to your work life. You can affirm your status as a reflective practitioner by staying alert to your practice. Although you need to have a degree of comfort and familiarity with your work setting so you don't 'become a nervous wreck', too much familiarity can blind you to what is around you. Stay alert to notice the details that can keep you entrenched in unexamined clinical procedures, patterns of human relating and power-plays. Work realities are complex and challenging, containing issues that relate to the need for ever-increasing technical knowledge, refinements of relationships and a constant critique of power within the organization in which you work. These issues present an immense challenge to stay alert to practice in order to monitor the moves and shifts in its nature and effects.

How do you stay alert at work? You cannot always predict how a shift at work may go. Sometimes it may be fast and action-packed and sometimes it may be slow and relatively uneventful. The point to consider is that the degree of busyness will not necessarily dictate your alertness. If you are busy you are most probably attentive to what you are doing and how you are doing it, but you may not necessarily be alert to the fine details of interactions and outcomes. This state of alertness comes when you make conscious attempts to tune in as you work. You have to be 'at the controls' and not cruising through the challenges on autopilot. Conversely, you may not be alert just because you have more time on a quiet shift. This may be the very time in which you go into a holding pattern and fail to see the fine aspects of your work, because it is 'uneventful'. The quiet shifts may be your richest times for reflection, in terms of being alert to the taken-for-granted ways of thinking, doing and being. In summary, every moment of practice is a potential source of reflection, so stay alert to these opportunities.

Reflector

Think of one example of an unexamined clinical procedure, a taken-for-granted pattern of human relating and an unchallenged work-based power-play. Why have these clinical phenomena become relatively invisible and strongly entrenched in your workplace?

Finding support systems

Try to ascertain whether there are other clinicians engaged in reflective practice. You may find that there are 'closet' reflective practitioners inside your ward or unit, hospital or health region. People begin reflection through many sources, such as tertiary study, professional development courses, organizational seminars and so on. To find these people, you may need to leave a message pinned on a staff notice board, indicating that you are trying to begin a support group for reflective practitioners. You could suggest a meeting time, place and agenda and leave your contact details for the RSVP. You may be surprised who emerges out of the system.

Alternatively, you could send out an invitation on email within your organization, or on the internet, to access people more broadly and set up electronic connections with other reflective practitioners. Check the listings already in use and you may find that you could join an established group within nursing and midwifery, or across health care professions and other disciplines such as education. This may lead on to organizing professional development seminars in your work setting in which to share your experiences or getting involved in research.

Reflector

When you locate other reflective practitioners in your workplace, how will you set up regular contact and discussion?

Sharing reflection

Why not share reflective experiences in your ward, department or organization, by organizing a professional development seminar or conference? There are many possibilities. You could focus on nurses and midwives and/or other health workers, locally, nationally or internationally. Start locally and within manageable proportions in your unit or hospital. If you decide to organize a seminar, here is a checklist of details to consider as you plan for the event:

- *Venue:* is it suitable and available?
- *Programme:* who will speak/present, for how long?

- *Catering:* will you provide meals and refreshments?
- *Papers:* will you provide participants with copies?
- *Promotion:* how will you invite attendance?
- *Sponsorship:* will you need to seek financial assistance?
- *Equipment:* will speakers need audiovisual aids?
- *Administration:* do you need a mechanism to budget and monitor numbers and costs?

Reflector

What avenues for sharing reflection are open to you? Use the checklist above to plan a seminar in your ward/unit at which you present your experiences of reflective practice.

Getting involved in research

Reflective processes work well in research projects (see Chapter 8) because the thinking required for research is similar to that required for maintaining reflective practice. Knowledge, research, thinking and reflection are related through the ways they engage people in cognitive processes.

There is wide scope for research incorporating reflective processes or centred on experiences of reflective practice. For example, you could use reflective processes as a method for data collection in the field notes of a journal, or you could construct a research proposal focused on the nature and effects of reflective practice in any work context. You could undertake research in your work setting at any level, such as a ward, department or organization. The project could involve nurses and midwives and other health workers. It could be planned to have a local, national or international focus and participation, depending on your knowledge and skills in establishing and maintaining research.

Reflector

Imagine a research project involving reflection. Use the formats in Chapter 8 to assist you in writing a research proposal.

Embodying reflective practice

As time passes, reflective practice will become a part of your life, so that it is in your daily repertoire. Just as you attend to the daily routines of life, so you will embody reflective practice, so that it becomes part of who and how you are. This may not mean that you remember to write in your journal or speak into an audiotape as a matter of daily routine, but it does mean that you do not lose your motivation to think reflectively and to be aware of the potential of making sense out of everyday events. You will remain aware of how life is constructed at home and work and why it might be so, and how it might be otherwise.

Your biggest challenge will be to remain aware of the danger of familiarity and the tendency to accept a given reality as though it is as it should be and could be no other way. Life will be seen as 'work in progress' in which nothing is perfect or complete and everything can be seen afresh constantly, to reveal new insights and possibilities for interpretation and adaptation. Your personal growth as a person and health professional will continue as you open yourself up to the value of your own reflections and those gained in collaboration with your colleagues. This is not to imply that life will be 'upwards and onwards' without a hitch, but you will be actively and consciously aware of the events which used to pass you by, and you will have some processes whereby you can make sense of them.

Reflector

What practical measures can you put in place to ensure that you remain aware of the danger of familiarity and the tendency to accept a given reality as though it is as it should be and could be no other way?

Practice story

Christina is a well-respected nurse with 30 years of experience in clinical practice, and in the last 10 years she has been actively engaged in regular reflection. She learned about reflective practice during her postgraduate studies in nursing, and because it fits so well with her practice intentions she continues to reflect on her work and life. At times, Christina has difficulties in maintaining reflective practice, because of all the other pressures and obligations in her life. Even so, she periodically reviews her reflective successes, in order to affirm herself as a reflective practitioner. As necessary, she responds to people who question the value of her reflective practice, by pointing out actual and practical ways in which it has helped her. Christina does not always manage to write in her journal or speak into her audiocassette daily, but she aims to average at least a weekly reflective habit when she is in a particularly busy phase of her life. Christina has learned how to see things freshly and stay alert to practice. To assist her in her resolve to maintain reflective practice, she formed a reflective practice group at her workplace, and the members convene a yearly conference at which they share their reflections and invite a guest speaker. Christina and her colleagues provide critical friend support for one another and they attempt to undertake a reflective research project every two years. Increasingly, Christina is embodying reflective practice, so that it has become part of her work and personal

> *life and she can barely remember a time when she was not actively reflecting on her practice.*

In this chapter I suggested that if you have found reflective processes useful for your work and life, you might like to consider letting other people know about them. To this end, I discussed the value of maintaining your reflective practice by affirming yourself as a reflective practitioner, responding to the critiques, creating a daily habit, seeing things freshly, staying alert to practice, finding support systems, sharing reflection, getting involved in research and embodying reflective practice.

I wish you well.

10 Conclusion

This book has described reflective practice for nurses and midwives, with a practical emphasis on how to undertake reflective processes. Central to the practice of reflection are the foundational ideas presented in this book.

Chapter 1 described the nature of reflection and practice. I defined reflection as the throwing back of thoughts and memories in cognitive acts such as thinking, contemplation, meditation and any other form of attentive consideration, in order to make sense of them, and to make contextually appropriate changes if they are required. Based on the work of Donald Schön, I supported his emphasis that reflection is a way in which professionals can bridge the theory-practice gap, based on the potential of reflection to uncover knowledge in and on action. Nursing and midwifery have used reflective processes for some time to improve practice, clinical supervision and research. Technical reflection, based on the scientific method and rational, deductive thinking, allows you to generate and validate empirical knowledge through rigorous means, so that you can be assured that work procedures are based on scientific reasoning. Practical reflection leads to interpretation for description and explanation of human interaction in social existence, and improves the way you communicate with other people at work, thereby improving your practice enjoyment and outcomes. Emancipatory reflection provides a systematic questioning process to help you to locate the bases of the problem, identify the political constraints and begin to address the issues, either alone or through collaborative action with other nurses or midwives.

Nursing and midwifery are person-focused helping professions requiring hard work and a strong knowledge and skill base from which to face the daily challenges of practice. Therefore, systematic approaches to reflection and action are needed. Cultural, economic, historical, political, social and personal constraints may affect the ways in which you are able to interpret and act at any given moment at work. Cultural constraints refer to the determinants that hold people in patterns of interaction within groups, based on the interpretation of shared symbols, rituals and practices. Economic constraints refer to workplace issues caused by a lack of money and the resources money can provide. Historical constraints are those factors that have been inherited in a setting, which remain unquestioned because of the precedence of time and convention. Political constraints are about the power, competition and contention in relationships in day-to-day life and work. Social constraints are the habitual features of a setting and the ways in which people define themselves through interactions in that setting. Personal constraints have to do with unique features about you as a person, shaped by influences in your life, into which you may or may not have insights.

When you shift the focus away from blaming yourself exclusively, to reflect on cultural, economic, historical, political and social constraints issues that may be affecting your practice, you begin to see that your work is complex and there are many reasons why things go wrong, and ways in which constraints may be identified, explored and changed. Issues faced by nurses and midwives that may benefit from reflection include engaging in self-blaming, wanting to be perfect and invincible, examining daily habits and routines, struggling to be assertive, struggling to be an advocate, differentiating between ideal and real practice expectations, playing the nurse/midwife–doctor game, managing collegial relations, dealing with organizational and health care system problems, and managing self-esteem and worthiness problems. Understood and practised, reflective processes have the potential to create a daily vigilance that keeps you alert to what is happening around you, and increases the likelihood that you will be able to be active and enthusiastic about developing and maintaining quality care in your practice.

In Chapter 2 I suggested ways of preparing for reflection. It takes time, effort, determination, courage and humour to initiate and maintain effective reflection. Reflection requires time and that is one of the main reasons why nurses and midwives do not make a commitment to creating a reflective work life. Life is full of activities, few of which happen if you do not make an effort, which you *will* make when you suspect that something is of value, reasonably easy and of benefit to you personally. Determination is needed for reflection, because it is easy not to begin or to give up regular reflective processes, due to tougher pressures that compete for your time and attention. You need courage to look at yourself and your practice, because it takes honesty and frankness to move outside your comfort zones and invest yourself in the depth of reflection needed to change dysfunctional procedures, interpersonal interactions and power relations at work. Even though reflection needs to be approached seriously, and has the potential to be complex and difficult, it is not always onerous and without some degree of fun.

There are many strategies you can use when engaging in systematic reflection, such as writing, audiotaping, creating music and so on. When you are reflecting, remember to be spontaneous, to express yourself freely, to remain open to ideas, to choose a time and place to suit you, to be prepared personally, and to choose suitable reflective methods. A good exercise to get you started on reflecting is to recall and record your childhood memories in relation to who you are now as an adult and a clinician, to discover some of your values and rules for living that influence your practice.

A critical friend can offer external perspectives to extend your reflective capacity, by asking important questions and making tentative suggestions to unseat your previous perceptions, to find other possibilities and insights. A critical friend realizes that they are not meant to be the person with answers to every dilemma, but rather the role is to encourage you to find the answers yourself. A critical friend hears what you have to say and lets you talk it out as fully as you can, while being non-judgemental about you as a person. One of the most important parts of a reflective story is its emotional content, because if you can identify your feelings, you can begin to reflect on why they are as they are, and what you can learn from them. One of the ways in which you can be encouraged to go beyond your initial interpretation of your work issues is to explore the answers to questions which trigger reflection.

Chapter 3 introduced the 'Taylor model of reflection' as a systematic flow approach to successful reflection. The model uses a mnemonic device of the word REFLECT, to represent Readiness, Exercising thought, Following systematic processes, Leaving oneself open to answers, Enfolding insights, Changing awareness and Tenacity in maintaining reflection, in and through practice, within the context of self in relation to other people, within the ground of internal historical, cultural, economic, social and political constraints, orbited by and in contact with external forces and influences.

Due to the ongoing severity of the insults and challenges on and in the sphere of practice, other means of help are necessary, so reflective processes do not claim to be the panacea for all of the ills and challenges of practice.

In Chapter 4 I introduced three main types of reflection. It is a tricky business to put ideas into neat, fixed categories, because concepts do not necessarily fit in 'boxes', however, when potentially complex phenomena are in focus, structures for thinking, such as theories, models and categories, can be used gainfully. Empirical knowledge comes from technical reflection, interpretive knowledge comes from practical reflection and critical knowledge comes from emancipatory reflection. It is important to consider these categories as ways of creating a temporary framework on which to hang certain broad principles, because it would be shortsighted to have an absolute conviction that there are only three forms of knowledge and reflection. The categories are ways of structuring your thinking until you have the confidence you need to disregard the conceptual boxes, so that you can roam freely in the open fields of uncategorized knowledge and reflection.

In Chapter 5 I described technical reflection through which questions about clinical procedures can be answered. For nurses and midwives, technical interest is associated with task-related competence, such as clinical procedures;

therefore technical reflection involves empirical knowledge, rationality, the scientific method, critical thinking and problem-solving. The evidence-based movement in nursing and midwifery is testing the validity of long-standing procedures, and is seeking to replace old untested and unproven approaches with newer research-based ones. In this book, technical reflection is based on Bandman and Bandman's (1995) view of scientific reasoning and the functions of critical thinkers, the features of critical thinking and thinkers described by van Hooft *et al.* (1995), and the problem-solving steps of the nursing process (Wilkinson 1996). 'Assessing and planning' is the part of the technical reflection process in which you set up the premises for rational thinking by making an initial assessment of the problem and begin planning for the development of an argument. 'Implementing' is the part in which you develop an argument by analysing the issues and assumptions operating in the situation. 'Evaluating' is the part in which you review the problem in the light of all the information gained through the process of technical reflection. The outcomes of technical reflection can be immediate, if the process has been shared with, and the findings endorsed by, the key people who are in a position to influence and ratify health care practice. In whatever situations you use it, technical reflection has the potential for allowing you to think critically and to reason scientifically, so that you can critique and adapt present procedures to better ones as necessary. You may also be able to predict likely outcomes for similar procedures and improve many work practices through objective and systematic lines of enquiry.

In Chapter 6 I described practical reflection, which is derived from the work of Smyth (1986a, 1986b) and Street (1991), with an adaptation to emphasize the communicative nature of this type of reflection. Practical reflection retains some of the questions used previously by Smyth and Street, within the process of experiencing, interpreting and learning.

Experiencing involves retelling a practice story so that you experience it again in as much detail as possible. Interpreting involves clarifying and explaining the meaning of a communicative action situation. Learning involves creating new insights and integrating them into your existing awareness and knowledge. Although change may not be an explicit aim of practical reflection, it is still possible through new insights that follow from raised awareness. Through the medium of language, practical reflection will help you to understand the interpersonal basis of human experiences and will also offer you the potential for creating new knowledge, which interprets the meaning of your lived experience, context and subjectivity.

In Chapter 7 I described emancipatory reflection. If you are thwarted by the power relationships within your practice and work setting, you may need to adopt emancipatory reflective processes to bring about transformative action. Emancipatory reflection is only as liberating as the amount of effort you are willing to invest in making a thorough and systematic critique of the constraints within your practice. Emancipatory reflection will help you to analyse critically the contextual features which have a bearing on your practice, whether they are personal, political, sociocultural, historical or economic. Of all the types of reflection, emancipatory reflection is the richest, but riskiest, in terms of what it tries to achieve and the courage required to use it effectively. Emancipatory reflection leads to 'transformative action', which seeks to free you from your taken-for-granted assumptions and oppressive forces, which limit you and your practice. Emancipatory reflection provides you with a systematic means of critiquing the status quo in the power relationships in your workplace and offers you raised awareness and a new sense of informed consciousness to bring about positive social and political change. Emancipatory reflection also offers you freedom from your own misguided and firmly-held perceptions of yourself and your roles, to bring about change for the better.

The process of emancipatory reflection for change is praxis, which offers clinicians the means for change through collaborative processes that analyse and challenge existing forces and distortions brought about by dominating effects of power in human interaction. Emancipatory reflection provides a process to construct, confront, deconstruct and reconstruct your practice. Construction of practice incidents allows you to describe, in words and other creative images and representations, a work scene played out previously, bringing to mind all of the aspects and constraints of the situation. Deconstruction involves asking analytical questions regarding the situation, which are aimed at locating and critiquing all the aspects of that situation. Confrontation occurs when you focus on your part in the scenario with the intention of seeing and describing it as clearly as possible. Reconstruction puts the scenario together again with transformative strategies for managing changes in the light of new insights.

In Chapter 8 I described reflective practice in research and scholarship. Reflective methods and processes not only guide practice, they can also provide evidence for supporting practice changes. It is advisable for a beginning researcher to reduce the complexity of research by thinking of three main types: empirico-analytical (quantitative), interpretive (qualitative) and critical (qualitative). Empirico-analytical (quantitative) research uses numbers and statistics as its main investigative tools, to observe and analyse through the scientific method. Qualitative research can be interpretive or critical and uses words and language as its main exploratory tools. Interpretive qualitative research aims mainly to generate meaning, that is, to explain and describe in order to make sense of phenomena of interest. Examples of interpretive qualitative research include historical methods, grounded theory, phenomenology and ethnography. Qualitative critical research also generates meaning and aims openly to bring about change in the status quo. Examples include action research, critical ethnography, feminist research and discourse analysis.

By working collaboratively with participants as co-researchers to systematically address research problems, qualitative researchers try to find answers and use them to bring about change. Reflective processes may be used solely as the research approach, or they may be integrated into other research approaches. The basic eight steps in the reflective research method are: identify the issue/problem/phenomenon for reflection; decide on the reflective method; clarify its intent; plan the stages in a research proposal; follow the method and use the process; generate insights, institute changes and improvements and continue to reflect on outcomes; report on outcomes; and use the outcomes in practice as evidence. Reflective processes can be used in conjunction with other research approaches, and there is no prescription as to how these might be used, as it is up to the researcher to make those choices, based on the fit of the approach to the research aims and objectives.

Reflective processes and action research combine well to create an effective collaborative qualitative research approach for identifying and transforming clinical issues, because reflection is part of the action research method of planning, assessing, observing and reflecting. The 13 steps to undertake action research and reflection are: find enough nurses or midwives to form a research group; ensure the nurses or midwives are ready to make a commitment to the group; decide on a venue and a regular meeting day and time; write a brief research proposal; check on ethics approval processes in your organization; get the project underway and decide who facilitates meetings; share the business of the first two meetings; share the first reflective task; share the practice stories; identify the thematic concern(s); generate the action plan and begin the action research cycles; write a research report; and disseminate the findings.

Scholarship in nursing and midwifery is generated through sharing disciplinary knowledge and skills, and the main modes of dissemination are professional conference presentations and publications.

You are now at a crucial point in your experience as a reflective practitioner, because you can decide to take on the ideas and use them actively, you can pay scant or no ongoing attention to them, or you can locate yourself somewhere along that continuum. How you approach the future is entirely up to you, but this book ends on a hopeful note, to encourage you to maintain reflective processes in your life and work.

Key points

- The maintenance of your reflective practices will require personal and group supports, so that your good intentions materialize into lifelong reflective approaches.
- Ways of maintaining reflective practice are by affirming yourself as

a reflective practitioner, by responding to the critiques, by creating a daily habit, by seeing things freshly, by staying alert to practice, by finding support systems, by sharing reflection, by getting involved in research, and by embodying reflective practice.

- When you resolve to maintain reflective processes, and your resolutions come to fruition, keep your resolution alive by holding on to the principle of the idea of reflection.
- Affirm your worth as a reflective practitioner by acknowledging your insights and how far you have come from who and how you were when you began, to who and how you are now.
- To be assured of the worth of reflection, you may need to respond to the critics, so that your investment in maintaining reflection does not suffer.
- To affirm your experience of reflection, it will be important to maintain the everydayness of your reflective practice, by using opportunities to take time out from the busyness of life to spend time in silence and quietness.
- Adopting a new way of seeing the events of everyday life can assist in maintaining reflective practice, by trying actively to keep a fresh perspective on ordinary aspects of life that you would otherwise have taken for granted.
- You can affirm your status as a reflective practitioner by staying alert to your practice and noticing the details that can keep you entrenched in unexamined clinical procedures, patterns of human relating and power-plays.
- Ascertain whether there are other clinicians engaged in reflective practice to encourage one another to maintain reflection.
- Share reflective experiences in your ward, department or organization, by organizing a professional development seminar or conference.
- There is wide scope for research incorporating reflective processes or centred on experiences of reflective practice.
- Just as you attend to the daily routines of life, so you may begin to embody reflective practice, so that it becomes part of who and how you are.
- This book described reflective practice for nurses and midwives, with a practical emphasis of how to undertake reflective processes.

References

Abdellah, F.G., Beland, I.L., Martin, A. and Matheney, R.V. (1960) *Patient-centred Approaches to Nursing*. New York: Macmillan.

Allen, D., Benner, P. and Diekelmann, N.L. (1986) Three paradigms for nursing research: methodological implications, in P.L. Chinn (ed.) *Nursing Research Methodology: Issues and Implementation*. Rockville: Aspen.

Anderson, J.M. (ed.) (1996) *Thinking Management: Contemporary Approaches for Nurse Managers*. Melbourne: Ausmed Publications.

Anderson, M. and Branch, M. (2000) Storytelling: a tool to promote critical reflection in the RN student, *Minority Nurse Newsletter*, 71: 1–2.

Argyris, C. and Schön, D.A. (1974) *Theory in Practice: Increasing Professional Effectiveness*. Washington, DC: Jossey-Bass.

Argyris, C., Putnam, R. and Smith, D.M. (1985) Quoted in H.S. Kim (1999) Critical reflective inquiry for knowledge development in nursing practice, *Journal of Advanced Nursing*, 29(5): 1205–12.

Atkins, S. (1995) Reflective practice, *Nursing Standard*, 9(45): 31–7.

Bandman, E.L. and Bandman, B. (1995) *Critical Thinking in Nursing*, 2nd edn. Norwalk, CT: Appleton and Lange.

Barrett, P. (2001) The early mothering project: what happened when the words 'action research' came to life for a group of midwives, in P. Reason and H. Bradbury (eds) *Handbook of Action Research*. London: Sage.

Baudrillard, J. (1988) (ed.) *Selected Writings Poster*. Stanford, CA: Stanford University Press.

Benner, P. (1984) *From Novice to Expert: Uncovering the Knowledge Embedded in Clinical Practice*. California: Addison-Wesley.

Benner, P. and Tanner, C. (1987) Clinical judgement: how expert nurses use intuition, *American Journal of Nursing*, 87(23).

Benner, P. and Wrubel, J. (1989) *The Primacy of Caring: Stress and Coping in Health and Illness*. California: Addison-Wesley.

Boud, D., Keogh, R. and Walker, D. (1985) *Reflection: Turning Experience into Learning*. London: Kogan Page.

Boyd, E.M. and Fales, A.W. (1983) Reflective learning key to learning from experience, *Journal of Humanistic Psychology*, 23(2): 99–117.

Brennan, B. (1987) *Hands of Light: A Guide to Healing through the Human Energy Field*. Toronto: Bantam Books.

Brennan, B. (1993) *Light Emerging: The Journey of Personal Healing*. New York: Bantam Books.

Brown, S. and Lumley, J. (1994) Satisfaction with care in labour and birth: a survey of 790 Australian women, *Birth*, 12: 4–13.

Burrows, D.E. (1995) The nurse teacher's role in the promotion of reflective practice, *Nurse Education Today*, 15: 346–50.

Burton, A. (2000) Reflection: nursing's practice and education panacea? *Journal of Advanced Nursing*, 31(5): 1009–17.

Capra, F. (1988) *Uncommon Wisdom: Conversations with Remarkable People*. London: Flamingo.

Capra, F. (1992) *Belonging to the Universe: New Thinking about God and Nature*. London: Penguin Books.

Carper, B. (1978) Fundamental ways of knowing in nursing, *Advances in Nursing Science*, 1(1): 13–23.

Carr, W. and Kemmis, S. (1984) *Becoming Critical: Knowing through Action Research*. Victoria: Deakin University Press.

Chein, I., Cook, S. and Harding, J. (1948) The field of action research, *American Psychology*, 3: 43–50.

Chenoweth, L. and Kilstoff, K. (1998) Facilitating positive changes in community dementia management through participatory action research, *International Journal of Nursing Practice*, 4: 175–88.

Chinn, P.L. and Kramer, M.K. (1991) *Theory and Nursing: A Systematic Approach*, 3rd edn. St Louis: Mosby.

Clegg, S. (2000) Knowing through reflective practice in higher education, *Education Action Research*, 8(3): 451–69.

Clouder, L. and Sellars, J. (2004) Reflective practice and clinical supervision: an interprofessional perspective, *Journal of Advanced Nursing*, 46(3): 262–9.

Cotton, A. (2001) Private thoughts in public spheres: issues in reflection and reflective practices in nursing, *Journal of Advanced Nursing*, 36(4): 512–19.

Couves, J. (1995) Working in practice, in L. Page (ed.) *Effective Group Practice in Midwifery: Working with Women*. Oxford: Blackwell Science.

Crookes, P.A. and Davies, S. (1998) *Research into Practice*. Edinburgh: Balliere Tindall.

Cruickshank, D. (1996) The 'art' of reflection: using drawing to uncover knowledge development in student nurses, *Nurse Education Today*, 16(2): 127–30.

Cunningham, J. (1993) Experiences of Australian mothers who gave birth either at home, at a birth centre, or in hospital labour wards, *Social Science of Medicine*, 36(4): 475–83.

Deery, R. and Kirkham, M. (2000) Moving from hierarchy to collaboration: the birth of an action research project, *Practising Midwife*, 3(8): 25–8.

Dick, R.A. (1995) A beginner's guide to action research, *ARCS Newsletter*, 1(1): 5–9.

Dilthey, W. (1985) *Poetry and Experience: Selected Works*, vol. V. Princeton, NJ: Princeton University Press.

Dreyfus, H.I. (1979) *What Computers Can't Do: The Limits of Artificial Intelligence*. New York: Harper & Row.

Driscoll, J. (1994) Reflective practice for practise, *Senior Nurse*, 13(7): 47–50.

Duffy, E. (1995) Horizontal violence: a conundrum for nursing, *Collegian*, 2(2): 5–17.

Ehrenreich, B. and English, D. (1973) *Witches, Midwives and Nurses: A History of Women Healers*. London: Writers and Readers Publishing Cooperative.

Evans, B. (2003) Reflection – who needs it? *Primary Health Care*, 13(9): 40–2.

Fay, B. (1987) *Critical Social Science: Liberation and its Limits*. Cambridge: Polity Press.

Foucault, M. (1982) Afterword: the subject of power, in H.L. Dreyfus and P. Robinow (eds) *Beyond Structuralism and Hermeneutics*. London: Harvester Wheatsheaf.

Fraser, D.M. (2000) Action research to improve the pre-registration midwifery curriculum Part 1: an appropriate methodology, *Midwifery*, 16(3): 213–23.

Frederick, H. and Northam, E. (1938) *A Textbook of Nursing Practice*. New York: Macmillan.

Freshwater, D. (1998) From acorn to oak tree: a neoplatonic perspective of reflection and caring, *Australian Journal of Holistic Nursing*, 5(2): 14–19.

Freshwater, D. (1999a) Clinical supervision, reflective practice and guided discovery: clinical supervision, *British Journal of Nursing*, 8(20): 1383–9.

Freshwater, D. (1999b) Communicating with self through caring: the student nurse's experience of reflective practice, *International Journal of Human Caring*, 3(3): 28–33.

Freshwater, D. (2001) Critical reflexivity: a politically and ethically engaged method for nursing, *NT Research*, 6(1): 526–37.

Freshwater, D. (2002a) Guided reflection in the context of post-modern practice, in C. Johns (ed.) *Guided Reflection: Advancing Practice*. Blackwell Science, Oxford.

Freshwater, D. (ed.) (2002b) *Therapeutic Nursing: Improving Patient Care through Reflection*. London: Sage.

Gadamer, H.-G. (1975) *Truth and Method*, eds and trans G. Barden and J. Cumming. New York: Seabury.

Ghaye, T. and Lillyman, S. (2000) Reflections on Schön: fashion victims or joining up practice with theory? in *Reflection: Principles and Practice for Healthcare Professionals*. Wiltshire: Quay Books.

Gilbert, T. (2001) Reflective practice and supervision: meticulous rituals of the confessional, *Journal of Advanced Nursing*, 36(2): 199–205.

Giroux, H.A. (1990) *Curriculum Discourse as Postmodernist Critical Practice*. Geelong: Deakin University Press.

Glass, N. (1997) Horizontal violence in nursing, *The Australian Journal of Holistic Nursing*, 4(1): 15–21.

Glaze, E. (2001) Reflection as a transforming process: student advanced nurse practitioners' experiences of developing reflective skills as part of an MSc programme, *Journal of Advanced Nursing*, 34: 639–47.

Glaze, J. (1999) Reflection, clinical judgement and staff development, *British Journal of Theatre Nursing*, 9(1): 30–4.

Greenwood, J. (1993) Reflective practice: a critique of the work of Argyris and Schön, *Journal of Advanced Nursing*, 18: 1183–7.

Habermas, J. (1972) *Knowledge and Human Interests*. London: Heinemann.

Handcock, P. (1999) Reflective practice: using a learning journal, *Nursing Standard*, 13(17): 37–40.

Hannigan, B. (2001) A discussion of the strengths and weaknesses of reflection in nursing practice and education, *Journal of Advanced Nursing*, 10(2): 278–83.

Heath, H. (1998a) Keeping a reflective practice diary: a practical guide, *Nurse Education Today*, 18(7): 592–8.

Heath, H. (1998b) Reflection and patterns of knowing in nursing, *Journal of Advanced Nursing*, 27(5): 1054–9.

Heath, H. and Freshwater, D. (2000) Clinical supervision as an emancipatory process: avoiding inappropriate intent, *Journal of Advanced Nursing*, 32(5): 1298–306.

Heidegger, M. (1962) Being and time, trans J. Macquarrie and E. Robinson. New York: Harper & Row.

Henderson, V. (1955) *Textbook of Principles and Practice of Nursing*. New York: Macmillan.

Houston, J. (1987) *The Search for the Beloved: Journeys in Sacred Psychology*. California: Crucible.

Hulatt, I. (1995) A sad reflection, *Nursing Standard*, 9(20): 22–3.

James, C. and Clarke, B. (1994) Reflective practice in nursing: issues and implications, *Nurse Education Today*, 14(2): 82–90.

Jarvis, P. (1992) Reflective practice in nursing, *Nursing Education Today*, 12: 174–81.

Johns, C. (1994) Nuances of reflection, *Journal of Clinical Nursing*, 3: 71–5.

Johns, C. (1995a) Framing learning through reflection within Carper's fundamental ways of knowing in nursing, *Journal of Advanced Nursing*, 22: 226–34.

Johns, C. (1995b) The value of reflective practice for nursing, *Journal of Clinical Nursing*, 4(1): 23–30.

Johns, C. (1996) Visualizing and realizing caring in practice through guided reflection, *Journal of Advanced Nursing*, 24: 1135–43.

Johns, C. (1999) Reflection as empowerment? *Nursing Inquiry*, 6(4): 241–9.

Johns, C. (2000) Working with Alice: a reflection, *Complementary Therapies in Nursing and Midwifery*, 6: 199–303.

Johns, C. (ed.) (2002) *Guided Reflection: Advancing Practice*. Oxford: Blackwell Science.

Johns, C. (2003) Easing into the light, *International Journal for Human Caring*, 7(1): 49–55.

Johns, P.R. (2000) *Becoming a Reflective Practitioner*. London: Blackwell Science.

Jourard, S.M. (1971) *The Transparent Self*. New York: D. Van Nostrand Co.

Judith, A. (1992) *Wheels of Life: A User's Guide to the Chakra System*. St Paul, MN: Llewellyn Publications.

Keatinge, D., Scarfe, C., Bellchambers, H., McGee, J., Oakham, R., Probert, C., Stewart, L. and Stokes, J. (2000) The manifestation and nursing management of agitation in institutionalised residents with dementia, *International Journal of Nursing Practice*, 6: 16–25.

Keleher, H. and McInerney, F. (eds) (1998) *Nursing Matters: Critical Sociological Perspectives*. Australia: Churchill Livingstone.

Kemmis, S. and McTaggart, R. (eds) (1988) *The Action Research Planner*, 3rd edn. Geelong: Deakin University Press.

Kenny, L.J. (2003) Using Edward de Bono's six hats game to aid critical thinking and reflection in palliative care, *International Journal of Palliative Nursing*, 9(3): 105–12.

Kermode, S. and Brown, C. (1996) The postmodernist hoax and its effects on nursing, *The International Journal of Nursing Studies*, 31(4): 1–10.

Kim, H.S. (1999) Critical reflective inquiry for knowledge development in nursing practice, *Journal of Advanced Nursing*, 29(5): 1205–12.

King, I.M. (1971) *Toward a Theory for Nursing: General Concepts of Human Behaviour*. New York: John Wiley.

Kinlein, M.L. (1977) *Independent Nursing Practice with Clients*, Philadelphia: Lippincott.

Kitzinger, S. (1991) Why women need midwives, in S. Kitzinger (ed.) *The Midwife Challenge*. London: Pandora.

Koch, T., Kralik, D. and Kelly, S. (2000) We just don't talk about it: men living with urinary incontinence and multiple sclerosis, *International Journal of Nursing Practice*, 6: 253–60.

Kuiper, R.A. (2004) Nursing reflections from journaling during a perioperative internship, *AORN Journal*, 79(1): 195.

Lau, A.K. (2002) Reflective practice in clinical teaching, *Nursing and Health Sciences*, 4(4): 201–8.

Leininger, M. (1985) *Qualitative Research Methods in Nursing*. New York: Grune & Stratton.

Lewin, K. (1946) Action research and minority issues, *Journal of Social Issues*, 2: 34–46.

Lian, J.X. (2001) Reflective practice: a critical incident, *Contemporary Nurse*, 3–4: 217–21.

Mackintosh, C. (1998) Reflection: a flawed strategy for the nursing profession, *Nurse Education Today*, 18: 553–7.

Markham, T. (2002) Response to 'private thoughts in public spheres: issues in reflection and reflective practices in nursing', *Journal of Advanced Nursing*, 38(3): 286–7.

Marriner-Tomey, A. and Alligood, M. (2002) *Nursing Theorists and their Work*, 5th edn. St Louis: Mosby.

McCool, W. and McCool, S. (1989) Feminism and nurse-midwifery: historical overview and current issues, *Journal of Nurse-Midwifery*, 345(6): 323–34.

McMorland, J. and Piggott-Irvine, E. (2000) Facilitation as midwifery: facilitation and praxis in group learning, *Systematic Practice and Action Research*, 13(2): 121–38.

Mezirow, J. (1981) A critical theory of adult learning and education, *Adult Education*, 32: 3–24.

Moore, B. (ed.) (1999) *The Australian Oxford Dictionary*. Oxford: Oxford University Press.

Munroe, J., Ford, H., Scott, A., Furnival, E., Andrews, S. and Grayson, S. (2002) Action research responding to midwives' views of different methods of fetal monitoring in labour, *MIDIRS Midwifery Digest*, 12(4): 495–8.

Newell, R. (1994) Reflection: art, science or pseudo-science? *Nursing Education Today*, 14: 79–81.

Nightingale, F. (1893) *Selected Writings of Florence Nightingale*, compiled by L. Seymer (1955). New York: Macmillan.

Noveletsky-Rosenthal, H. and Solomon, K. (2001) Reflections on the use of Johns' model of structured reflection in nurse-practitioner education, *International Journal for Human Caring*, 5(2): 21–6.

Oakley, A. and Houd, S. (1990) *Helpers in Childbirth: Midwifery Today*. USA: Hemisphere Publishing.

Orem, D. (1959) *Guides for Developing Curricula for the Education of Practical Nurses*. Washington, DC: Government Printing Office.

Orlando, I.J. (1961) *The Dynamic Nurse-Patient Relationship*. New York: Putnam.

Palmer, A., Burns, S. and Bulman, C. (1994) *Reflective Practice in Nursing: The Growth of the Professional Practitioner*. Oxford: Blackwell Science.

Parse, R.R. (1985) *Nursing Research: Qualitative Methods*. Bowie, MD: Brady.

Paterson, J. and Zderad, L. (1976) *Humanistic Nursing*. New York: Wiley.

Pearson, A. (ed.) (1988) *Primary Nursing*. London: Croom Helm.

Pearson, A., Borbasi, S., Fitzgerald, M., Kowanko, I. and Walsh, K. (1997) *Evidence Based Nursing: An Examination of Nursing Within the International Evidence Based Health Care Practice Movement*. Sydney: RCNA Discussion Document no. 1, *Nursing Review*.

Peplau, H.E. (1952) *Interpersonal Relations in Nursing*. New York: Putnam.

Platzer, H., Blake, D. and Ashford, D. (2000a) Barriers to learning from reflection: a study of the use of groupwork with post-registration nurses, *Journal of Advanced Nursing*, 31(5): 1001–8.

Platzer, H., Blake, D. and Ashford, D. (2000b) An evaluation of process and outcomes from learning through reflective practice groups on a post-registration nursing course, *Journal of Advanced Nursing*, 31(3): 689–95.

Polit, D., Beck, C. and Hungler, B. (2001) *Essentials of Nursing Research: Methods, Appraisal, and Utilization*. Philadelphia: Lippincott.

Posner, G. (1989) Why and how should you reflect on your field experience, in G. Posner, *Field Experience: Methods of Reflective Teaching*, 2nd edn. New York: Longman.

Pryce, A. (2002) Refracting experience: reflection, postmodernity and transformations, *NT Research*, 7(4): 298–311.

Roberts, K. and Taylor, B. (2001) *Nursing Research Processes: An Australian Perspective*, 2nd edn. Melbourne: Nelson ITP.

Rogers, M. (1961) *Educational Revolution in Nursing*. New York: Macmillan.

Rolfe, G. (2003) Is there a place for reflection in the nursing curriculum? A reply to Newell, *Clinical Effectiveness in Nursing*, 7(1): 61.

Rosenau, P. (1992) *Post-modernism and the Social Sciences: Insights, Inroads and Intrusions*. Princeton, NJ: Princeton University Press.

Rothwell, H. (1996) Changing childbirth – changing nothing, *Midwives*, 109(1306): 291–4.

Roy, C. (1976) *Introduction to Nursing: An Adaptation Model*. Englewood Cliffs, NJ: Prentice-Hall.

Rubenfeld, M.G. and Scheffer, B.K. (1995) *Critical Thinking in Nursing: An Interactive Approach*. Philadelphia: Lippincott.

Sargent, M. (2001) Move with the times – reflection is here to stay in nurse education, *Nursing Standard*, 16(13–14–15): 30.

Schön, D.A. (1983) *The Reflective Practitioner: How Practitioners Think in Action*. New York: Basic Books.

Schön, D.A. (1987) *Educating the Reflective Practitioner*. London: Jossey-Bass.

Seymer, L. (1955) (compiler) *Selected Writings of Florence Nightingale* [F. Nightingale (1893)]. New York: Macmillan.

Shorten, A. and Wallace, M. (1997) Evidence based practice: the future is clear, *Australian Nursing Journal*, 4(6): 22–4.

Smith, A. (1998) Learning about reflection, *Journal of Advanced Nursing*, 28(4): 891–5.

Smyth, W.J. (1986a) *Reflection-in-action EED432 Educational Leadership in Schools*. Geelong: Deakin University Press.

Smyth, W.J. (1986b) The reflective practitioner in nursing education, unpublished paper to the Second National Nursing Education Seminar, SACAE, Adelaide.

Stein, L. (1967) The doctor–nurse game, in R. Dingwall and J. McIntosh (eds) *Readings in the Sociology of Nursing*, Edinburgh: Churchill Livingstone.

Stickley, T. and Freshwater, D. (2002) The art of loving and the therapeutic relationship, *Nursing Inquiry*, 9(4): 250–6.

Street, A. (1991) *From Image to Action: Reflection in Nursing Practice*. Geelong: Deakin University Press.

Street, A. (1992) *Inside Nursing: A Critical Ethnography of Clinical Nursing*. New York: SUNY.

Streubert Speziale, H. and Rinaldi Carpenter, D. (2003) *Qualitative Research in Nursing: Advancing the Humanistic Perspective*. Philadelphia: Lippincott.

Stringer, E.T. (1996) *Action Research: A Handbook for Practitioners*. Thousand Oaks, CA: Sage.

Sullivan, D. and Weitz, R. (1998) *Labour Pains: Modern Midwifery and Homebirth.* New Haven, CT: Yale University Press.

Taylor, B.J. (1997) Big battles for small gains: a cautionary note for teaching reflective processes in nursing and midwifery, *Nursing Inquiry*, 4: 19–26.

Taylor, B.J. (2000) *Reflective Practice: A Guide for Nurses and Midwives.* Buckingham: Open University Press.

Taylor, B.J. (2001) Identifying and transforming dysfunctional nurse-nurse relationships through reflective practice and action research, *International Journal of Nursing Practice*, 7(6): 406–13.

Taylor, B.J. (2002a) Technical reflection for improving nursing and midwifery procedures using critical thinking in evidence based practice, *Contemporary Nurse*, 13(2–3): 281–7.

Taylor, B.J. (2002b) Becoming a reflective nurse or midwife: using complementary therapies while practising holistically, *Complementary Therapies in Nursing and Midwifery*, 8(4): 62–8.

Taylor, B.J. (2003) Emancipatory reflective practice for overcoming complexities and constraints in holistic health care, *Sacred Space*, 4(2): 40–5.

Taylor, B.J. (2004) Technical, practical and emancipatory reflection for practising holistically, *Journal of Holistic Nursing*, 22(1): 73–84.

Taylor, B.J., Bulmer, B., Hill, L., Luxford, C., McFarlane, J. and Stirling, K. (2002) Exploring idealism in palliative nursing care through reflective practice and action research, *International Journal of Palliative Nursing*, 8(7): 324–30.

Taylor, C. (2003) Issues and innovations in nursing education – narrating practice: reflective accounts and the textual construction of reality, *Journal of Advanced Nursing*, 42(3): 244.

Thorpe, K. and Barsky, J. (2001) Healing through self-reflection, *Journal of Advanced Nursing*, 35(5): 760–8.

Todd, G. and Freshwater, D. (1999) Reflective practice and guided discovery: clinical supervision, *British Journal of Nursing*, 8(20): 1383–9.

Travelbee, J. (1971) *Interpersonal Aspects of Nursing.* Philadelphia: F.A. Davis.

van Hooft, S., Gillam, L. and Byrnes, M. (1995) *Facts and Values: An Introduction to Critical Thinking for Nurses.* Sydney: Maclennan and Petty.

Watson, J. (1981) Nursing's scientific quest, *Nursing Outlook*, 29(7): 413–16.

Wiedenbach, E. (1964) *Clinical Nursing: A Helping Art.* New York: Springer Publishing.

Wilkin, K. (2002) Exploring expert practice through reflection, *Nursing in Critical Care*, 7(2): 88–93.

Wilkinson, J.M. (1996) *Nursing Process: A Critical Thinking Approach.* Menlo Park: Addison-Wesley Nursing.

World Health Organization (1985) *Having a Baby in Europe: Report on a Study.* Copenhagen: World Health Organization.

Young, A., Taylor, S.G. and McLaughlin-Renpenning, K. (2001) *Connections: Nursing Research, Theory, and Practice.* St Louis: Mosby.

Index

Page numbers in *italics* refer to figures, tables, 'practice stories' and 'critical friend responses'

abstracts, research
    preparation of, 187
action research
    and reflection as research methodology,
        177–85
    use within clinical settings, 20–21
advocacy, 37–8, *37–8*
alertness, professional
    importance to practitioners,
        200–201
Allen, D., 90
analysis, data, 171
Anderson, M., 13
Argyris, C., 8
art, as reflective strategy, 55–7
articles, research
    preparation of, 191–4
assessment, 124–5, 126–8
assertiveness, role and management, 36–7,
    36–7
assurance, quality of care, 44–5
audiotaping
    as reflective strategy, 53–4
    see also music; poetry; videotaping
awareness, changed
    following reflection, 81–2, *82*

Bandman, E.L. and B., 105, 108
Barrett, P., 20, 178
Bill, practice story, 37–8
blame (self blame), 32–3, *32–3*
Branch, M., 13

budgeting, as element in research planning,
    172
bullying, 41–2, *42*

care, patient
    quality assurance measures, 44–5
Carper, B., 9, 88
Cathy
    critical friend response, 134–5
    practice story, 134
Cheryle, practice story, 66–8
Chinn, P.L., 88–9
Christina, practice stories, 39, 203–4
clarification, as element in research
    planning, 169
clinical settings
    action research within, 20–21
    and role of reflection, 9–11
Clegg, S., 13
Clouder, L., 12
colleagues
    as fellow reflective practitioners,
        201–2
    relationships with, 40–42, *42*
    see also culture, health care; friends
conferences, as research dissemination
    venues, 186–91
collection, research data, 171
confrontation, emancipatory reflection
    procedures, 154, 158–61
constraints, employment and organizational
    within health care, 22–31, 42–3, *43*

construction and deconstruction, 152–3,
157–8
see also reconstruction
context (concept)
element of interpretive knowledge, 93, 136
courage
critical thinking requirement, 107–8
successful reflection requirement, 49–50,
50
creativity, as source of reflection, 16–17
critical knowledge, 95–100, *97*, 150–51
critical research, 166–7
critical social theory (Allen), 90
critical social science, 150
see also elements, e.g. critical thinking;
emancipation and emancipatory
interests; empowerment; false
consciousness; hegemony; reification
critical thinking
definition and characteristics, 105–7
importance, 120–21
relationship to reflection, 109
skills and attitudes required, 107–9
critics
practitioner responses to, 197–8
responses to practice stories, 75, 76, 79, 80,
81, 82, 90, 118–19, 123–4, 134–5, 149,
155–6
role in reflection process, 64–5, *65*
Cruikshank, D., 12
culture, health care
as constraint within health service,
22–4

dancing
as reflective strategy, 55
see also music
data collection and interpretation, 171
De Bono, E., 13
decision-making (methodological)
as element in research planning, 169
deconstruction and
construction
emancipatory reflection procedures,
152–3, 157–8
see also reconstruction
determination, successful reflection
requirement, 49
Dilthey, W., 92–3
doctors, midwife/nurse relationships, 40–42,
42

drawing
as reflective strategy, 55–6
see also painting

education, nurses
and role of reflection, 12–14
effort, personal
successful reflection requirement, 49
emancipation and emancipatory interests,
95, 96, 99–100, 150
emancipatory reflection
applicability within research, 168, 175–6,
176
characteristics, 15–16, 76–7, 147–9, *148–9*,
151
examples of, 148–9, 155–61
importance of, 103
process of, 151–61, *155–6*
empathy, critical thinking requirement,
107–8
empirical knowledge, 91–2, *91–2*,
119–20
empirico-analytical
paradigm of knowledge (Allen), 90
research, 165
employment, health care
as source of reflection, 200–201
constraints, 22–31
see also relationships, health care
empowerment, 96, 150
epistemology, 88
esteem (self), 44
Esther
critical friend responses, 149, 155–6
practice stories, 148–9, 155
evaluation, technical reflection procedure,
126, 130–31
evidence-based practice, 44
expectations, self, 33–5
experiencing, process of
practical reflection procedure, 138–9,
141–4
see also learning, process of
expression (individual free expression)
successful reflection requirement,
60

fair-mindedness, critical thinking
requirement, 108
false consciousness, 95–6, 150
Fay, B., 95, 150

finance
  as constraint within health care provision,
    24–5
  as element in research planning, 170–72
findings, research
  dissemination, 171, 173
  see also conferences; publications
Fraser, D.M., 21, 178
free expression (individual)
  successful reflection requirement, 60
Freshwater, D., 9, 10, 11, 13
friends, role as reflection facilitator and critic,
    64–5, *65*

Ghaye, T., 14, 198
Gilbert, T, 11–12
Glaze, J., 10
Greenwood, J., 14, 197
groups (action research groups), 179–85

Habermas, J., 86, 90, 98–100, *101,* 121
habits
  as source of reflection, 16
  maintenance of reflection habits, 198–9
  reflective examination of, 35–6, *35*
health care service and provision
  action research within, 20–21
  and role of reflection, 9–11
  constraints within, 22–31, 42–3, *43*
  see also staff, health care
Heath, H., 9–10, 11
hegemony, 96, 150
Heideggerian phenomenology (Allen),
    90
historical practice and precedence
  as constraint within health care, 26–8
humility (intellectual)
  critical thinking requirement, 107–8
humour, successful reflection requirement,
    50–51

ideas and insights
  enhanced, following reflection, 80–81, *81*
  generation in research planning, 172–3
identification, as element in research
    planning, 168–9
implementation, technical reflection
    procedure, 125–6, 126–7, 128–30
insights and ideas
  enhanced, following reflection, 80–81, *81*
  generation in research planning, 172–3

integrity, critical thinking requirement,
    107–8
interest, human
  and critical knowledge, 98–100
interpretation
  of research data, 171
  practical reflection procedure, 139–40,
    141–4
interpretive
  knowledge, 92–4, *94,* 135–7
  research, 166–7
intersubjectivity (concept)
  element of interpretive knowledge, 94,
    136
invincibility (personality trait)
  role and management, 33–5, *34*
  see also self-blame

Jocelyn, practice story, 35
John
  critical friend responses, 75, 76, 79, 80, 81,
    82
  practice stories, 32–3, 74, 75, 78, 80, 81,
    82
Johns, C., 10
Jourard, S.M., 30
Julia, practice story, 36–7

Kenney, L.J., 13–14
Kim, H.S., 8–9, 12
knowledge (concept)
  approaches within nursing and midwifery,
    88–90, *89–90*
  categorization and characteristics, 86–8,
    98–100, *100*
  see also critical knowledge; empirical
    knowledge; interpretive knowledge
'knowledge-constitutive interests'
    (Habermas), 86, 100, *101*
Kramer, M.K., 88–9

learning, process of
  practical reflection procedure, 140
  see also experiencing, process of
Lewin, K., 177
Lillyman, S., 14, 198
literature reviews, 170–71
'lived experience', 92–3, 135–6
location of reflection experience
  availability of as successful reflection
    requirement, 61

McMorland, J., 21, 178
Marcia
    critical friend response, 123–4
    practice story, 122–3
Mary, practice story, 43
Meg, practice story, 32–3
methodologies, research, 175–85, *176*
Michael
    critical friend response, 118–19
    practice story, 117–18
midwifery
    definition and characteristics, 18, 20–21
    employment constraints, 22–31 .
    history, 26–7
midwives
    doctor relationships, 40–42, *42*
    responses to critics, 197–8
mistakes, fear of, 33–5, *34*
models of reflection *see* Taylor model
montage
    use of as reflective strategy, 55–6
    see also painting
music
    use of as reflective strategy, 54
    see also dancing; singing

Nancy, practice story, 104
Nightingale, F., 20, 27
Nurse/midwife-doctor game (Stein), 40, 41
nurses
    doctor relationships, 40–42, *42*
    education *see* education, nurses
    responses to critics, 197–8
nursing
    definition and characteristics, 18, *19*
    employment constraints, 22–31
    history, 27–8

observation, action research process, 183
ontology, 88
openness of mind, successful reflection
    necessity, 60, 79–80, *80*

painting
    as reflective strategy, 56–7
    see also montage
participatory action research, 20, 178
patient care, quality assurance measures,
    44–5
perception, critical thinking requirement,
    108

perfection (personality trait)
    role and management, 33–5, *34*
perseverance, critical thinking requirement,
    107–8
personality, individual
    and constraints within employment,
    30–31
perspectives, on daily living
    affirmation in reflective practice, 196–7
    importance of renewal for practitioners,
    199–200
Peter, practice story, 50
phenomenology, Heideggerian (Allen), 90
philosophies of knowledge, as sources of
    reflection, 16
Piggott-Irvine, E., 21, 178
planning
    action research process, 182–3
    as element in research, 167–74, *174*
    within technical reflection, 124–5, 126–8
Plato, 17
Platzer, H., 13
poetry
    use of as reflective strategy, 57
    see also writing
political structures (organizational and
    individual)
    constraint within health care, 28–9
pottery, creation of as reflective strategy,
    57–8
power (concept)
    constraint within health care, 28–9
    see also empowerment
practical reflection
    applicability within research, 168, 175–6,
    176
    characteristics, 15, 76–7
    example of, 134–5, 140–45
    importance of, 102, 133–7, *134–5*
    process of, 137–45
practice, professional
    definitions of ideal and real, 38–40, *39*
practices, health care
    constraint of inherited practices, 26–8
praxis, 8, 151
presentations, research
    preparation, 186–91
problem-solving
    critical thinking requirement, 107
publications, research
    preparation, 191–4

qualities, personal
    required for successful reflection, 48–51,
    50, 59–62
qualitative research, 166–7, 175–6,
    176
quality of care, assurance measures, 44–5
quantitative research, 165, 175–6, *176*
questioning, reflective
    encouragement of, 65–8, *66–8*
    process and meanings, 76–9, *78–9*
quilting, use as reflective strategy, 58

Rachael, practice story, 42
reasoning, as component of critical thinking,
    106–7
reconstruction, 154–6, *155–6*, 161
    see also construction and deconstruction
reflection
    applicability and planning in research,
        167–74, *174*, 175–6, *176*, 184–5
    definition and characteristics, 8–14
    exercises in, 62–3
    limitations of techniques, 14–16
    qualities required for success, 48–51,
        59–62
    relationship with critical thinking,
        109
    sources and value, 16–18, 103–5, *104*
    strategies, 51–9, 196–204, *203–4*
    see also action research; emancipatory
        reflection; practical reflection; Taylor
        model of reflection; technical reflection
reification, 96, 150
relationships, health care
    management of, 40–42, *42*
    see also culture, health care
religion, as source of reflection, 17
research
    applicability and project planning,
        167–74, *174*
    dissemination of, 186–94
    methodologies, 175–85, *176*
    types of, 165–7
    see also action research
reviews, literature, 170–71
rituals, as source of reflection, 16
Rosie, practice story, 174
routines
    as source of reflection, 16
    maintenance of reflection routines, 198–9
    reflective examination of, 35–6, *35*

Schön, D., 8, 197
scientific reasoning, as component of critical
    thinking, 107
self-blame, 32–3, *32–3*
self-esteem, 44
self-expectations, 33–5
self-worth, sense of, 44
Sellers, J., 12
silence, importance within reflection, 199
singing
    as reflective strategy, 58
    see also dancing
Smyth, W.J., 148
social settings, health care
    constraint within, 29–30
    management of relationships, 40–42,
        42
spirituality, as source of reflection, 17
spontaneity, successful reflection
    requirement, 60
staff, health care
    as fellow reflective practitioners, 201–2
    relationships with, 40–42, *42*
    see also culture, health care; friends
Stein, L., 40–41
Stewart
    critical friend response, 90
    practice stories, 89, 94
stories (practice stories)
    critical friend responses, 75, 76, 79, 80, 81,
        82, 90, 118–19, 123–4, 134–5, 149, 155–6
    narratives, 32–3, 34, 35, 36–7, 37–8, 39, 42,
        43, 50, 65, 66–8, 74, 75, 78, 80, 81, 82,
        89, 91–2, 94, 97, 104, 117–18, 122–3,
        134, 148–9, 155, 174, 203–4
Street, A., 148
subjectivity (concept)
    element of interpretive knowledge, 93–4,
        136
supervision, clinical
    and role of reflection, 11–12

taping (audio and video)
    as reflective strategy, 53–4, 58–9
Taylor, B.J., 11, 31, 71–85, *72, 74–5, 76, 78–9,
    80, 81, 82,* 184–5
Taylor, C., 14, 198
Taylor model of reflection, 71–85, *72, 74–5,
    76, 78–9, 80, 81, 82*
technical interests
    and theory of critical knowledge, 98–9, 121

technical reflection
    applicability within research, 167, 175–6,
        176
    characteristics, 15, 76–7
    examples of, 117–19, 122–4, 126–31
    importance of, 101–2, 116–22, *117–19*
    process of, 122–31, *122–4*
tenacity, successful reflection requirement,
        82–3
Thea, practice story, 65
thought
    essentiality of for reflection, 75–6, *75–6*
    independence of as critical thinking
        requirement, 107–8
    ways of thinking in reflection, 109–11
    see also critical thinking
time
    as element in research planning, 172
    availability of for successful reflection, 48,
        61

Todd, G., 11
traditions
    as source of reflection, 16
    see also habits

Van Hooft, S., 105–6, 108–9, 120–21
videotaping
    as reflective strategy, 58–9
    see also audiotaping; music; poetry
Virginia, practice story, 65

Wilkin, K., 11
Wilkinson, J.M., 106, 107–8
work, health care employment
    see employment, health care
worthiness, sense of, 44
writing
    as reflective strategy, 52–3
    as research dissemination medium, 191–4
    see also poetry

Related books from Open University Press
Purchase from www.openup.co.uk or order through your local bookseller

PSYCHOLOGY FOR NURSES AND THE CARING PROFESSIONS
SECOND EDITION

Jan Walker, Sheila Payne, Paula Smith and Nikki Jarrett

- In what ways does psychology contribute to health and health care?
- How can psychology be applied in different health and social care contexts?
- What are the current psychological approaches used in health and social care?

This book introduces students and practitioners to psychological knowledge and understanding, and helps them to apply sound psychological principles in clinical contexts.

The text retains the emphasis of the previous edition upon the application of fundamental psychological principles in health and social care settings but is extensively revised to give increased attention to the developing evidence base within the psychology of health and illness. New to this edition are:

- Key questions for each chapter
- Research-based applications to practice
- Inclusion of a family scenario, used throughout the book to focus on professional, patient and carer perspectives
- Revised glossary explaining important terms

The book provides clear and concise descriptions of psychological theories, research-based evidence, and practical examples of applications across the lifespan in different health and social care settings.

Psychology for Nurses and the Caring Professions is essential reading for all students undertaking diploma or degree level courses in nursing and health care, including nurses, midwives, occupational therapists, physiotherapists and radiographers. It is also a useful introduction to the application of psychology to health for professionals working in social care.

Contents
Series editor's preface – Preface – What is psychology? – The perception of self and others – Memory, understanding and information-giving – Learning and social learning – Development and change across the lifespan – Social processes in health care – Stress and coping – Psychology applied to health and well-being – Case study – Glossary – References – Index.

232pp   0 335 21462 2 (Paperback)   0 335 21501 7 (Hardback)